Copyright and Tradem:

IMPORTANT NOTE TO OUR READERS

Disneyland
DETECTIVE

An INDEPENDENT Guide to Discovering Disney's Legend, Lore, and Magic!

Kendra Trahan

Portrait Illustrations: Brian McKim
Illustrations: Karl Yamauchi
Photography: Dave Hawkins
& Debbie Smith

PermaGrin
Publishing, Inc.

Disneyland Detective: An INDEPENDENT Guide to Discovering Disney's Legend, Lore, and Magic! by Kendra Trahan

Published by
PermaGrin Publishing, Inc.
27758 Santa Margarita Parkway #379
Mission Viejo, CA 92691
www.permagrinpublishing.com

Cover art by Lightbourne, Inc. based on a photograph by Dave Hawkins.

See page i for additional copyright and trademark information.

Publisher's Cataloging in Publication Data
Library of Congress Control Number: 2002090535
Trahan, Kendra D.
      Disneyland Detective: An INDEPENDENT Guide to Discovering Disney's Legend, Lore, and Magic! / by Kendra Trahan
      p. cm.
      Includes bibliography and index.

      1. Disneyland (Calif.)—History 2. Amusement Parks (Calif.). I. Trahan, Kendra D., 1967- II. Title

ISBN 0-9717464-0-0

Printed in the United States of America
15 14 13 12 11 10 9 8 7 6

ACKNOWLEDGMENTS

• •

There are so many knowledgeable people about Disneyland that it was a little intimidating admitting that I had written a book. Fortunately, these wonderful people made me feel welcome as they do with every Disney fan. I'm proud to call these dynamic and enthusiastic people friends.

Strong contributors who reviewed the content are: Doug Marsh, Bill & Tanya Guy, Wally and Kaye Malins, Susie Langdale, Michael Broggie, Dennis Tanida, Billy Smith, Heather Dagle, Melissa & John Henry, Lorene Ritchert, Danny Gossett, Suzanne Bennett, Rod & Sandy Trahan, Gary Marliss, Loys Hawkins, Mary Parker, Roger Morgan, Rosa Tycksen, Brandi Randall, Robbin & Terry Lynn, Louis Boish, Brian Thomas, Louis Garcia, Debbie Smith, Fred Lack, Chris & Kathy Prewitt, Dan DeMeyere, Dennis Emslie, and GG Misa. A special thanks to David DeVries and the Kalamazoo Public Library.

Thanks to my copy editors Robert Goodman, and Tom and Sara Graves who helped make the book more reader friendly. Bob Swingle at Lightbourne who shares two alma maters, and designing the interior and developing a fabulous cover.

A special thank-you to photographer Dave Hawkins who has an amazing talent with the camera and with his artistic eye. Thank you to Debbie Smith who has the patience and love of making photos that filled in with other critical prints.

To the Disney Legends and family members who graciously shared their stories, time, and support. You're the inspiration for writing this book.

To my husband Russell who never tires of my enthusiasm, and screwball adventures—Thank you! The journey would not have been as sweet without you.

This book is dedicated
to my husband Russell,
the love of my life since
once upon a dream.

Contents

As swarms of people enter Disneyland every day, a few will find Hidden Mickey and even fewer can call themselves Disneyland Detectives.

Introduction

Disneyland is not just a remarkable amusement park. Behind the scenes and beneath the surface lie a world of details and features that add layer upon layer of enjoyment for both casual and veteran visitors. The depth of these details is extraordinary. Visitors to the park can enjoy just being there, or they can explore the subtleties that add so much to the experience.

This book is a guide to the riches that lie just beyond the obvious. Disneyland is ever changing, and treasures are constantly being added and removed. That in itself is good because it constantly renews the park and reinvigorates the magic of the kingdom. No book can capture a moving target, but I hope this one helps you appreciate the existing points of interest and look for some of the new ones on your own. Enjoy discovering these treasures, and when you do, take a moment or two to think of the talented craftsmen who put them there.

How to use this book

There are several ways to use this book. For some, reading straight through from the first page to the last is the only way to satiate a healthy Disneyland appetite. For others, identifying and searching out every detail is a fun way to read. Parents and teachers may use the *Lesson to Learn* sections to inspire the young readers or the young at heart to learn more about true life characters. Still others may carry the book with them in the park to make the waiting in line pass more quickly. Ultimately, I hope this book becomes a permanent reference in any Disneyland book collection.

Things to look for

HIDDEN MICKEY

Hidden Mickeys are scattered throughout the park. The Hidden Mickey is a symbol—usually three circles forming the shape of Mickey's head and ears. The ear circles are equal in size, while the head circle is larger than the two ear circles. Hidden Mickeys are official parts of an attraction. An Imagineer put them there intentionally. Occasionally, Disneyland cast members may also create Hidden Mickeys. There are websites dedicated to Hidden Mickeys, but this book mentions only those I have personally confirmed. Hidden Mickeys first appeared in the 1980s at EPCOT and MGM Studios in Florida. Once people started noticing them, finding the Hidden Mickeys has become a fun activity for many visitors.

The most common shape of a Hidden Mickey sprinkled throughout the park.

TREASURE & TRIVIA

You'll find information about movie props, stories, and interesting facts here. You can spend a whole day scavenging in the park for Treasures and Trivia or just brush up on special sites to see while standing in line.

LESSON TO LEARN

Although Disney has a Norman Rockwell-like approach to history that glosses over politically incorrect subjects, there are still a lot of springboards for learning. Inspired by or based on real history, *Lessons to Learn* are topics you can take home and read more about. These lessons may refer to people, places, or events. These sections are especially useful for teachers and parents and for anyone who loves to read and learn.

"E" Ticket Attractions–Early visitors to Disneyland received books of tickets that could be exchanged for rides. The tamest rides usually called for an "A" ticket, while the top attractions cost an "E" ticket, which was valued at 50 cents. Before it was discontinued in 1982, the famous "E" ticket quickly earned its place as an American slang phrase meaning the ultimate thrill. Today, these pieces of paper are quite valuable to collectors of Disneyana.

Disney Legends—The Walt Disney Company honors individuals who have made major contributions to the company. Disney has a number of ways of bestowing these honors, but this refers to the official title of "Disney Legend." The first Disney Legend designation was bestowed in 1987. Disney honors important people in a number of ways, including dedicating windows in the park to them, which you'll read about later. There are no references in the park to Disney Legends. They are at Disney-MGM Studios in Florida. These legends and honors are mentioned here as a courtesy.

DISNEY MYTH vs DISNEY URBAN LEGEND

It's important to distinguish between Disney myth and Disney urban legend. The Disney myth is a story created by the Imagineers to set the theme or mood for an attraction. The Haunted Mansion and Big Thunder Mountain both have Disney myths associated with them. An urban legend is a popular belief that is simply not true or difficult to prove. There is an urban legend, for example, regarding the hearse outside of the Haunted Mansion. It is reported having carried the coffin of Brigham Young. This is simply not true, since Young was carried by hand to his grave.

Although we may not know where urban legends are started, they are fun and part of the storytelling that makes Disneyland special.

BECOMING A TRUE DISNEYLAND DETECTIVE

As a final reminder to the new generation of Disneyland Detectives, the park is always changing. A new Hidden Mickey may appear while another one is removed. A new window is dedicated while another attraction may be completely overhauled. I mention this for two reasons. First, this book may become dated the minute it goes to press. Every effort has been made to focus on the current state of the park. You won't find information about the Monsanto House of the Future or Adventure Thru Inner Space as these attractions were closed a long time ago. Future editions of the book will strive to represent current attractions to visitors of the park. Second, we all too often resist change. But change is the reason to come back to the park. Imagine Disneyland without Indiana Jones, Splash Mountain, Big Thunder Mountain, or Space Mountain. Even though Walt Disney died before any of these attractions were added, these are often mentioned as guest favorites. So, discover the changes for yourself, and accept that improvements are eminent. Seeing what's new is a great reason for returning to Disneyland because Disneyland is a living tribute from one man to the world.

Photos used by permission of Milt Albright

In 1954, Walt Disney took an orange grove in Anaheim, Calif., and developed

Chapter 1

THE CASE HISTORY OF
Disneyland

Walt Disney wanted his guests to enjoy their visit to Disneyland and also to leave with some knowledge they didn't have when they woke up that morning. He was passionate for authenticity, good taste, quality, and design. Walt didn't try to educate people about anything directly, but believed his audience would always know the difference between good and bad.

As early as 1948, Walt had written about a little "Mickey Mouse Park" he wanted to build across the street from his new motion picture studio in Burbank, Calif. On March 27, 1952, the *Burbank Daily Review* printed the first public announcement of Walt's plans to build Disneyland. It described the site as a 16-acre plot of land on Riverside Drive, which later became part of the Ventura Freeway. On May 1, 1954, however, the *Anaheim Bulletin* broke the news that Disneyland would be built in Anaheim, 38 miles south of Burbank.

Walt had decided to pursue his dream of building a park independently when Roy Disney, his brother and financial partner, refused to take him seriously. The $10,000 Roy offered for research and development would hardly do justice to Walt's dreams for the project. So, Walt borrowed on his life insurance and sold Smoke Tree Ranch, a vacation home he had built in Palm Springs, Calif. By this time Roy could see that Walt was very serious about his park and decided to help him see it through. Walt gathered some of his artists and animators along with art directors and developed WED Enterprises, named for his initials, Walter Elias Disney. (In 1984 the name was changed to Walt Disney Imagineering.) WED began to develop a model for the park. The team visited amusement parks, fairs, and carnivals, finding the same problems wherever they looked — seamy characters running the rides, tawdriness, greasy foods, rip-off games, and nothing for parents to enjoy. Walt wanted something different.

Herb Ryman recalled that one Saturday morning in 1952 he received a call from Walt asking him to come to the studio. When Herb arrived, Walt was waiting outside the studio for him, where he began to describe his newest project — Disneyland. Roy Disney would be going to New York on Monday to raise money for the park and needed plans to show the lenders. Herb said, "Great, I'd love to see them," not realizing that Walt was asking him to make the plans. After some coaxing and a promise to stand by his side, Walt and Herb spent a marathon weekend drawing the first concept art of Disneyland. Over the next months Walt recruited many more people from his movie studio to develop the plans.

In 1941, Walt had released the movie *The Reluctant Dragon* as a movie studio tour; now he wanted California visitors to experience Disneyland as a three-dimensional movie tour. His first written description of the park stated "Disneyland will be something of a fair, an exhibition, a playground, a community center, a museum of living facts, and a showplace of beauty and magic . . . " Walt instructed his designers to build every attraction with the goal that people would leave with a smile on their face. Walt's personal interests and his thoughts about what guests would enjoy gave direction to the designers. Lending institutions, in general,

typically avoided funding amusement parks. At that time, most amusement parks were considered dirty, unsafe, and often run by unsavory characters. Coney Island-style amusement parks were going out of business all over the country.

At the same time, Hollywood questioned Walt's judgment for getting involved with television. The movie-making town distrusted it, fearing it would do to the movie industry what the movie industry had done to vaudeville. Roy and Walt, however, found the financing salvation of Disneyland in television. Television was new in the 1950s, and networks were eager to find programming and big-name talent. Leonard Goldensen at ABC agreed to invest $500,000 in Disneyland and to guarantee loans up to $4.5 million. In return, the network received about one-third stake in Disneyland and all of the profits from concessions for 10 years. Roy secured a seven-year contract with ABC to develop television shows in exchange for the initial financing of Disneyland. On October 1, 1953, initial ideas were outlined for four shows: The Walt Disney Show, later named Walt Disney Presents Disneyland, The True Life Show, The World of Tomorrow and The Mickey Mouse Club. The Disneyland show was an instant success, creating a sensation with three Emmy-winning episodes about Davy Crockett. The Mickey Mouse Club was also a success. Together these two shows ensured the financial backing for the park.

Construction costs would eventually spiral out of control. Additional financial backing came from Western Printing and Lithographing, which had long published Disney books. Both ABC and Western Printing made its investment on the understanding that Disney would have the right to buy them out if the park was a success. This right was exercised not long after the park opened. Banks and other financial institutions were prepared to lend the rest. Eventually, institutional lessees were brought in to pay for their own exhibits and staff. Companies, such as Eastman Kodak, Upjohn, Swift & Company, and Carnation, signed contracts with Disneyland.

Walt Disney planned a gala ceremony to announce the ground breaking for Disneyland on July 21, 1954. The ceremony was never held—Walt and the crew were too busy building the park for a grand opening less than a year away.

The original cost to build Disneyland was $17 million. Although far from complete, the park opened for the press preview day at 10 a.m. on July 17, 1955. The public opening was on July 18, although historians still consider July 17 "opening day."

From groundbreaking to opening, within one short year, the park had 20 attractions ready.

Construction of Disneyland required 32,000 sacks of cement, 3.5 million board ft. of lumber, and 5 million square ft. of pavement, and 300,000 cubic yards of earth had been moved.

Black Sunday

Six thousand invitations had been mailed for press preview day, but many more tickets were counterfeited. There is no way to be certain, but an estimated 28,154 guests actually came. One person was caught with a ladder, charging people $10 to climb over the berm. The park had broken ground with a staff of 21 and 5 consultants; by opening day Disneyland had 850 employees.

Walt dedicated Disneyland on opening day with these words:

"To all who come to this happy place –Welcome! Disneyland is your land. Here age relives fond memories of the past . . . and here youth may savor the challenge and promise of the future. Disneyland is dedicated to the ideals, the dreams and the hard facts that have created America . . . with the hope that it will be a source of joy and inspiration to the entire world."

ABC-TV broadcast the opening with Art Linkletter, Bob Cummings, and Ronald Reagan hosting the ceremonies. Opening day was later referred to as "Black Sunday" because of all the mishaps that occurred. Power went out on several of the attractions in Fantasyland, restaurants ran out of food and beverages, the Mark Twain Steamboat threatened to sink from overcrowding, and women stepped out of their high-heeled shoes because the asphalt was still soft on Main Street. A plumber's strike forced Walt to choose between drinking fountains and restrooms. Guests complained of thirst. ABC's broadcast reflected the chaos and created some of its own. Walt missed the dedication of Tomorrowland. Fess Parker in his Davy Crockett garb was referred to as Cinderella. Disneyland borrowed character costumes from the Ice Capades because of budget and time shortages.

Over 90 million viewers witnessed the live coverage. Numerous celebrities were on hand, including Frank Sinatra, Sammy Davis Jr., Kirk Douglas, Danny Thomas, Debbie Reynolds, Charlton Heston, Maureen O'Hara, and others. The Mouseketeers were there, even though Mickey Mouse Club wouldn't air until October of that year.

The following day, Roy Disney purchased the first public ticket. Not every glitch was solved. Some of the attractions, such as Casey Jr., were closed for refining and reworking. Autopia had only three surviving cars from the previous day. Nevertheless, from that first day, the public has embraced the park and returned to see it grow and develop.

The First Half Century

Many television shows have featured Disneyland, from holiday parades, talk shows, and sit-coms, but only two movies have been filmed there. In 1962, the comedy *40 Pounds of Trouble,* starring Tony Curtis and Suzanne Pleshette, featured an elaborate chase staged all over the park. In 1996, *That Thing You Do,* starring Tom Hanks and Tom Everett Scott, featured a short Matterhorn segment that harkened back to 1964 when the action in the movie took place.

By the time Michael Eisner joined Disney in 1984, Disneyland had become a local theme park, drawing 10 million residents of the Los Angeles Area. It was a one-day experience that relied heavily on new attractions, parades, and shows to keep guests coming back. During the '80s, however, Disney had very few movie successes on which to model new attractions. Re-energizing the park meant finding new, well-known characters that attractions could be built around. Partnering with George Lucas and Michael Jackson, Disney built attractions such as Star Tours, Captain EO, and Indiana Jones until Disney could create new characters and stories.

TREASURE & TRIVIA

Disneyland saw its one-millionth guest just two months after it opened. Guests continued to visit the park as fast as one fast-food chain sold hamburgers.

- Elsa Marquez was the 1 millionth guest on September 8, 1955.
- Leigh Woolfenden was the 10 millionth guest on December 31, 1957.
- Dr. Glenn C. Franklin was the 25 millionth guest on April 19, 1961.
- Mary Adams was the 50 millionth guest on August 12, 1965.
- Valerie Suldo was the 100 millionth guest on June 17, 1971.
- Gert Schelvis was the 200 millionth guest on January 8, 1981.
- Claudine Masson was the 300 millionth guest on September 1, 1989.
- Minnie Pepito was the 400 millionth guest on July 5, 1997.
- Mark Ramirez was the 450 millionth guest on March 15, 2001.
- Bill, Anne Marie & daughter Aspen Trow were the 500 millionth guests. They walked through the gates on January 8, 2004.

TREASURE & TRIVIA

In 1959, Premier Nikita Khrushchev of the Soviet Union was denied a visit to Disneyland. The U.S. State Department felt there were too many security precautions for Disneyland to handle. The Soviet leader's negative reaction caused an international incident.

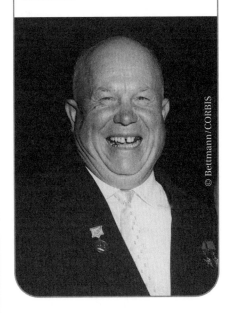

© Bettmann/CORBIS

OPERA HOUSE

THE WALT DISNEY STORY
FEATURING GREAT MOMENTS WITH MR. LINCOLN

Photo by Debbie Smith

Main Street U.S.A. is an idealized version of Walt's boyhood home in Marceline, Mo. The opulent facade of the opera house hid the lumber mill inside during the early years of Disneyland.

Chapter 2

MAIN STREET
Motives

Walt's hometown, Marceline, Mo., was the inspiration for Disneyland Main Street, U.S.A. He lived there from 1906 to 1910, but the town and the times made a powerful impression. Walt's Main Street is his ideal of the town at the turn of the century.

The designers built Main Street U.S.A. using forced perspective, a movie-making trick that gives a fantasy look and makes small places seem large. Many people claim that Main Street was designed to get narrower as you approach the castle in order to make the castle appear farther away. Some quick measurements will show that this is a myth.

The ground floors were built to full scale. The succeeding floors are built proportionately smaller. There are a lot of theories on the scale for Main Street, but actually it is built with several scales in mind. The second and third floors windows are smaller and narrower, tricking the eye into believing that the building is full size. The second floor rooms are only about three feet deep, perfectly wallpapered and furnished appropriately for the era. Items at a distance always appear smaller. Even the trees are trimmed to stay in proper perspective.

Turn-of-the-century music is piped in over the street. The songs are a combination of Victorian era favorites, Disney movie songs, and Broadway Show tunes. Favorite songs from "Oklahoma," "Hello Dolly," "The Music Man," or Disney's "The Happiest Millionaire," and "Summer Magic," grace the streets all day long. The music in the morning is upbeat with a fast tempo, as the day progresses, the music slows down to keep pace with the energy of the guests.

Town Square: The two authentic 19th century cannons that decorate the square were built in Paris for the French Army. Fortunately, the cannons have never been fired in adversity. Marceline, Mo., has cannons in its Town Square, so it is only fitting that Town Square in Disneyland has the same. The

Disneyland Band plays here daily, keeping the flag-raising and lowering ceremonies alive.

The 65-ft. flagpole at the base of Town Square was recovered from Wilshire Boulevard in Los Angeles. Disney Legend Emile Kuri passed an accident in which a car knocked over the streetlight. He bought the pole for $5 and brought it to Disneyland. The gas lamps are over 150 years old; they once lit the cities of St. Louis and Baltimore. Walt purchased the 500-pound gas lamps for 8 cents per pound. In the early days of Disneyland, these gas lamps were individually lit each night by a lamplighter in a turn-of-the-century costume.

TREASURE & TRIVIA

There are several popcorn vendors throughout the park. Each cart is assigned to a specific area; it's easy to tell where each belongs because of the character in the upper left window turning the kernels. The one on Main Street is dressed as a Dapper Dan.

Empty Building: This building was once the Police Station. The light poles in front still resemble a typical police station. Guests often came to this building for information, so the staff became proficient at telling people to go next door to "City Hall." Early in his career, this building was an office for Marty Sklar, the vice chairman and principal creative executive of WED Imagineering.

TREASURE & TRIVIA

Marty Sklar is the current vice-chairman and principal creative executive of WD Imagineering. He was a writer for early publicity for the park. He is the first author to write a "serious" book about Disneyland. It was written to coincide with the Tencennial. He joined Disney in 1955 and is the only remaining employee on the payroll who has been to the opening of every Disney theme park. He was named president in 1987 and promoted to vice chair when Imagineering merged with Disney Development Company in 1996. He was honored with the Disney Legends Award on December 5, 2001, the 100th anniversary of Walt Disney's birth.

The first office for Marty Sklar was in the police station building. Marty is the last employee to have attended every Disney Park opening.

City Hall: You can obtain maps, schedules, tours, and information about Disneyland here at City Hall. Harper Goff, a 1993 Disney Legend, drew the original design of the building. City Hall is modeled after the county court house in Goff's hometown of Fort Collins, Colo. You can read more about Harper at the window dedicated to him in Adventureland.

The offices upstairs once belonged to some original WED employees: Bill Cottrell, Marvin Davis, Dick Irvine, Bill Martin, and Goff. Every Saturday morning the group would join Walt to walk the park and look for ways to improve it. Sometimes young Marty Sklar would join them with a cameraman.

Planted in 1910, the giant eucalyptus trees behind City Hall are as old as Main Street is supposed to be. Today, they act as background foliage for Adventureland and Main Street, but originally the trees provided a windbreak for the orange orchard that once stood there.

Fire Department: This building was constructed in 1955. The Disneyland version of an early model fire engine features a honking horn instead of a siren. The Fire Wagon, too, was one of the attractions on Opening Day in 1955. Although Main Street depicts America circa 1890-1900, the fire engine is a 1928 model. (This is just one of a very few anomalies in the park.)

The fire truck was added in 1958 at the suggestion of a young Imagineer Bob Gurr. He imitated Walt in front of the founder with a knee slapping "you know what we haven't got?" Walt was less than amused, but he listened to Bob's suggestion. It didn't seem that way at first. Instead of an answer, Bob received the raised eyebrow that was Walt's quintessential disapproving look. A few minutes later, though, the accounting department called

City Hall and some of the oldest trees in the park. City Hall is modeled after the Fort Collins, Colo., Courthouse.

and authorized Bob to design a fire truck. It's a classic design, handmade with a 12-hp, two-cylinder engine.

Bob drove the finished fire truck from the studio in Burbank to Disneyland. Since the truck was built to travel slowly up Main Street, it couldn't keep up with the Los Angeles traffic. While he was driving the fire truck on the far right side of the road to allow cars to pass, a little boy yelled to him, "Hey mister, by the time you get there, it'll be burned down!"

The apartment over the fire station on Main Street was Walt's. It was finished before the park so that Walt could stay close to the project and ensure it would be completed on time. The original designer was Emile Kuri, who was a set designer for many Disney films. Lillian Disney loved to collect antiques, so the room was designed with the ornate flower-patterned furniture and rose-colored carpeting and drapes that were so typical of the Victorian style. It served as a home and office for Walt and his family. The apartment was not designed for extended living, but the Disneys often stayed there and entertained celebrities and friends. The apartment is not open to the public, but at City Hall you can get a copy of *Room with a View* by Anne K. Okey, an article that describes the furniture and the apartment. The eternal light that burns in the window is a memorial to Walt.

The family spent many nights at the Firehouse, where they were lulled to sleep by the "wild animals" sounds in the Jungle Cruise. Cast members always knew when Walt was in the apartment—the fire station doors were closed to keep people from honking the horn while he was working or resting.

In the back left corner of the fire station is a fireman's pole that Walt might have used to get from his apartment to the Fire Station. Reportedly, a guest once climbed the pole and entered the private apartment. Shortly after that, access between the two rooms was closed.

The Carriage Place/ Emporium Annex/Emporium:

The largest store on Main Street, it features Disneyland merchandise for the crowds of last-minute shoppers. It was part of the opening-day ceremonies. What makes this store special are the windows facing Main Street. Elaborate dioramas tell the story of the most recent Disney film.

New Century Jewelry/ New Century Timepieces: This

building was originally the Upjohn Apothecary. Its windows were festooned with antique pharmacy bottles, and vitamins were handed out to guests. The only remaining evidence of the building's past life is the window dedication upstairs. Sponsored first by Elgin, the clock shop opened in January of 1972.

Today, the shop features one-of-a-kind, hand-painted watches of Disney characters.

TREASURE & TRIVIA

Pictures of Walt line the wooden, antique cabinet. The antique-looking frames hold some Disney family photos.

Carnation Café: This patio restaurant opened in March of 1997. Carnation is one of the few corporate sponsors that have been with Disneyland from opening day. Carnation also sponsors the Plaza Gardens.

Oscar's Choice is a menu tribute to a longtime cast member and cook at the Carnation Café. The potatoes are made from his original recipe, and the designation "Oscar's Potatoes" was made to celebrate his 45th year with the company.

Blue Ribbon Bakery: This bakery replaced the *Sunkist* Citrus House in April of 1990. Sponsored by Nestlé Toll House, it serves fresh muffins, scones, and sticky buns daily over the counter. The store also offers sandwiches made with fresh-baked bread. This is a great place to get a latte and plan your route. During the holidays,

you can even get eggnog and peppermint lattes.

According to Disney mythology, German immigrants operate the Blue Ribbon Bakery. The wife opened the Carnation Café outside on the street to showcase her tempting hot dishes.

Old Fashioned Frozen Yogurt/ Gibson Girl Ice Cream Palace:

This store is hosted by and features Nestlé Ice Cream. Stand in front of the windows, beneath the awning, and inhale. Air ducts under the window blow a vanilla scent to tempt you via your olfactory senses. The canopy helps circulate the scent. You'll encounter this effect again in front of the Candy Palace.

The back bar in the Ice Cream Parlor was salvaged from the former Carnation Ice Cream Parlor that was once next door. If you appreciate depression-era and colored glass, notice the King's Crown or Thumbprint glass on the back wall shelves. U.S. Glass (Tiffin) Company produced glass like this as early as the late 1800s.

The dining room in the back with the crystal elephant was the Main Street Shooting Gallery, then it became a video game arcade. The crystal elephant looks like an ice sculpture, but is reminiscent of the Crystal Arcade.

Penny Arcade: The Penny Arcade was one of the opening-day

Oscar, the only cast member with his name on the menu.

attractions. It features Muta-scopes and Cail-o-Scopes. These hand cranked, moving-picture machines were first introduced around 1900. They cost a penny to operate. You'll see other antique interactive games here as well. Check out the penny presses, too. When you insert a penny (and a few other coins to operate the amusement), the penny will be flattened and imprinted with a Disney image.

Few people notice the giant Indian Chief penny in the Penny Arcade. The year on the giant Penny is consistent with the era of Main Street, 1901.

Photo by Dave Hawkins

HIDDEN MICKEY
Esmerelda, the woman who tells your fortune, uses Mickey Mouse cards.

Candy Palace:
This shop, also known as Candyland, opened one week after the park. Employees make fresh fudge and chocolate-dipped strawberries every day. The large windows allow you to watch and smell the process. Below the windows, near the ground, are air vents that blow a vanilla scent. The canopy above the window helps circulate the scent.

Coca-Cola Refreshment Center:
The Coca-Cola Company is another of the remaining opening-day sponsors at Disneyland. It's a great place to rest with plenty of tables, shade, and piano accompaniment.

Plaza Pavilion:
At the time of this printing, the Plaza Pavilion was closed except for busy days in renewing annual passes. The building was designed and used as a buffet-style restaurant. Early in Disneyland history, guests could enjoy their meals on the terrace overlooking the Jungle Cruise.

Carnation Plaza Gardens:
This entertainment area opened near the castle in August of 1956. The band shell was once located here. The Osmond Brothers made their professional debut in 1961 here at the Carnation Gardens.

Partners Statue:
The statue was dedicated on Mickey's birthday, November 18, 1993, and rededicated at the anniversary of Walt Disney's 100th birthday on December 5, 2001. Walt was never comfortable

with the idea of his likeness in the park, so it wasn't until 1993 that Lillian Disney finally agreed to allow a life-sized bronzed statue of Walt to be placed in Disneyland. The design of Walt holding hands with Mickey Mouse was created by Disney Legend John Hench. Another Disney Legend, Blaine Gibson, a longtime artist and sculptor for the Walt Disney Company, did the actual sculpting. The statue is called "Partners." You'll see it at the hub of Disneyland, where all the lands come together. A similar statue is in Walt Disney World's Magic Kingdom.

Look for three initials that resemble a cattle brand on Walt's tie. Walt wore his STR tie in many pictures and films. The STR stands for Smoke Tree Ranch, a favorite vacation spot in Palm Springs.

Mickey Mouse is always drawn with both ears in full circle. Blaine Gibson was challenged to find a way to sculpt Mickey that accomplished the same effect. Blaine created the statue with the idea of showing Walt admiring the park and sharing the idea, "look what we've done," with Mickey.

Plaza Inn: This, too, was an opening-day restaurant once called Red Wagon Inn. You can enjoy a Carnation Ice Cream sundae or a meal here. This buffet-style restaurant is a great place for watching the parades. Carnation is also one of the remaining original corporate sponsors.

This was Disneyland's original fine dining restaurant. There was a private dining room where Walt could take guests as well as an employee dining room. The "Inn Between" restaurant for cast members is still located there.

In 1965, the restaurant was extensively remodeled and renamed the Plaza Inn. The buffet service was instituted then. According to some sources, Roy O. Disney was particularly fond of the split roast chicken served here.

Photo by Dave Hawkins

The Partners Statue was designed by John Hench and sculpted by Blaine Gibson.

Red Wagon: The Red Wagon is the only place in the park where you can buy a fresh, hand-dipped corn dog. The little truck is named in tribute to the original Red Wagon Inn.

Disneyland First Aid: Registered nurses are always on duty here to assist with medical needs. You can store medications that need to be refrigerated. You can also lie down if you feel ill.

The first baby born in Disneyland was on July 4, 1979. Rosa Salcedo went into labor while riding the Submarine Ride. She quickly tried to exit the park with her family. With the help of park nurses, she gave birth to her baby on a park bench on Main Street.

In 1984, two park nurses helped a pregnant Margarita Granados deliver her baby girl. Margarita was waiting for her husband and two sons to ride Space Mountain when she went into labor.

The most recent baby born in Disneyland was March 30, 2002. Austin Ray Mirlo decided to join his family and the world just after his family entered the park. Mother Wendy Wood-Mirlo was taken to the Main Entrance Lead Office where nurses and paramedics delivered the baby.

Disneyland Baby Center: The center is hosted by Carnation. It provides changing tables, high chairs, a nursing area, and toddler's toilets.

You can warm baby food and buy baby powder, diapers, formula, and food. Napping facilities and baby-sitting services are not available.

TREASURE & TRIVIA

Inside the Disneyland Baby Center is a picture of Walt Disney when he was 10-months old.

Main Street Photo Supply Company:

Taking pictures is an important part of any trip to Disneyland. This shop, sponsored by Kodak, features film and equipment for the photographer in the group. You can also pick up character photos here, all printed on Kodak paper of course. This is the pickup area for the photos taken by cast members, too.

The window display includes an authentic, turn-of-the-century office. Everything facing the castle in this window is an antique, from the desk and phone to the fan and clock. The authentic-looking water-marks on the ceiling, however, are fake.

China Closet: Originally this location was Ruggles China and Main Street Intimate Apparel Shop. The opening day guide book refers to it as "Corset Shop, V-Ette (Hollywood-Maxwell.)" This is where the infamous "Wizard of Bras" Show was presented. The entrance was through the porch of the house between the China Shop and Silhouette Studio.

Silhouette Studio: Silhouettes were one of the novel advances of the early 1900s. For a small fee, you can experience this century technology and have a silhouette of yourself or your loved ones made.

TREASURE & TRIVIA

Silhouettes were popular in Europe earlier than the turn of the century. The term is taken from Etienne de Silhouette, the French Minister of Finance in 1859.

Crystal Arts: (by the giant Timex clock): This Old World Glass Cutter's Shop is leased by the Arribas Brothers, an outside vendor whose craftsmanship is worthy of the Disneyland affiliation. The Arribas Brothers also lease the store in New Orleans Square where you can get hand-blown figurines and have your name cut into glassware.

The permanent display of the crystal castle here is hand-blown. If you can wait several months, you can order one. According to one shopkeeper, the store has sold three crystal castles since their

opening. Be advised: they are not your run-of-the-mill souvenirs. The first one sold for $5,000. The store priced the second one at $10,000. When it sold, the price went up again to $15,000. The fourth and most recent will cost you $20,000.

TREASURE & TRIVIA

Outside the store is a free-standing clock on the sidewalk. This location was the original clock store, sponsored by Timex. Walt's boyhood town of Marceline, Mo., built a similar clock on its Main Street.

Castle Brothers Collegiate Fashions/Chester Drawers Togs for Toddlers:
The Castle Brothers Store sells Disney clothing for men and women. In back is the children's store. The name, Chester Drawers, is a pointer to the beautiful wardrobe behind the cash register. Inside the closet and throughout the shop are antique toys.

Disney Clothiers LTD: To encourage visitors to buy sweatshirts and warm clothing, this store is kept a few degrees cooler than the other stores. Cast members call it the "coldest store in the park." It used to be the Hallmark Card Store until it was remodeled and re-opened in March of 1985. In the back of the store, you'll find a selection of nightwear and bath accessories.

Main Street Cone Shop: You'll seldom have much of a wait for the delicious cones served at the counter of this concession run by Nestlé Ice Cream.

Main Street Lockers: You can rent different sizes of lockers here for $3 a day with unlimited access. Because they are so convenient for storing coats and packages, most of the lockers are taken by noon, which is yet another reason to arrive at Disneyland early.

Hotel Marceline: The hotel façade features sounds made by the pseudo-guests. It is named for Marceline, Mo., the small town where Walt spent his years between 1906 and 1910.

Market House: This store was once an old general store with displays typical of a general store at the beginning of the 20th century. The shelves, counters, chairs, checkerboard, and potbelly stove look like they came straight out of history. There are several old fashioned phones in the store. Pick up one of the receivers; you'll be listening in on a "party line." At the turn of the century, phones weren't available in private households, so people often gathered at the general store to use the phone. Those families who were fortunate to have a

phone usually were connected to a party line they shared with their neighbors. The phones at the market house let you hear what a typical party line conversation sounded like. One tip: don't say anything you don't want someone else to overhear!

Disneyana: This shop opened January 9, 1976, selling only Disney logo merchandise. Eventually it became a haven of limited editions and collectible merchandise in response to the ever-growing demand from collectors of Disneyana.

Author Cecil Munsey coined the term "Disneyana" in 1974. The original Disneyland shop was located in the Emporium, and sold only vintage memorabilia.

Main Street Cinema: The Main Street Cinema was one of the opening day attractions. It plays cartoon films continuously. These historic cartoons change periodically, except for *Steamboat Willie*, which was the debut film for Mickey Mouse. *Steamboat Willie* was released on November 18, 1928. It was the first animated film with synchronized sound. Disney actually made two other Mickey Mouse films before *Steamboat Willie*, but since sound was novel to the motion picture industry, Walt decided to hold the other two films back until he could add sound. Those two films were eventually released as *Plane Crazy* and *Gallopin' Gaucho*.

TREASURE & TRIVIA

There's a bit of irony here as the "silent" movie theater shows Mickey Mouse cartoons. Mickey Mouse cartoons were the first to feature sound.

TREASURE & TRIVIA

Steve Martin worked here before his acting career took off. He spent a lot of time with Disney Legend Wally Boag at the Golden Horseshoe Revue.

HIDDEN MICKEY

The lights that illuminate the steps are the shape of a famous mouse.

New Sounds for a New Century, 20th Century Music Company:

Walt originally intended for this to be a tobacco store with a carved wooden Indian in front. The Native American wears a U.S. coin and his rifle is turned backwards, both symbols of peace. Cast members have named the three wooden Indians in the park. This one is Chief Stands A Lot. In Frontierland you'll find Chief Leans A Lot. Chief Waves A Lot can be seen riding his horse from the Mark Twain Steamboat and the Railroad.

Main Street Magic Shop:
This shop opened in 1957. It is filled with magic tricks, disguises, and costume makeup. Bring the kids! The hosts of the store often put on free magic shows.

Main Street Hotel/Disney Showcase/The Great American Pastime:
Keeping with the turn of the century theme, this store takes a nostalgic look at sports. It is a collector's haven. The walls and shelves are lined with replicas of uniforms worn by past and current sports heroes. Although the name, *The Great American Pastime*, refers to baseball, other sports memorabilia includes autographed trading cards, Michael Jordan basketballs, Mighty Ducks team hockey sticks, and much more.

Yet another fascinating "shop" is the current pin patio. The façade behind this area was built as a temporary construction fence in 1955. It is still in use today.

Mad Hatter Shop:
Here you can buy hats and have your names embroidered on them. The location has been moved around, but this shop has been in the park since 1958.

The Mad Hatter appeared in the animated feature, *Alice In Wonderland*. That "10/6" tag on his hat is the price—10 shillings sixpence. Actor Ed Wynn provided the voice.

Opera House: The Opera House dates back to 1955. It hosts *The Walt Disney Story, featuring Great Moments with Mr. Lincoln* (an exhibit that was built for the 1964-1965 New York World's Fair). This attraction is exclusive to Disneyland. It was moved to Disneyland and opened on the 10th anniversary of the park on July 17, 1965. The technology was updated in 1984 and again in 2001. At its most recent refurbishing (on the 46th anniversary of the park), actor Martin Landau dedicated the opening and read the Gettysburg address while a 14-piece civil war band played "The Battle Hymn of the Republic."

The supplemental exhibits depict the history of Walt Disney and Disneyland. Walt's awards, personal correspondence, and memorabilia are on display, as is a recreation of his offices. The lobby pays tribute to the accomplishments of Walt Disney. In 1973, his actual offices were carefully photographed, dismantled in Burbank, and reassembled in the Opera House. The same papers and projects that Walt was working on at the time of his death are on his desk and in his briefcase. The last script he worked on, *The Happiest Millionaire*, sits on the desk with his notes in the margins. Many of his personal effects are in the room, including his briefcase and photographs.

There are actually two offices here, both imported from the movie studio. The formal office was used for special guests. The baby grand piano was used to play some of the pieces proposed for film and television. Leopold Stokowski previewed some of the music for *Fantasia* there.

The map of Disneyland on the wall is frozen in the year 1966. The aerial photo shows New Orleans Square and Pirates of the Caribbean still under construction. The Haunted Mansion appears in the photo, but sits empty. The window in Walt's office overlooks a backdrop of the Disney Studio. The background through the window is a photograph of the view from his studio office.

As you walked in the main entrance to the Opera House, you may have noticed portraits of Walt and Roy Disney. Roy is Walt's older brother and the co-founder of the Disney Company. Roy provided the financial genius to supplement Walt's creative genius. He managed the growth of licensed consumer products, formed the Buena Vista Distribution Company, and supervised the building of Walt Disney World Florida, a project that cost $400 million dollars in 1971 with no

TREASURE & TRIVIA

Norman Rockwell drew the pencil drawing of Walt's daughters Sharon and Diane that sits behind his desk in the left office.

TREASURE & TRIVIA

On the grand piano is a statue of the mermaid in the Copenhagen Harbor. She symbolizes Walt's interest in the Hans Christian Andersen story that would be made into the Disney classic, *The Little Mermaid*, 20 years after Walt's death.

TREASURE & TRIVIA

On the coffee table in the left office is a small bird in a cage. Walt and Lilly purchased this whistling antique bird while touring Europe in 1948. Fred, Harriet and Wathel studied it carefully to discover how it worked. The mechanisms they uncovered were later developed into Audio-Animatronics.

LESSON TO LEARN

The Original Reuge Singing Birdcages were first invented in 1780 in Switzerland by clockmakers. The birds realistically bob and turn while singing authentic bird songs and are painstakingly feathered by hand. The collector piece is still manufactured today and quite expensive.

TREASURE & TRIVIA

The model airplane in the front left corner of the right-hand office is of Walt's private plane.

debt. (For more information about Roy, see Bob Thomas's excellent biography *Building a Company*.)

After getting your headset and enjoying the pre-show you'll be asked to enter the theater. The theater seats 500 guests, but it wasn't always so opulent. For the first five years of Disneyland, the Opera House was the lumber and sawmill. In 1961, it housed the sets from the movie *Babes in Toyland* as an attraction. In 1962, the television show The Mickey Mouse Club taped science segments here. For a couple of years the building served as a "Mickey Mouse Headquarters" where kids could get autographs from the Mouseketeers.

The Abraham Lincoln in this exhibit was the first human Audio-Animatronics character. A Disney animator once said, "We weren't creating a mechanical man, we were creating the illusion of a man—an illusion of Abraham Lincoln." At the World's Fair a reporter once said "Lincoln looks so real he even perspires" which was true because of a migratory oil on the surface of the skin.

The animated Lincoln was built by Disney for the New York World's Fair because, as Marty Sklar explained, "The World's Fair was a chance to experiment with someone else's money." Imagineers spent more than five months researching Lincoln's exact measurements and appearance. Lincoln stands an accurate 6 ft. 4 in. tall. The museum-quality craftsmanship is based on photos, paintings, and written descriptions. Lincoln's face is molded from actual masks of Abraham Lincoln. One mask dates back to 1860 (without a beard) and the other to 1865. Imagineers even tracked down samples of 1860 cloth for his suit. The black suit, high collar shirt, vest, string tie, and watch chain are his-torically accurate enough to satisfy any museum. Lincoln's hair is tousled and his clothes are wrinkled, just as they may have appeared in Gettysburg after Lincoln's train ride from Washington to be part of the dedication ceremony of the cemetery.

The exhibit was refurbished in 2001. At that time, a new show was created to introduce guests to a Union Soldier who actually met President Lincoln. Lincoln himself gives only his most famous speech, *The Gettysburg Address*. The exhibit also introduces other famous characters, including photographer Matthew Brady and leader Frederick Douglass.

LESSON TO LEARN

Abraham Lincoln (1809-1865) remains perhaps the most respected figure in American history. He was born in a humble, Kentucky log cabin and went on to become the 16th president of the United States. He taught himself to read and write. In 1832, he ran for the Illinois House of Representatives and lost. In 1834, he ran again and was elected, then re-elected three times. He became a licensed attorney during that time and later ran for the U.S. House of Representatives. He became a forceful spokesman against slavery, especially in the debates with Senator Stephen Douglas that earned him national recognition. In 1860, he was elected president of the United States and faced the enormous challenge of the American Civil War almost immediately after he took office. Following the Battle at Gettysburg, he gave a short speech, *The Gettysburg Address*, to honor the men who died in battle. That speech is reproduced in this exhibit. Lincoln was murdered by a disgruntled political opponent before his term expired.

LESSON TO LEARN

One of the noblest speeches and moving expressions in American history is *The Gettysburg Address*. Although the battle at Gettysburg was fought in July 1863, Lincoln did not give his famous address until the dedication of the cemetery at the battle site in November, while the war still raged. According to legend, Lincoln composed the address on the back of a used envelope while he rode the train to Gettysburg.

LESSON TO LEARN

Matthew Brady (1823-1896) was an American photographer noted for photographing more than 3,500 battle sites and soldiers engaged in daily activity during the American Civil War. He was born in Warren County, New York. At his photography studio in New York, he photographed many of the famous people of his time, including Abraham Lincoln. The photos inside the Disneyland Opera Theater are reprints of Brady's photographs.

LESSON TO LEARN

Frederick Douglass (1817-1895) was an African-American abolitionist, orator, and writer. He was born a slave in Tuckahoe, Md., and escaped by moving to Massachusetts. He later encouraged others to escape and assisted the Underground Railroad, one of the most important networks of escape for slaves both before and during the Civil War. He helped recruit black soldiers for the Massachusetts 54th and 55th regiments. Douglass was a symbol of freedom for people of all colors. His intellect and oratory skills were so impressive that his opponents refused to believe he was a former slave. In response, he wrote his biography in 1845, later revising it in 1882 with a new title, *Life and Times of Frederick Douglass*. He held a number of government appointments, including U.S. District Marshall in the District of Columbia.

Bank of Main Street: The bank was once an actual branch of Bank of America and one of the only branch offices to have regular Sunday and holiday hours. It was also one of the longest running institutions at Disneyland. Walt depended on Bank of America for finishing *Snow White and the Seven Dwarfs* and *It's a Small World*. A branch of the Bank of America operated in this building from 1955 until 1993. Today, the "bank" is used for processing annual passes, exchanging foreign currency, selling Disney Dollars, and ATM transactions.

Transportation: All the vehicles on Main Street travel at about 4 mph. Each has its own loading and unloading station for the one-way trips from one end of Main Street to the other. Originally, each ride cost 10 cents or an "A" Coupon. For most visitors, the importance of these vehicles is that they make Main Street complete. National Car Rental, the official rental car agency for Disney Resorts, sponsors all the transportation vehicles on Main Street U.S.A.

Horse-Drawn Streetcars: Inspired by 19th century photographs, the Horse-drawn streetcars take guests on a one way ride along the 1,830-ft. route to either end of Main Street. Designed and built in Burbank, all are original Disneyland rides dating from 1955.

Sixteen horses pull the streetcars. Most are Belgian and Percheron draft horses. Each stands 17 to 18 hands tall and weighs about a ton. The horses work four-hour shifts, four days a week. They are trailered both to and from work. A polyurethane coating on their shoes gives them better traction and adds to the clip-clop sound they make as they walk along Main Street. Look for the ceremonial "D" on each of the harness. It stands, of course, for Disney.

Two cars are in use at any given time. They load and unload passengers simultaneously at opposite ends of Main Street, and each car departs at the same time. From a distance it appears that the cars will collide as they approach each other, but they run over a guided, spring-loaded switch that causes each car to veer right just in time. If one streetcar happens to be delayed along the route, the other will wait at the midpoint for the switching.

Horseless Carriages: These were inspired by turn-of-the-century automobiles. The vehicles appear old and rickety, but they were actually designed that way, the red one in 1955 and the yellow one two years later. Authentic antiques could not have survived the daily demands of Disneyland. Disney enhanced the maintenance, safety, reliability, and seating when he built the cars.

If you have any doubts that these are not original carriages, look carefully. They were built with off-the-shelf parts from the mid 1950s. The Yellow Tonneau has a Jeep rear end, a Model A front end, a 1950 Imperial steering assembly, and brakes from a 1952 Mercury. The two-cylinder engines use a Hercules water pump for realistic shaking, sound, and hood vibration.

TREASURE & TRIVIA

Bob Gurr has readily admitted that, "if it moves on wheels at Disneyland, I probably designed it." Bob Gurr was an Imagineer and Mechanical Designer who started his career in 1954 working on the Autopia cars. His training in automotive design soon evolved to mechanical engineering and attraction development in the critical days prior to the park opening. When he started his career he gave himself the title "Director of Special Vehicle Development." His designs include Autopia cars, Matterhorn Bobsleds, Monorail, Horseless Carriages, "Doom Buggies," and even the parking lot trams. Toward the end of his career he was introduced as the guy who had the same title for 27 years.

Bob Gurr, creator of all Disneyland Gurr-mobiles.

Disneyland Railroad: This original attraction was built in 1955. Walt had a life-long fascination with trains. Their presence in the park is significant. Walt's uncle was an engineer in Missouri for the Missouri Pacific. At the age of 14, Walt took his first job as a news butcher on Missouri Pacific. (A news butcher sold candy, magazines, fruit, cigars, and soft drinks to passengers.) Many people know that Mickey Mouse was created on a train from New York City to Los Angeles. Many others believe that Disneyland was created as a place for Walt to house his trains for others to enjoy.

Two of his key animators, Ward Kimball and Ollie Johnston, were also train hobbyists. Walt consulted both before investing in his trains. He built his own miniature railroad, the Carolwood Pacific, in the backyard of his private home, naming the engine "Lilly Belle" in honor of his wife, Lillian. That was a fair trade— the Carolwood Pacific ran though Lilly's flower garden. Walt even had his lawyer draw up a contract giving him "right of way" through the garden. Walt's model is a one-eighth-scale working miniature patterned after an 1872 diamond-stacked, wood-burning engine, the first steam locomotive built in California. The Carolwood caboose was hand-built. Walt fitted the interior with small bunk beds, clothes lockers, a desk lamp, washstand, magazine rack, and a potbelly stove. The Carolwood Pacific model train may have been the real inspiration for Disneyland. It made its maiden backyard run on May 7, 1950. Roger E. Broggie, Disney Studio Machine Shop Head, directed the engine construction.

TREASURE & TRIVIA

Roger E. Broggie started his career at Disney in 1939 in the Camera Department and later the studio machine shop. Roger's interest in trains gave him the opportunity to engineer the layout for the scale-model train in Walt's backyard and build the Lilly Belle. He led the manufacture of the first two train engines at Disneyland, which are also model trains and the refurbishment of engines three and four. Roger is considered the first Imagineer. He went on to head MAPO and worked on many projects at Disneyland and Walt Disney World. There is no dedication at Disneyland for Roger, but he was celebrated with a window and an engine in Walt Disney World. Roger retired in 1975 and was named a Disney Legend in 1990. Roger died in 1991. His son Michael Broggie wrote the difinitive book of the Disney trains titled Walt Disney's Railroad Story.

LESSON TO LEARN

Walt's fascination with trains inspired another side business. When train enthusiasts learned of Walt's miniature Lilly Belle and potbelly stove, they wanted to own their own as well. Walt built a small barn at his Carolwood home to use as a workshop where he could tinker with the trains and build miniature train parts. On weekends Walt operated his miniature railroad for guests. Walt's idea for Disneyland is thought to have come to him in the barn. The barn still stands, but not at Carolwood. It was moved to Griffith Park's Los Angeles Live Steamers Facility. The barn is open to tour on the third Sunday of each month. For more information about events and barn tours, check out the club's website at www.carolwood.com.

The Main Street Train Station is 270-ft. long, but it uses forced perspective to make it seem even larger. It holds 300 people. There is a collection of pictures of Walt running the Lilly Belle and several of the people responsible for the railroad's creation on the back right wall. In front of the station is a sign that reads 138 feet above sea level and an ever-increasing population, roughly reflecting the number of guests to the park to date. The station originally had a built-in display case for the Lilly Belle. It was located in the diagonal wall where the photos and clock are currently displayed. Note the wainscot running across this section is lower than the rest of the waiting room. It was simply sealed up when the Sante Fe ceased to sponsor the Steam Trains. It is almost certainly true that the original empty display case is still sealed up in the wall.

Until 1981, Retlaw owned the trains and monorails. Retlaw, which is Walter spelled backwards, is one of the Disney family's personal companies. Because the train employees worked for Retlaw, they worked directly for Walt. The employees of attractions owned by Retlaw were therefore on Walt's payroll and issued different checks than the other cast members of the park. For each of these Retlaw attractions, Walt paid for the design and construction out of his own pocket.

The voice saying, "Your attention please. The Disneyland Railroad now arriving from a trip around Walt Disney's Magic Kingdom . . . " is actor Pierre "Pete" Renoudet, a long-time studio employee who could sound perfectly like a droll station master announcing trains.

The railroad tracks were laid along the side of the berm. Each steam engine is either an antique or modeled after one. There are four engines: *E.P. Ripley* and *Fred Gurley* (the ones with the small, narrow smoke stacks), *C.K. Holliday* and the *Ernest S. Marsh* (with tall, wide-mouthed stacks). Powered by oil-fueled boilers, each engine must stop several times a day to take on water. The engineers and firemen on board stoke the fire and keep constant watch on the gauges and water levels.

The train makes a 20-minute loop around the perimeter of the park. There are four stops to board and de-board the train: Main Street U.S.A.,

Engine #1 steams through Frontierland as seen from the Mark Twain. This train is a larger version of the Lilly Belle.

Photo by Dave Hawkins

New Orleans Square, Mickey's Toontown: and Tomorrowland.

For almost 20 years the train was called The *Santa Fe and Disneyland Railroad*. When the *Santa Fe Railroad* ended its passenger train service in the 1970s, *Santa Fe* pulled out of the park. The name of the railroad changed, but the engine names remain the same.

When the park opened, it had only two engines, six passenger cars, a caboose, and freight cars. The price for the railroad was in excess of $240,000 in 1955. Each locomotive cost in excess of $40,000 to build. Walt sometimes engineered the train, unbeknownst to his guests.

Engine No. One, *C.K. Holliday*, was named after Cyrus Kurtz Holliday, the founder of the Atchison, Topeka & Santa Fe Railroad in 1859. The first train to whistle into the Main Street Station was Engine No. Two, *E.P. Ripley*, named for Edward Payson Ripley (1845-1920), an early president of Atchison, Topeka,

Ks., & Santa Fe's after the company was reorganized in 1895. (In Marceline, Mo., the Town Square is named Ripley Park, after the same E.P. Ripley. By coincidence, E.P. Ripley was also a relative of past Disney Chairman, Donn B. Tatum.) Both trains were built in the Walt Disney Studio from scratch under the direction of Roger Broggie just before the park opened in 1954.

Engine No. Three, the *Fred G. Gurley*, was named after the Santa Fe Chairman of the Board in 1958, when the engine became part of the Disneyland fleet. It was originally built by Baldwin Locomotive Works in Philadelphia in 1894. When Disney found it, the engine was being used in Louisiana to transport sugar cane. Walt purchased the engine for $1,500 and spent another $35,000 to refurbish it. Surprisingly the *Holliday* and *Ripley* built at 5/8 scale are larger than the full size 25-ft. 4-in. *Gurley*.

In 1994, the park celebrated the train's

Photo by Dave Hawkins

100th year and added a commemorative plaque on the side of the engine. Special pins were handed out to guests to celebrate the event.

Engine No. Four, *Ernest S. Marsh*, was named in honor of the Santa Fe Railroad president in 1959. This 1925 Baldwin locomotive worked a rock and sand quarry in New Jersey before coming to Disneyland. It hauled sand from the river to receiving yards outside of the small town of Raritan. When Disney ordered the train to be shipped to California, it literally "missed the train" and ended up outside of Pittsburgh. Walt called on friend Ernest Marsh, who quickly solved the problem and got the locomotive back "on track."

TREASURE & TRIVIA

The Kalamazoo handcar near the Train Station was donated to Walt by the Kalamazoo Manufacturing Company in Michigan. Track inspectors and track laborers used handcars like this to commute to their work sites. It was possibly donated to Walt in September 1964 when he visited Donald S. Gilmore of Upjohn Pharmacy.

Grand Canyon Diorama: Riding the train between Tomorrowland and Main Street, you'll see the Grand Canyon Diorama, which was built in 1958. It is the longest diorama in the World. The seamless canvas is 306-ft. long, 34-ft. tall, and covered with 300 gallons of paint. It

Photo by Dave Hawkins

Engine # 4 enters Main Street Station. This train was named for the 1959 Santa Fe Railroad president who found the lost engine and sent it on to Disneyland.

took more than 80,000 hours to build and cost over $367,000, not including the sound system that was added to the trains. The music you hear as you look over the South Rim of the Grand Canyon is "On the Trail," from Ferde Grofe's *Grand Canyon Suite*. At the opening ceremony for the diorama, 96-year-old Hopi Indian Chief Nevangnewa blessed the trains that carried visitors past the diorama.

Walt wanted the train to have a finale, so he asked Claude Coats to tie the project together based on the 1958 Academy Award-winning short subject, *Grand Canyon*. Throughout the rest of the park are artificial animals that sing and move. Here, there are real animals that don't sing and don't move.

Primeval World Diorama: The Primeval World actually debuted at the Ford Pavilion of the New York World's Fair. The diorama was inspired by Stravinsky's "Rite of Spring" featured in the 1940 film, *Fantasia*. Dinosaur enthusiasts can identify the edaphosauruses, brontosaurus, pteranodons, triceratops, ornithomimuses, stegosaurus and tyrannosaurus. It was added to the Disneyland Railroad in 1966.

After the fair, Walt named the three baby brontosaurus figures "Huey, Dewey, and Louie." In New York, the diorama included human figures, but Walt was unimpressed with these primitive Audio-Animatronic humans. He instructed that the cavemen be removed from the scenes. For some time after that, Imagineers found new uses for the figures. The prehistoric heads and hands often appeared in cupboards or desks around the office.

HERE YOU LEAVE TODAY
AND ENTER THE WORLD
OF YESTERDAY, TOMORROW
AND FANTASY

The careful design of the park doesn't reveal Main Street U.S.A. until you cross under the tunnel.

ELIAS DISNEY

CONTRACTOR
EST. 1895

The windows above Main Street U.S.A. are the theme park's version of movie credits. Here is Walt's tribute to his father, who actually worked as a contractor in 1895. A lantern burns eternally for him in the Elias Disney window.

Chapter 3

ABOVE
Main Street

Recreating a turn of the century advertising practice, the second floor windows above Main Street U.S.A. are painted with the names of people and businesses. Although the businesses are fictional, the names are not. They honor people for instrumental efforts in the construction and operation of Disneyland. Some of the "businesses" provide a clue to the personal interests or roles the honorees played. On the day of a window dedication, employees gather minutes before the opening of the park at a ceremony to honor the person receiving the window. Each cast member so honored receives a copy of the window to keep.

The term "Disney Legend" is a separate honor from the window dedication. Beginning in 1987, the Disney Company began honoring individuals who made major contributions to the company over the years by naming them "Legends."

THE LEFT SIDE OF MAIN STREET TO THE REFRESHMENT CENTER

City Hall
J.B. Lindquist, Honorary Mayor of Disneyland: "Jack of all Trades, Master of Fun: Jack was Disneyland's first advertising manager. He began working in this capacity in 1955, though he later took on other marketing positions. In 1971, he became marketing director of both Disneyland and Walt Disney World. In October of 1990, he was named president of Disneyland. This window was dedicated in honor of his retirement in 1993.

Jack Lindquist

He became a Disney Legend the following year. Among his contributions are: the Magic Kingdom Club, Disney Dollars, Grad Nights, and the Ambassador Program. Prior to his Disney career, Jack was an actor who played an extra in

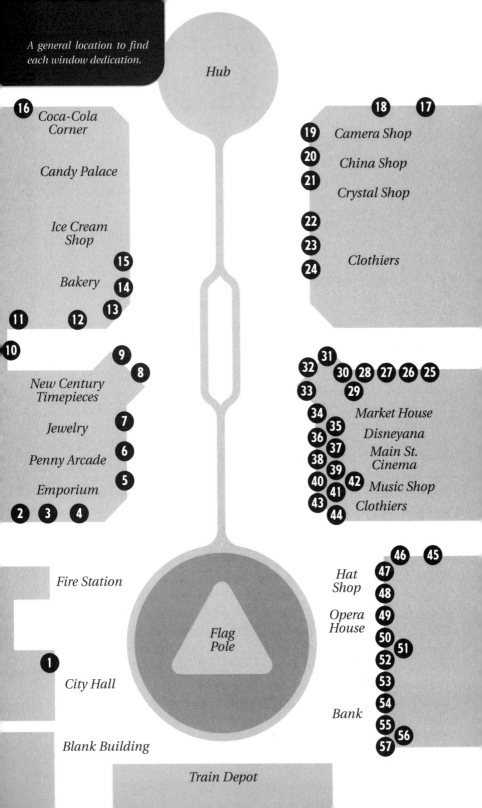

A general location to find each window dedication.

Hub

16 Coca-Cola Corner

Candy Palace

Ice Cream Shop

15
Bakery
14

13

11   12

10

9
8
New Century Timepieces

7
Jewelry

6
Penny Arcade

5
Emporium

2   3   4

18   17

19 Camera Shop

20 China Shop

21 Crystal Shop

22

23

24 Clothiers

31
32   30 28 27 26 25
33   29

34   Market House

36 35 Disneyana
     37 Main St.
38   Cinema
     39
40   42 Music Shop
   41
43   Clothiers
  44

Fire Station

Flag Pole

46   45

47
Hat Shop
48

49
Opera House
50
     51
52

53

54
Bank
55
   56
57

1

City Hall

Blank Building

Train Depot

Disneyland Credit Directory

1 JB Lindquist
2 Harriet Burns
3 Charles Boyer
4 Claude Coats
5 Elias Disney
6 Wathel Rogers
7 Mary Anne Mang
8 Dr. Patterson
  Dr. Allen
9 Dr. Gilmore
  Dr. Upjohn
10 Christopher Miller
11 Fred Joerger
12 Ed Winger
13 Renie Conley
14 Royal Clark
15 Wally Boag
16 Bob Penfield
17 Alexander Irvine
18 Herb Ryman
  John Hench
  Peter Ellenshaw
19 Renie Bardeau
20 Cicely Rigdon
21 Edward Meck
22 C. Randy Bright
23 H. Draegart Barnard
24 Jim Cora
25 W.H. Dennis Cottrell
26 Orlando Ferrante
27 Jack Rorex
  Ivan Martin
  Cash Shockey
28 Robert Wisky
29 Seb Morey
30 George Whitney

31 Chuck Boyajian
32 Emile Kuri
33 Ron Dominguez
34 George Mills
  Ray Conway
  Charles Alexander
35 L.H. Roth
36 Ken Anderson
37 Bruce Bushman
38 Don DaGradi
39 Gordon Youngman
  Leopold
40 Gunther Lessing
41 Marc Davis
42 Van France
43 Hideo Amemiya
44 Dick Nunis
45 John Louis Catone
46 Ray Van De Warker
47 X Atencio
48 Milt Albright
49 Blaine Gibson
50 Bill Evans
51 Main Street Elec.
  Parade, Robert Jani
52 Wade Rubottom
  George Patrick
53 Gabriel Scognamillo
  Wilson "Bill" Martin
54 Richard Irvine
  Marvin Davis
55 Frank Wells
56 J.S. Hamel
57 William Wheeler
  John Wise

Our Gang as a child, and a dancer in *Best Foot Forward* with Lucille Ball.

Blank Building
The Artisans Loft; Handmade Miniatures by Harriet Burns: Harriet started her career with Disney working on the sets and props for the Mouseketeer Television show in 1955. Walt told her that since the television show didn't shoot all the time, would she help work on Disneyland. Harriet was the first and only woman to work in WED (Imagineering) for quite some time. She worked in the model shop, which did more than just make models. Once an attraction has designed on paper, Harriet would make a 3D miniature model of the façade and every room. From the model the life-size features of the attraction were built. Sculpting, casting, and painting, dressing were the normal part of her day. Harriet worked with paint, clay, ink, wood, chemicals, fabric, feathers, makeup, blowtorches, power tools and whatever else she could find. She affectionately calls Imagineering the Oddball/Screwball Department because of the variety of things Walt would ask her to do. Harriet worked on virtually all of the early attractions, such as Matterhorn, Submarine Ride, Tiki Room, Lincoln, It's a Small World and Pirates of the Caribbean. Sometimes she was asked to help with movie or television props or effects like in the film *Darby O'Gill and the Little People, Babes in Toyland, and Shaggy DA*. Thanks to Harriet, and her 31-year career, the fantasy is a little more believable. Each tiki bird breathes naturally, the human Audio-Animatronics have realistic-looking skin, and the pirates have hairy faces, arms and legs.

Harriet Burns worked in the model shop and was the first female Imagineer.

Partners Portrait Gallery
Charles Boyer, Master Illustrator: Charles received his window on July 17, 1999. He is best known for his Norman Rockwell-type triple self-portrait. He started in 1960 as a portrait sketch artist and was soon transferred to marketing. He retired from the park 39 years later after creating nearly 50 collectible lithographs as well as artwork for magazine covers, flyers, in-park packaging, merchandise, and corporate-sponsored oil portraits for retiring employees.

Charles has created over 50 collectible lithographs that are very popular with the Disneyana collectors.

Emporium

Coats & Co., Claude Coats Proprietor: Big and Tall Sizes for Gentlemen: Claude was one of the few Disney employees to receive a 50-year service award. His career with Disney lasted 54 years. He began in 1935 as a background painter on *Snow White and the Seven Dwarves*. He later contributed to *Fantasia, Dumbo, Saludos Amigos, Make Mine Music, Lady and the Tramp, Cinderella,* and *Peter Pan*. He transferred to WED Enterprises in 1955, where he helped design Pirates of the Caribbean, Haunted Mansion, Submarine Voyage, dioramas, and many of the attractions at

Claude's window makes reference to his height as Claude stood 6 feet 6 inches. Walt often teased him that he was out-of-scale next to some of the attractions.

Walt Disney World. Claude became an early black-light expert, painting the backgrounds for Mr. Toad's Wild Ride, Snow White Scary Adventures, Peter Pan, and the Alice in Wonderland dark rides. He painted the Grand Canyon diorama as well as several three-dimensional constructions and models. Coats retired in 1989 and became a Disney Legend two years later. He passed away in 1992.

Elias Disney, Contractor, Est. 1895: Elias was the father of Roy and Walt. Born in Bluevale, Ontario, Canada, on February 6, 1859, Elias married Flora Call in Steuben, Ohio. Together they

Elias Disney

had several children. Elias actually opened a Chicago contracting office in 1895. He tried many occupations, including building contracting, farming, running a newspaper delivery business, and working in a jelly factory. He died in September 1941. Although he never saw Disneyland, the lamp in his window is always lit in his honor.

New Century Jewelry

"You'll cut a Fine Figure" Menswear, Wathel Rogers: Wathel began his career in 1939 in the animation department. He helped animate all the features between *Pinocchio* to *Sleeping Beauty* and created props and miniatures for some of Walt Disney's other films and television shows, including the Mickey Mouse Club. In 1954, he was one of the three original members of the WED Model Shop, where he helped build architectural models of Disneyland. He was a major contributor to the development of

Audio-Animatronics, and over the years, he participated in all the processes associated with Audio Animatronics. He manufactured, programmed, and developed the system controls for Lincoln, Tiki Room, Pirates of the Caribbean, and Haunted Mansion, often completely covering himself with machinery to record his movements (which may explain why his window refers to men's wear and cutting a fine figure). He appeared with Walt in a television program introducing Audio-Animatronics. He retired in 1987 and became a Disney Legend in 1995. Wathel died August 25, 2000, in Sedona, Ariz.

Wathel Rogers started the model shop at WED and was instrumental in perfecting Audio-Animatronics.

Good Neighbor Foundation, "Caring and Giving Come From the Heart"; Mrs. M.A. Mang, Director: Even in her youth in Des Moines, Iowa, Mary Anne loved Disney and would often draw the characters. In 1960, she moved to California and wrote a letter to Walt Disney requesting a job. Writing the letter wasn't so unusual as Walt Disney received a lot of letters, but Mary Anne's letter was so special that she was offered a position in sales promotion at the Disneyland Hotel. In May 1961, she moved over to the park as a Convention & Tour sales administrator. In 1972, she was the first woman promoted to manager. As the public relations manager, she hosted kings, queens, presidents, emperors, celebrities, shahs, and other special guests to the park. Her window "Good Neighbor Foundation" refers to her role in making Disneyland a strong community supporter. Mary Anne has said that this was the most meaningful aspect of her position. Walt Disney was clear about being

Mary Anne Mang stands in front of her favorite Disneyland place, the Partners Statue.

involved with the community and giving something back and making community relations the focal point of Disney's public relations. The "caring and giving come from the heart" reference is fitting of Mary Anne's heartfelt compassion and devotion. Imagineers did something a little different with her window name. Staying consistent with the era of early 1900s women were never allowed to have their first name in print. Just a little leeway was given by using her initials M.A. Thankfully Imagineers discontinued this practice of not using women's first names. Mary Anne was honored with the window dedication when she retired in July of 1994.

New Century Timepieces/Clocks

C.V. Patterson, M.D., W.F. Allen, M.D.: This window is a set along with D.S. Gilmore and E.G. Upjohn. When the park opened there was an authentic turn-of-the-century store on Main Street called Upjohn Pharmacy. Historians at the Upjohn Company designed the late 19th century drugstore. Over 1,000 antiques were used to reproduce the store accurately. In 1970, the museum-type store was removed. C.V. Patterson started his career at Upjohn Company as a traveling sales representative

C.V. Patterson

and worked his way up to vice-president over the next 26 years. It is most likely that he was involved with the decision-making process of building the pharmacy in Disneyland.

W. Fred Allen also started his career with Upjohn Company as a sales representative after becoming a registered pharmacist. He took promotions to sales management, marketing, director of sales, director of marketing, vice president, and eventually member-of-the-board. His career lasted 44 years, and he died in December 1975.

W.F. Allen

D.S. Gilmore, M.D., E.G. Upjohn, M.D.: Walt Disney was a good friend with Donald S. Gilmore, the Chairman of the Board and Managing Director of Upjohn Company, a pharmaceutical company founded in 1885 by Dr. W.E. Upjohn and his older brother Dr. Henry Upjohn. The Gilmores were part-time neighbors to Walt Disney at Smoke Tree Ranch, which explains his association and participation in Disneyland. Donald Gilmore attended Yale, but was never a medical doctor. He received an honorary doctor of law degree from Kalamazoo College in 1956. Gilmore was both a son-in-law and stepson of W.E. Upjohn, the entrepreneurial and inspirational leader of the Upjohn Company. The company has since been bought out by Pharmacia and Pfizer. Although Donald Gilmore lacked medical training, he became a dominating force at Upjohn and with the guidance of Dr. Lawrence Upjohn; the son of Dr. Henry Upjohn and president and chairman of the company; Donald foresaw the contribution of research in the pharmaceutical industry. Under his direction during World War II, the company increased production of penicillin and heparin, which saved thousands of lives and kept the company from going bankrupt as over 3,500 other drug companies did. His greatest success and risk came in the early 1950s by committing to a major investment in the development of hydrocortisone and other steroid drugs. Donald Gilmore was a generous and enthusiastic supporter of the arts. His involvement with Walt would explain the generous donation by Disney to the Kalamazoo Art Center for some Chinese Art Objects. Just days after Walt Disney died, the Gilmore Art Center in Kalamazoo established a Walt Disney Children's Scholarship Fund.

Donald S. Gilmore was a good friend and neighbor to the Disneys.

Dr. E. Gifford Upjohn, the son of Dr. Lawrence Upjohn and grandson of co-founder Dr. Henry Upjohn, was the chairman and president of Upjohn Pharmaceuticals during the 1950s and 1960s. He had brought back news from a medical meeting that patients receiving cortisone for arthritis were throwing their *E. Gifford Upjohn* crutches away. This led to the investment in steroid research. He had gone to college and medical school at the University of Michigan, so he was well prepared to establish medical liaisons with practicing doctors and to arrange clinical testing of new product candidates. Dr. Upjohn had many business successes, including taking the company into international markets, but was equally philanthropic, serving on a myriad of foundations, boards, and National Associations. He was president of the National Vitamin Foundation, which may explain the distribution of vitamins at the Upjohn Pharmacy at Disneyland. He was born in Kalamazoo, MI., in October of 1904 and died there December 20, 1993.

Carnation Café

Christopher D. Miller, Massage Parlor: Walt was a very proud grandfather. Christopher is Walt's first grandson, the son of Ron Miller and Diane Disney Miller. A professional athlete at the time of Christopher's birth, Ron later became president of Walt Disney Productions. Diane and Ron had seven children altogether. Chris worked as an assistant director at Walt Disney Productions.

Decorative Fountains and Waterworks Fred Joerger:

Fred was a model maker and designer whose contributions include Storybook Land and the Matterhorn. He also worked on a number of the waterways in the park. As art director, he was known for special finishes, such as distressed timbers and faux rocks. Joerger became a Disney legend during the celebration of Walt Disney's 100th birthday in December 2001.

Fred was one of the initial people to work in the model shop.

Blue Ribbon Bakery

Milady Fashions Renie: Dressmaking, Hemstitching & Picating: Renie Conley was the original costume designer for Disneyland. Today, there are more than 12,000 costumes for both cast members and Audio-Animatronic figures.

Old Settler's Gold Dredging: Ed Winger, Proprietor:

Ed was Supervisor for the Paint Department, Mill, and Sign Shop. He modeled for the moonshiner who once sat in front of the burnt cabin on Tom Sawyer Island. Ed was a member of the 55 Club, working for Disney during its opening in 1955.

United Audit: Bookkeeping, Accounts, Audit, Royal Clark, Mgr.:

Royal "Mickey" Clark is a younger brother to Les Clark, one of Walt's "Nine Old Men" (see page 56). Royal was born in 1918, the seventh of 12 children and named Mickey by a toddler sister who couldn't pronounce his name. A popular song of the time served as her inspiration, 10 years before the famous mouse was created. Mickey Clark started with Disney in 1941 in the shipping and receiving department. He went onto the mailroom, the camera department and joined the service during WWII. After

Royal "Mickey" Clark

the war he returned to Disney in accounting and entered accounting management. In 1952, he joined WED with key people like Bill Cottrell and Dick Irvine. Mickey worked his way up to executive vice president of Retlaw, and WED Enterprises. He also served as Walt Disney's personal family accountant. Mickey retired in June of 1984 after 43 years of service.

Theatrical Agency: Golden Vaudeville Routines, Wally Boag, Prop.: Wally Boag is best known for his Comic Traveling Salesman and Pecos Bill characters in the Golden Horseshoe Revue. Before joining Disney, he played vaudeville for 20 years throughout the United States, Europe and Australia. Signed by "Uncle Walt" two weeks before the Park opened in 1955, he retired 27 years later in 1982. These shows earned him a place in the *Guinness Book of World Records* for the most performances of a show. He also voiced "Jose" the parrot in the Enchanted Tiki Room, stunt-doubled for Fred MacMurray in both *The Absent-Minded Professor* and *Son of Flubber*, and had cameos in other Disney movies including *The Love Bug*. Additionally, he wrote portions of Enchanted Tiki

Legendary Wally Boag, a former entertainer at the Golden Horseshoe.

Room and the Haunted House. He became a Disney Legend in 1995.

Candy Palace ABC Typing, Acme Business College, ABC Shorthand: In 1954, the American Broadcast Company (ABC) Television Network invested $500,000 and guaranteed loans for an additional $4.5 million to build Disneyland in exchange for a one-third ownership of Disneyland. In return, Walt Disney agreed to produce four weekly television series for ABC; The True Life Show, The World of Tomorrow, The Mickey Mouse Club, and The Walt Disney Show. Walt and ABC promoted Disneyland on the shows during the construction, introducing the park to thousands of people before the gates even opened.

On opening day, July 17, 1955, ABC produced a live television broadcast featuring the grand opening of the park. Walt's contract with ABC lasted until 1961, when the Walt Disney Company bought out ABC's park investment for about $7.5 million. Ironically, in 1995 ABC merged with The Walt Disney Company to make Disney Enterprises, Inc.

Coca-Cola Refreshment Center Club 55 School of Golf, Bob Penfield, Instructor: Bob Penfield was the last of the original Disneyland opening day cast members to retire. He retired on July 31, 1997, after more than 42

years of service. Bob was honored with a window to commemorate this event. The window placement has a lot to do with a television show that centered on his retirement. Publicity placed the value at $2 million in advertising. Another

Photo courtesy of of Bob Penfield.

Bob Penfield leads the Club 55 members to their annual golf tournament.

interesting fact is that WED Imagineering named the building front for Bob and gave him an original painting by Kim Irvine.

Bob started his career in operations, and transferred to the Maintenance Division in 1966 (now called Facilities). He finished his career as a supervisor in Project Management working on construction, rehabilitation, etc. Club 55 refers to the cast members who started their career in 1955, of which Bob is a member. In 1990, Bob helped develop an annual golf tournament for Club 55 members.

TREASURE & TRIVIA

Club 55 is a group made up of people who started at Disneyland in 1955. One of the rarest Disneyland items is a 15-year service pin distributed to Club 55 Members. A little bar that says "Charter" hangs from the pin.

ACROSS THE STREET AND BACK TOWARD THE TRAIN STATION

Disneyland Baby Center

Alexander R. Irvine, M.D.: Alexander Irvine is an ophthalmologist and father of Richard F. Irvine (See the Bank of Main Street window).

Main Street Photo Supply Company

Plaza School of Art: Instructors: Herbert Ryman, John Hench, Peter Ellenshaw: In 1938, Walt Disney convinced Herb Ryman to join Disney Studios. He left the studio for a period, but returned in 1953 to draw the original concepts of Disneyland. He became the illustrator of what had been, until then, only a dream in Walt's mind. Roy Disney used Ryman's illustrations to help convince investors to buy into the project. Ryman designed Sleeping Beauty Castle and worked on a number of other projects for Imagineering. He retired in 1971, but continued consulting for Disney on plans for Euro Disneyland until his death in 1989.

In 1990, he was named a Disney Legend. Herb Ryman was a mentor to many Disney artists. The Ryman foundation supports art students, making the window dedication all the more fitting. His biography, *A Brush with Disney,* includes many of the beautiful drawings that reflect his diversity of style. (See Sleeping Beauty Castle for more about Herb Ryman).

Legend Herb Ryman was a mentor to many Disney artists.

John Hench started his career in the Disney Story Development in 1939, contributing to the atmosphere, mood, color, and lighting of Disney projects. He painted the background for *Nutcracker Suite* in *Fantasia* and worked on *Cinderella* and *Alice in Wonderland.* In 1955, he transferred to WED Enterprises to work on Tomorrowland and later

Senior vice president of Walt Disney Ima-gineering, John Hench is the only person to work full time for Disney for over 50 years.

Snow White Grotto and the Monorail. In 1972, he became executive vice president of WED. Hench has been involved in the creative development of every Disney Theme Park. He painted the company's official portraits of Mickey Mouse for his 25th, 50th and 60th birthdays. Hench so resembled his employer, especially when he wore a hat during the 1960s, that he was occasionally confused for Walt Disney. In 1990, he was named a Disney Legend. In 1999, he celebrated his 60th year with the company as the master artist and senior vice president of Walt Disney Imagineering. John was known to the Imagineers as the resident color expert. John died February 4, 2004.

Peter Ellenshaw won an Oscar for special effects on the film Mary Poppins.

British born, Peter Ellenshaw was first asked by Walt Disney to paint the mattes for *Treasure Island* in the late 1940s. Matte paintings create scenes for films that would be too expensive or impossible to recreate on sound stages; they are usually seen as backgrounds. Ellenshaw has worked on numerous Disney live-action films such as *20,000 Leagues Under the Sea, Darby O' Gill and* the Little People, *Pollyanna, Swiss Family Robinson* and many other recognizable titles. While Disneyland was in the planning stages, Walt asked Peter to create a concept painting showing the entire park as envisioned. He painted a spectacular 4-ft. x 8-ft. aerial view which, on occasion is on display at the Disney Gallery. Peter has received an Oscar for Special Visual Effects in *Mary Poppins* and was nominated four other times for production design and visual effects. In 1993, he joined the prestigious ranks of Disney Legends. His autobiography, *The Garden Within*, contains a beautiful collection of his landscape art. Many admirers find his work so breathtaking that it can easily be confused with a photograph. He continues to travel the world for inspiration, painting nearly every day of his life.

Kingdom Photo Services
The Magic Eye to the World— Renie Bardeau: For more than three decades, Renie Bardeau was the official photographer for Disneyland. His works include many pictures of Walt Disney in Disneyland, including

Renie was the official photographer for Disneyland for more than 30 years.

a famous shot of Walt walking through the arch of the castle.

China Closet
The Disneyland News; Edward T. Meck, Editor-in-Chief In 1919, Edward Meck began his career in the entertainment industry at Pathé News Service in Chicago in the publicity and promotion department. In 1922, he transferred to the San Francisco Pathé Office where he became acquainted with two very influential men in the entertainment field—Lloyd Pantages and his son, Rodney Pantages. They remained close friends and business associates throughout his whole life.

In 1930, he came to Hollywood and joined the Publicity Department of Columbia Studio where he rose to the position of publicity director. While at Columbia, he was a key factor in the promotion and success of Harold Lloyd films, Frank Capra films, e.g. *It Happened One Night* and *Mr. Deeds Goes to Town*, the *Our Gang* series, and Three Stooges films. In 1940, Eddie Meck became Director of Publicity for RKO. Although he worked out of his offices in the RKO and Pantages Theaters, he was responsible for promoting the movies distributed to all the RKO theaters that were released from the RKO, Samuel Goldwyn, Universal International and Disney Studios.

During Word War II, Ed Meck was a member of the United States

Government's War Activities Committee Motion Picture Industry. The Secretary of the Treasury Department in 1945 awarded him a citation in recognition of his outstanding service on behalf of the War Finance Service. He organized and promoted events with Hollywood stars and celebrities to sell war bonds that helped finance the war.

Ed Meck was successful in any and everything he did. He was especially known for being personable, having creative ideas, being sincere and honest with a "soft sell" approach. He was loved and respected by members of the press from all over the United States, as well as the celebrities in the film industry.

In 1954, Walt Disney asked Ed Meck to help him promote a new Disney venture—Disneyland. Ed was the twentieth employee hired for Disneyland. Since Disneyland was at that time a muddy field and a few remaining orange groves, Ed sold Disneyland to the members of the press across the country with artists' renderings and drawings of the different "Lands" and rides on positive-negative stills. Opening day was a great success with a sell-out crowd, but also a major challenge for the Operations Department. Thanks to the efforts of Ed Meck, the park was filled with members of the press and Hollywood's "A List."

His office and staff were housed

in the City Hall on Main Street—about two minutes from the entrance turnstiles. Ed always greeted members of the press and celebrities visiting Disneyland with a special welcome and his personal attention during their visits. Throughout his career in publiciz-

Photo used with permission of Mary Agnes Meck.

Walt hired Edward T. Meck because he was the best publicist in Hollywood in the 1930s and 1940s. Walt needed his help to promote Disneyland while it was still in conceptual form.

ing both movies and Disneyland, Ed was always successful in getting the writers of both magazines and newspapers to write personal accounts and/or stories about their ideas or experiences. The special stories had unique interest and were far better promoters for what Ed Meck wanted the readers to know about Disneyland. He did not believe that paid advertising reaped the same results as a story with the personal touch.

During his years at Disneyland, Ed had access to Ear Force One (the Disney company plane), and he sent it all over the United States to pick up members of the press and their wives or husbands for a week at Disneyland and the Disneyland Hotel. Ed Meck retired from Disneyland in 1972, just after organizing the Publicity Department at Walt Disney World. He died a year later. He was named a Disney Legend posthumously in 1995. His daughter and three sons received the honor in his name. His window on Main Street refers to Disneyland News. This is a tribute to his work with the press and his efforts in generating news about Disneyland. It should not be confused with what is known as the *Disney News Magazine*, which was not started until the 1960s. Ed Meck's Disneyland News window was dedicated and presented to him at his retirement dinner in 1972.

Disney Clothiers LTD

Photographic Studio: C. Randy Bright, Proprietor. Photographic Studio, Bright Views to Order: C. Randy Bright began his Disney career as an attractions host, in the early days dressing up as an astro-naut in Tomorrowland. He also worked at the Monorail and Columbia Sailing Ship. Eventually he became vice president of Concept Development at Walt Disney Imagineering. Bright was instrumental in developing the simulator ride for Star Tours. His favorite hobby was photography.

Real Estate—Houses Bought and Sold, H. Draegart Barnard: Walt's early window dedications went to people he wanted to honor. H. Draegart Barnard was Walt's ear, nose, and throat specialist. Walt was a heavy smoker and probably sought out Dr. Barnard's services often as they developed a relationship that was window-worthy.

Global Exports and Expats. Specializing in Land and Sea Operations. Our motto: The sun never sets on our Magical Kingdoms. Jim Cora, Master Operator: This window was dedicated on April 26, 2002. With this ceremony, Jim Cora is the only person to have a window in each of Disney's Magic Kingdom parks. Jim started his career with Disney in 1957 as an hourly cast member polishing 3D glasses for the Mickey Mouse Theater in Fantasyland. At a chance meeting with Walt, Jim shared some of his story ideas for the Matterhorn attraction. Walt was impressed with Jim's initiative and suggested he meet Van France. At this meeting, Van liked Jim's ideas and began mentoring him and four other young cast members to be part of a new training concept. Jim continued to prove himself in the training field and rose through the managerial ranks. In the late 1960s/early 1970s, he passed on a transfer to Florida, but assisted in the training of the opening crew for the Magic Kingdom and hotels in Walt Disney World. In 1979, he accepted a promotion as managing director of operations for Tokyo Disneyland, believing the position would be temporary. His responsibility was to train and develop the staff for the opening of Tokyo Disneyland. He was allowed to choose an out-of-the-way office whereever he liked while in California, so he brilliantly chose the recently vacated apartment in New Orleans Square that was built for Walt and Roy, but never occupied by them. Today, the office is the Disney Gallery. There and overseas he worked closely with the Oriental Land Company's (OLC) nine executives and 95 other OLC staff. In 1982, he was promoted to vice president, Walt Disney Productions Japan and relocated full-time to Tokyo. After Tokyo Disneyland was opened and running, Jim returned to the U.S. with no new position and new management in place as Michael Eisner and Frank Wells were just brought in. In his first meeting with Michael and Frank he created his own position and was given the go ahead to move forward with the Euro Disney

project. For the next decade, Jim and his team worked on the master planning and site research for Disneyland Paris and eventually became the executive vice-president and chief operating officer of Disneyland Paris. With Disneyland Paris open and running, the Japanese were reluctant to sign the contracts for the second Disney Park. Jim approached Frank Wells who was negotiating with OLC and promised the contract would be signed in three weeks. Frank commented that he'd be surprised if it was signed in three years, but Jim stood fast. Frank Wells tragically died during that three-week period, but Jim held true and met the deadline anyway. Jim was named president of Disneyland International with responsibility for development and creative direction of Tokyo Disneyland and Tokyo DisneySea. Jim was promoted to chairman of Disneyland International in 1999 and retired in 2001 after 43 years of service. Jim is involved in volunteer work with St. Joseph Hospital, the Special Olympics, and other worthy causes. The window, Exports and Expats, is a tease to signify his expatriate work overseas, although Jim kindly detests the word Expats. The term is used for anyone who works outside of his or her home country. He challenges that his patriotism was always intact. The Land and Sea reference is simply for Disneyland (California, Florida, Tokyo and Paris) and

Disney Sea (Tokyo).

Jim Cora, the only person to have a window in each of the four Magic Kingdom parks.

Hotel Marceline

This small façade is Walt Disney's tribute to his hometown of Marceline Mo. Main Street was modeled after a turn-of-the-century Marceline as Walt lived there in 1906. Times were tough for the Disney family as Elias struggled to make ends meet, but Marceline became the source of Walt's happiest memories. Marceline is where Walt began to draw. Listen carefully you can sometimes hear conversations of the fictitious hotel guests.

Market House

W.H. Dennis "Bill" Cottrell, Detective Agency, Private Investigator. "We Never Sleep": Bill Cottrell was president of Retlaw Enterprises from 1964 until his retirement in 1982. He was the first person to receive a 50-year Disney Service award. He began his Disney career in 1929 as cameraman, then he worked as a cutter and animation director before moving into the story department. He was the sequence director for *Snow White and the Seven Dwarfs*, and he worked on *Pinocchio, Saludos Amigos, Victory Through Air Power, The Three Caballeros, Melody Time, Alice in Wonderland*, as well as *Peter Pan*. In 1952, he became vice president/treasurer of Retlaw. Since Walt was the president, Bill was referred to as "assistant to the president." He later became president of WED Enterprises. He assisted Walt in the planning and construction of Disneyland. Bill was named a Disney Legend, a year before his death in 1994. Bill was a collector of Sherlock Holmes memorabilia, which is why he is honored as a detective on the window. He was also Walt's brother-in-law and a close friend. Walt once brought him a deer-stalker hat on a trip from England. On another trip Walt bought him a pipe.

Bill Cottrell was the first employee to reach the 50 years of service mark. He helped form and manage WED and Retlaw, Walt's personal companies.

The Pico Organization Installation and Coordination of World Class Projects. "We never sleep in *any* time zone." Orlando Ferrante

Founder: Before joining the Walt Disney Company Orlando had a successful football career earning a full football scholarship to USC where he earned a bachelor's of business administration. He served two years in the U.S. Navy and then played professional football as an offensive guard for the Los Angeles Rams and San Diego Chargers in 1960-1961. By 1962, Orlando joined his former USC teammates Dick Nunis and Ron Miller at WED Enterprises.

His first project was to serve as expeditor on the Enchanted Tiki Room. He was responsible for overseeing the installation of the first Audio-Animatronic attraction. Five years later, he was responsible for relocating and installing the Disney attractions from the 1964-1965 New York World's Fair to California. At that time he created a new department called Project Installation Coordinating Office (PICO), which is referenced in his window. He went on to oversee the installation *of* Haunted Mansion, Pirates of the Caribbean and the Walt Disney World Project in Florida.

Orlando was named general manager of administration in 1972 and then vice president of administration and production overseeing Imagineering. In 1979, he served as vice president of manufacturing and production followed by vice president of engineering and production. In 1990, he moved to France to manage the installation of Disneyland Paris. Later, he oversaw the building of Tokyo DisneySea which opened in 2001. Before he retired, he moved to Italy to help launch the second Disney Cruise Line ship in 2002. Since he has worked all over the world, his window makes reference to "world class projects" and "any time zone." Orlando was given his window dedication upon retirement after 40 years on March 18, 2003, and named a Disney Legend later the same year.

Buena Vista Construction Co:

Jack Rorex, Ivan Martin, Cash Shockey: Jack Rorex was in charge of studio construction. Ivan Martin was a prop maker who worked for Jack Rorex. Cash Shockey was in charge of the Disney Studio's Paint Department. Cash worked at the studio before helping out at the park. His department would paint the base coats before the artists would add the special touches. He died in July of 1982. Harriet Burns is known for winning over Cash with homemade gingersnaps on his birthday. At the time of press no other information could be found on Ivan Martin or Cash Shockey.

Seb Morey, Taxidermist: Seb Morey was the original taxidermist for Disneyland. He was kept very busy by the Jungle Cruise and Grand Canyon diorama.

Robert Wisky, Stone Mason: Robert "Bud" Wisky did concrete and plaster work as head of the Staff Shop. Later he became

Disneyland's building manager. Once, when the park was under construction, Walt saw a huge pile of cement under a tarpaulin. "What's all this?" he asked. Bud explained that the buildings were unlike movie sets because they had to be built to withstand millions of guests. Walt was afraid that all his money was being wasted underground and no funds would be left for the structures above the foundation.

Geo. Whitney, Guns: George was the only member of the original Disneyland design team who had ever previously worked for an amusement park. Later in his career, he became the manager of Fantasyland, but he started out by designing the original Shooting Galleries in Frontierland. This, and his private gun collection, explains the window's reference.

Royal Care Co. "We Keep Your Castle Shining." Chuck Boyajian, Prop.: Chuck was the superintendent of Disneyland's first janitorial department.

Emile Kuri, Interior Design: Emile joined Disney in 1952 as his head decorator. He won two Oscars in his lifetime; one for his work on *20,000 Leagues Under the Sea* and another for *The Heiress*, a non-Disney film. He also won an Emmy for *Walt Disney's Wonderful World of Color.* He supervised the set decoration on *Mary Poppins*, *Bedknobs And Broomsticks*, and the *Absent-Minded Professor.* He was the primary decorator for Main Street U.S.A., the Sailing Ship Columbia, and New Orleans Plaza Inn. He helped decorate company executive offices and the Disney apartment over the fire station, and he contributed to the 1964 World's Fair projects. Kuri died in October 2000.

Orange Grove Property Mgt.

"We'll Care For Your Property As If It Were Our Own." Ron Dominguez, Owner: Ron started his career four days before opening day as a Ticket Taker at the Main Gate. Two weeks later, he transferred to the railroad and within the first year he was trained on every attraction. At one point he was dressed up as Davy Crockett on the Keel Boats, but he wasn't fond of constantly having his picture taken in the height of the Davy Crockett craze. His experience of working all over the park later proved helpful as it gave him a better understanding of the park's operations and the many people who ran it. He became

Ron Dominguez grew up surrounded by the orange groves that later became Disneyland.

Assistant Supervisor and later Supervisor of Adventureland, Frontierland and Tomorrowland. By 1971, Ron was promoted to director of operations and later vice-president of Disneyland and Chairman of the Park Operating Committee. Like many of his colleagues, Ron worked when everyone else (guests) played. One characteristic that made Ron stand out was his people skills. He made an effort, no matter how busy, to know his staff personally, always take time to listen, treat them well, and give them acknowledgement. In 1990, his managerial style and proven track record ascended him to the ranks of executive vice president of Walt Disney Attractions - West Coast.

Ron's window is a special tribute because his family was one of the 17 who sold their property to Walt Disney in 1953 to build Disneyland. Ron grew up in a house which was between the current site of Pirates of the Caribbean and Café Orleans. His family was the last to leave the property, because their new home wasn't ready until August of 1954. Keep in mind that this was a month after construction of Disneyland began and the entire park was built in only one year. The Dominguez home was later moved and joined to another to become the first Disneyland Administration building. It has since been replaced by a more functional building.

Ron was rewarded with his window upon retirement in August of 1994. What started as a summer job at Disneyland lasted 39 years. Ron was named a Disney Legend in 2000. Due to his approachable style, he is still well recognized by former cast members and keeps in touch with many of his former Disney colleagues.

Carpenters and Joiners; George Mills, Ray Conway, Charles Alexander: Not a lot is known about George, Ray and Charles, although George Mills ran the mill. Ray Conway was in charge of construction. Charles Alexander was the field supervisor for the Disneyland Construction Department.

Surveying & Engineering—L.H. Roth: L.H Roth helped in the construction of buildings and attractions. He was an assistant to Admiral Joe Fowler (see Fowler Harbor in Frontierland).

Ken Anderson Bait Co.: Architect Ken Anderson began his Disney career in 1934 as an artist. He was art director for *Snow White and the Seven Dwarfs*; developed character designs for Shere Khan in *Jungle Book* and Elliott in *Pete's Dragon*; was production designer on *Sleeping Beauty, 101 Dalmatians, The Aristocats*; and designed several areas of Disneyland, including much of Fantasyland and the Storybook Land Canal Boats. In the early stages of park development, Ken was on Walt's personal payroll and sketched ideas solely for Walt. He is one of the first Imagineers. In 1949, he accepted a project from Roger Broggie (see Main Street) to develop a new form of dimensional animation, a miniature "dancing man." He developed a prototype that moved by metal cams located beneath the figure. Many years later, this original concept evolved to become Audio-Animatronics. The window is a backhanded gag—Ken was an avid fly-caster and Walt found fly-fishing dull. (No bait is used in fly fishing.) Ken became a Disney Legend in 1991. He died in 1993.

Ken Anderson was one of the first Imagineers to do some early work on what was later to become Audio-Animatronics.

Ship Models: Bruce Bushman & Don DaGradi, Manufacturers:

Bruce Bushman was a Longtime Studio Art Director. He was responsible for much of the ambience of Fantasyland attractions.

Don DaGradi was a storywriter and stylist for *Pinocchio, Bambi, Fantasia, Dumbo, Alice in Wonderland, Peter Pan, Lady and the Tramp,* and *Sleeping Beauty.* (A stylist visualizes the whole concept to make it attractive and fresh and establish the overall integrity of the design of both characters and locale.) He co-wrote with Bill Walsh the scripts for *Mary Poppins, Son of Flubber, Bed knobs and Broomsticks,* and other famous titles. His stories inspired many of Fantasyland's attractions. He was honored posthumously in 1991 as a Disney Legend.

Don DaGradi

Disneyana

Youngman & Leopold: Youngman and Leopold were members of Gunther Lessing's legal team. Gordon Youngman was a legal counsel who served on the board of directors.

Gunther R. Lessing, Esq.: A lawyer at Disney Studios in 1930, Gunther became general counsel in 1952 and served on the board of directors. His legal team was instrumental in the early negotiations for Disneyland. According to legend, before he joined Disney, Gunther gave legal services to

Legendary Gunther Lessing was legal counsel for Disney Corporation.

Pancho Villa, the famous Mexican Revolutionary.

Far East Imports Exotic Arts: Marc Davis, Proprietor: Walt named his key animators in the 1950s "Disney's Nine Old Men." Marc Davis was the only one to move over to WED. He began his career in 1935 at the studio, working on *Snow White and the Seven Dwarfs*. He is better known for creating some of Disney's most memorable characters, including Cinderella, Tinker Bell, Sleeping Beauty, Maleficent, Cruella De Vil, and others, giving him the reputation of being "a ladies man." He was one of the leaders in planning the Tiki Room and all four Disney New York World's Fair Attractions. Many Disneyland attractions, including Pirates of the Caribbean, Haunted Mansion, Jungle Cruise and It's a Small World, feature humorous touches that were added by Marc. Marc retired in 1978 and was named a Disney Legend in 1989. He died in January 2000. Alice, his wife of 43 years, also worked for Disney. She designed and created many of the Pirates costumes and outfits for It's A Small World. Together they have a

Through his drawings Marc Davis gave a great deal of humor to every attraction he touched.

large collection of native New Guinea Art, which explains the Far East Exotic Art reference in the window.

LESSON TO LEARN

Walt's Nine Old Men were called that after Franklin D. Roosevelt referred to the Supreme Court as "Nine Old Men." Walt's nine were his key animators during the 1950s: Marc Davis, Frank Thomas, Ollie Johnston, Ward Kimball, Wollie Reitherman, Les Clark, Eric Larson, Milt Kahl and John Lounsbery.

Main Street Hotel

Van Arsdale France, Founder and Professor Emeritus, Disney University: In 1955, Van France taught guest services to all the cast members who opened the park. Later this would come to be known

Van France, the creator of Disney University and later the Alumni Club for retirees.

as the Disney University. After his retirement in 1978, he started the Disneyland Alumni Club for former employees. Because he was a chain smoker, his window was placed above the old tobacco shop. His biography, *Window on Main Street,* is his account of the opening and development of Disneyland. He was named a Disney Legend in 1993 and died in 1999.

Happiest Dreams on Earth, International School of Hospitality, Hideo Amemiya, Headmaster, "We put people first.":

Hideo Amemiya was senior vice president of the Disneyland Resort Hotels when he passed away at the age of 56 on February 19, 2001. He started his career with the Walt Disney Company in 1971 as a hotel cast member in Florida. He had a remarkable career in Florida, Japan, and eventually California. He dedicated a lot of energy toward the Disneyland Resort Expansion, the refurbishing of the Disneyland Hotel, the conversion of the Disneyland Pacific Hotel to the Paradise Pier Hotel, and the grand opening of the Grand Californian Hotel. His window was dedicated on September 25, 2001.

Senior Vice President of the Disneyland Resort Hotels, Hideo Amemiya.

Disney Showcase

TREASURE & TRIVIA

Hideo's window, along with Walt Disney's and a few others are always lit. The everburning flame is to honor those cast members who died while employed at Disney.

Coast-to-Coast People Moving, Dick Nunis, Proprietor, Founded in 1955, Anaheim, Orlando, Tokyo, Paris:

Dick Nunis was a member of the USC football team and a classmate of Ron Miller (Diane Disney's husband and former CEO of Walt Disney Corporation.) He began his career at Disney in 1955, assisting Van France with the first cast-member orientation training. He worked his way up the ranks from area supervisor to supervisor to the mailroom and steno pool. Later, he became director of Disneyland Operations and vice president of Disneyland Operations. He became executive vice president of Disneyland and Walt Disney World in 1972 and president in 1980. In 1981, he became a member of the Disney Board of Directors and was named chairman of Walt Disney Attractions in 1991. He left the company in 2000.

Cast members use insider lingo that are known as "Nunis-isms." One of the better known was first uttered 12 hours before Walt Disney World's Magic Kingdom opened. Dick recruited anyone with a pulse to shovel dirt, plant shrubs, and lay sod.

One young supervisor who had never laid sod before stopped Dick to ask for help. Dick said, "It's easy—green side up."

Dick Nunis started with Disneyland just before it opened and stayed for an illustrious career. He was well known for making cast members smile with his "Nunis-isms".

China Shop

Ambassador Finishing School: Cicely Rigdon, Instructor.: Cicely Rigdon began her career with Disneyland in 1957 as a ticket seller. In 1959, she joined the Tour Guide Department and was responsible for initiating its growth and development. She eventually became supervisor of Guest Relations and in 1967 took the additional responsibility for the ticket sellers, ticket takers, and guest relations. From 1982 until her retirement in 1994, Cicely lead and developed the Ambassador Program. During her tenure, she had the privilege of working with 12 outstanding Disneyland ambassadors and the opportunity to represent Disneyland around the world. Cicely says that one of the highlights of her 37-year career at Disneyland was traveling with Walt to the 1964 World's Fair in New York. Cicely was presented her window in April 1994.

Mad Hatter Shop

John Louis Catone—Locksmith: Catone literally held all of the keys to the Magic Kingdom. He served many years at Disneyland in the Communications Services department.

Ragin' Ray's River Rafting Expedition, "Experienced Guides Since '55":

Ray Van De Warker, Owner, Guide: Ray began his career at Disneyland in 1955 as a raft driver. He retired in 1996 as Manager of Office Support Services, responsible for the mail room, key control, and central files.

The Musical Quill; Lyrics and Librettos by X. Atencio:

Xavier or "X," as his friends called him, began his career in 1938 as an inbetweener on *Pinocchio* and later became an assistant animator on *Fantasia*.

Photo by Penny Crawford

Cicely Rigdon

Later he became an animator on several short subjects including the Academy Award-winning *Toot, Whistle, Plunk, and Boom.*

In 1965, at Walt's request, he moved to WED Enterprises. Although he was an artist, Walt asked him to write the dialogue and lyrics for the Pirates of the Caribbean. This was a new adventure for him. His first song, "Yo Ho, A Pirate's Life for Me" is one of the most memorable and loved songs at Disney- land. Teaming up with musical director, Buddy Baker, his next song, "Grim Grinning Ghosts" for the Haunted Mansion, had equal success. As a team, X and Buddy went on to do several shows for EPCOT and Walt Disney World.

The window is a tribute to X's lyrical talent. Retiring in 1984, X was appropriately named a Disney Legend in 1996.

Artist and Disney Legend X. Atencio never knew he could write lyrics until Walt asked him. Today, "Yo Ho, A Pirate's Life For Me," and "Grim Grinning Ghosts" are two park favorites.

Milt Albright, Entrepreneur: No Job Too Big, No Job Too Small: Like Walt, Milt left rural Missouri for new challenges and a new life in California. Milt's life was forever changed in December 1937, when he bought a copy of TIME magazine with Walt on the cover. His goal became clear, but the studio wasn't hiring . . . especially people with no artistic talent. After many rebuffs, he was finally hired in 1947 as a junior accountant. He later got acquainted with Walt and Roy through his job as paymaster for the confidential payroll.

With lots of ambition and some skill, he built a prototype car for the proposed Autopia attraction at Disneyland. Walt liked the initiative shown, and Milt's requested transfer to Anaheim was okayed. Building attendance became an obsession with Milt, one that endured for 35 years. In 1957, he was named group sales manager by Walt. He retired in 1992. His goal established early on by Roy Disney, was "maximum utilization of the existing facility," which meant concentrating on off-season, and off-hours. It became the "MUEF" philosophy.

Group Sales at other parks (many were successful) originated mostly from picnic grounds (which were usually free-no charge). Walt personally visited several prior to 1957, including Copenhagen and sent Milt to others, and was influenced. So he built Holidayland, which Milt calls "Walt's only failure in the outdoor-family entertainment endeavor." Its basic concept was flawed. Unlike all the visited parks, it couldn't compete

Milt Albright designed the first prototype for the Autopia cars. In his words, "as a ruse" to get Walt's attention, to be transferred to the park. Amazingly, it worked!

with the next-door wonders of Disneyland. Holidayland was a "gold-plated" picnic facility and as such was expensive for the sponsoring organization. In Fall 1959, the big striped tent fell victim to Santa Ana winds and closed permanently.

Group Sales then moved quickly to further the MUEF concept in new and mostly successful ways. Magic Kingdom Club—offered a better ticket in the off-season, but no cash discount. This was a huge success and was recently replaced by the Disney Club. The first one sold to United California Bank in September 1960. The organization contracted to buy exclusive use of the entire park for say, 7,000 people minimum. This program was well accepted.

Grad Nites. Exclusive use of the park from about 11 p.m. until 5 a.m. The first Grad Nite was in 1961, and was very successful. The Grad Nite tradition is still active

today. Youth groups—highly popular and managed by a youth administrator, were personally recruited by Walt.

In the early years, group sales accounted for nearly 25 percent of total attendance in the off season (about eight months each year). For this, a career committed to the Disney challenge of making the impossible happen, Milt earned his window on Main Street.

The Busy Hands School: Sculpting, Whittling, Soap Carving. Blaine Gibson, Head Master, "The Eternal Pursuit of the Artist's Craft"

Blaine Gibson is an artist and a sculptor. He joined Disney in 1939 as an "in-between" and assistant animator on *Pinocchio;* he continued working on features up to *101 Dalmatians*. In 1954, he

Blaine Gibson headed the sculpting department and was responsible for most of the Audio-Animatronic heads for the Haunted Mansion and Pirates of the Caribbean.

began doing projects for WED Enterprises in his spare time, joining them permanently in 1961. He headed the sculpting department and was responsible for most of the Audio-Animatronic presidents, ghosts, and pirate heads. His statue, "Partners," graces the hub at the end of Main Street in front of the castle *(see page 16)*. He retired in 1983 and was made a Disney Legend a decade later.

Opera House

Evans Gardens: Exotic & Rare Species, Freeway Collections, Est. 1910, Morgan (Bill) Evans, Senior Partner: Bill Evans is an expert in rare plants and those not native to California. In the early 1950s, he and his brother Jack designed the landscaping for Walt's private home. Walt asked Bill to continue landscaping at Disneyland. In a matter of months, in spite of a very tight budget, he gave each area of Disneyland its unique yet appropriate landscaping.

The California Department of Transportation allowed Bill to take trees that were in the way of the new freeway system. All Bill had to do was remove them. This is why his window says "Freeway Collections." As he walked through the park, he often pointed out a tree from Ventura, another from Santa Monica, or another from San Diego. (Bill was referring to the freeways, not the cities.)

He is also well known for his last-minute creativity during the final preparation of Disneyland. His budget was exhausted, so he tagged weeds with jaw-breaking Latin names in the hope of passing them off as plants. Later, when timelines weren't so critical and budgets weren't so tight, he introduced topiaries, floating gardens, and parterre to the park and forever influenced the landscaping industry.

As Director of Landscape Design for WED Enterprises, he contributed to each of the Disney parks, consulting even after his retirement in 1975. In 1993, he was honored as a Disney Legend and he died August 10, 2002, at the age of 92.

Bill Evans

Main Street Electrical Parade World Headquarters: Robert "Bob" F. Jani, Master Showman: During the dedication of this window in January 1997, Vice President Mike Davis commented, "This is the first time a window has been dedicated to an Entertainment experience—the Main Street Electrical Parade—and a person Bob Jani." As director of Entertainment for Disneyland and Walt Disney World until 1978, Bob was the creative force behind the Main Street Electrical Parade and other events.

The Main Street Electrical Parade, which began in 1972, was one of the most beloved Disneyland traditions. It ran intermittently for 25 years. This unique nighttime parade featured half a million tiny lights on moving floats. The synthesizer music played a piece called "Baroque Hoedown" into which themes from a number of Disney movies were woven, including *Pete's Dragon, Dumbo's Circus, Cinderella,* and *Snow White and the Seven Dwarves.*

Bank of Main Street

Wade B. Rubottom and George Patrick: Wade Rubottom and George Patrick were art directors. Wade worked on Main Street U.S.A. and George contributed to Frontierland.

Gabriel Scognamillo, Wilson "Bill" Martin: Gabriel Scognamillo was an art director who worked on Tomorrowland.

Wilson "Bill" Martin began as the art director for Fantasyland and soon became the art director for all of Disneyland. An art director takes actual designs of construction projects and integrates into them Disney stories, ideas, and film themes. Bill is the artist and architect who developed the track layouts for all the original dark rides. His major contributions relate to the layouts of areas and attractions. He planned the layout for the 1959 Tomorrowland remodel where the Submarine, Monorail, Matterhorn, Autopia and Motorboats were fit into a small area. He also designed the layout for New Orleans Square, Pirates of the Caribbean, and Haunted Mansion. At some point in their development, though, he worked on every attraction at Disneyland. Every Saturday morning for 13 years, he walked the park with Walt and a handful of other WED people.

Bill Martin walked the park every Saturday morning with Walt to look for ways to improve it.

Richard "Dick" Irvine and Marvin Davis, Architects and Associates: In the 1940s, Dick Irvine was an art director at Disney. He was twice nominated for Academy Awards for Set Design. In 1953, he led the team of designers, artists, architects, and engineers in the planning and developing Disneyland. He headed WED Enterprises until he retired in 1973. Even then, he continued in charge of development for all new attractions in Disneyland and Walt Disney World. He died on March 30, 1976, and was named a Disney Legend in 1990.

One of the stern-wheel steamboats in Florida's Magic Kingdom, a replica of the Mark Twain, is named after him.

Richard "Dick" Irvine led the designers, architects and engineers to build Disneyland in 1953.

Marvin Davis was an architect and set designer who joined WED Enterprises in 1953 to assist in developing some of the early Disneyland layouts. He worked mainly on outdoor areas, positioning lands and buildings. After Disneyland opened, he returned to television and became art director for *Davy Crockett, Zorro,* and *Babes in Toyland.* He won an Emmy in 1964 for the art direction and scenic design of Walt Disney's Wonderful World of Color. In 1965, he returned to WED as Project Designer for Walt Disney World. He retired in 1975. He became a Disney Legend in 1994 and died four years later. Marvin was married to Walt Disney's niece, and his father-in-law was Disney Legend Dennis "Bill" Cottrell.

Marvin Davis joined WED in 1953 to develop the concepts and architectural designs for Disneyland. He was a master planner and decided where each of the "lands" would be positioned.

Seven Summits Expeditions, Frank G. Wells, Proprietor: *"For those Who Want To Do It All":* In 1984, Roy Disney asked his friend, Frank Wells, to join Michael Eisner in one of the two top positions at Walt Disney Company. Frank and Michael are responsible for one of the most productive decades in Disney history. Frank served as president until his untimely death in a helicopter accident April 3, 1994. His window refers to the book he co-wrote about climbing the highest mountain on each of the seven continents in one calendar year. He was honored posthumously in 1994 as a Disney Legend. He earned a window and a "Wells Expedition" crate on the Matterhorn.

Frank Wells on his first attempt to climb Mt. Everest in 1982.

J.S. "Sam" Hamel, Consulting Engineer: Jacob Samuel "Sam" Hamel was a civil and electrical engineer who started working at Disneyland in 1954. Walt assigned him the task of building all the waterways in the park down to the pipes and sluice gates that keep the water moving and fresh. One of his most remarkable projects is Schweitzer Falls in the Jungle Cruise.

William T. "Bill" Wheeler and John Wise, Structural Engineers: Bill Wheeler was a partner in Wheeler & Gray, a structural engineering firm. He was contracted to build the support structures for the buildings in the park.

John Wise accompanied Bill Wheeler to the park. He later joined WED where he held a number of engineering positions, including chief engineer at Disneyland. He has continued with Disney since 1954, most recently completing the realignment of the monorail track around Indiana Jones.

ELIAS DISNEY

CONTRACTOR
EST. 1895

NOVELTIES

SOUVENIR

Keep a sharp eye out for Disney's theme park credits on the second floor windows.

The view of Disneyland from the Tarzan's Treehouse is worth the climb.

Chapter 4

MYSTERIES OF
Adventureland

During the 1950s, Walt's studio produced Disney's True-Life Adventure Series. This television series inspired Adventureland. In fact, Adventureland was almost named "True-Life Adventureland." Walt wanted to capture the feeling of areas of the world most people may never see. He succeeded in Adventureland. Brimming with exotic plants, this area is built around Polynesian, Asian, and African cultures. Exotic mystery is the driving motif behind Adventureland. Stand at the hub of the park and look toward each of the lands. Adventureland is the only land not to show something moving. It creates a mystery that beckons you to enter.

Enchanted Tiki Room
(1963)

This was once owned by WED Enterprises. When it first opened, it cost an additional 75 cents to enter.

During the 1960s, people were fascinated by Pacific Island culture thanks to cultural icons such as Elvis Presley movies that were set at Waikiki. The Enchanted Tiki Room was designed to be a Polynesian restaurant where meals would be choreographed to the choir of Audio-Animatronic flowers, birds, and tiki gods. Polynesian food was perfect for the Disneyland experience—it was so new few people had much expectation about how it should taste or be presented. The restaurant idea was abandoned at the last minute, but guests still sit on the restaurant chairs. The coffee service station in the middle of the room is now the stage for the fountain finale. United Airlines, which provided extensive service to the Hawaiian Islands, was the original sponsor of the attraction. Later, Dole Pineapple became the sponsor because of its close association with Hawaii. Dole Pineapple also hosts the Tiki Juice Bar that offers a sweet taste of the islands.

Three-dimensional Audio-Animatronic birds surprise and entertain guests. This was the first attraction to feature Audio-Animatronics. The advent of

Audio-Animatronics started a new era for attractions at Disney. Hosts Fritz, Michael, Pierre, and Jose introduce more than 200 birds, flowers, and tikis. The Audio-Animatronic cast includes 54 orchids, four tiki poles, 12 tiki drummers, 24 singing masks, seven birds of paradise, eight macaws, 12 toucans, nine forktail birds, six cockatoos, and 20 tropical birds.

The synchronized sound and movement of the three-dimensional creatures foreshadowed the later development of Great Moments with Mr. Lincoln, Pirates of the Caribbean, Haunted Mansion, and many other attractions that have become synonymous with Disney.

In the early days, Audio-Animatronics was so new and innovative that it was difficult to describe.

TREASURE & TRIVIA

Brothers Robert B. and Richard M. Sherman became Disney icons and legends. Together they've written some of the most recognizable Disneyland tunes. Their score for the Enchanted Tiki Room was the very first ever written for Audio-Animatronic characters. The Enchanted Tiki Room opened in 1963 and is the longest running show in Disneyland. Some of the Sherman Brothers' other works around the park include "There's a Great Big Beautiful Tomorrow," "It's a Small World" and the songs as well as atmosphere music for The Many Adventures of Winnie the Pooh attraction. Their first major film at Disney was *The Parent Trap* where they wrote the music and lyrics. They went on to write scores for 28 more films including *The Jungle Book*,

Aristocats and *Bedknobs and Broomsticks*. Their biggest hit was *Mary Poppins* for which they won two Oscars: one for Best Score and another for the Best Song "Chim Chim Cher-ee." For more information about the long careers of the Sherman Brothers, pick up their autobiography, *Walt's Time– (from before and beyond.)*

Legends Richard M. (right) and Robert B. Sherman (left) are the composers of the music for many Disneyland attractions.

Imagineers placed José, the Audio-Animatronic-talking macaw, on a perch outside the entrance of the attraction. He attracted such a crowd of people that the path became congested and José had to take an early retirement. You can see José's twin at the Opera House.

HIDDEN MICKEY

You can see this only from inside the queue area of the Enchanted Tiki Room. Stand near the refreshment stand and look up at the side of the Adventureland sign. By looking straight on at the sign you shouldn't be able to see the letters very clearly for Adventureland. The ends of the three bottom poles of the sign form a Hidden Mickey.

TREASURE & TRIVIA

Disney Legend Wally Boag is the voice of José and Fulton Burley is the voice of "Michael." Thurl Ravenscroft voices "Fritz."

HIDDEN MICKEY

On one of the perches in the Enchanted Tiki Room a feather is suspended from a bamboo Hidden Mickey.

HIDDEN MICKEY

While inside the Enchanted Tiki Room, look for four large cages with five to six limbs and a bird on each limb. The birds hang on a piece of thick material. Follow the thick string that hangs the birdcage about halfway up it makes a circle. The circle above Pierre Parrot forms a Hidden Mickey.

HIDDEN MICKEY

You can see another Hidden Mickey two perches toward the exit door from Michael the Irish parrot.

Jungle Cruise

The opening of this ride on July 17, 1955, was one of the most eagerly awaited events at Disneyland because of the publicity Walt gave it during his pre-opening television shows. (Actually, very little else was far enough along for him to show.) In many ways, the Jungle Cruise defines Disneyland as the cinematic experience it was meant to be. It is an art director's dream, composed of curves and well-placed switchbacks and covered with landscaping that hides different parts of the set from each other and preserves all the illusions. Harper Goff modeled the Jungle

LESSON TO LEARN

The falls are named after Dr. Albert Schweitzer, the 1953 Nobel Peace Prize recipient. Schweitzer was an author, a musician, a church pastor, and a professor of philosophy. At the age of 30, he devoted his life to the medical needs of the underprivileged communities in Africa, where he eventually built a hospital.

Cruise after the film, *African Queen,* with Humphrey Bogart and Katherine Hepburn. The waterway is known as "Rivers of the World" and includes elements of Burma's Irrawaddy River, Cambodia's Mekong, Africa's Nile and Congo Rivers, and the Rapids of Kilimanjaro.

Originally, Walt wanted live animals for the attraction. He had to be talked out of it. The large and exotic animals would have to be fed and they might run away or sleep during the day while guests were visiting. Visitors would get different rides; one person might see dozens of animals, but another might not see any. Walt finally agreed that live animals might not be the best way to give everyone their money's worth. The seven original boats on the Jungle Ride were Congo Queen, Swanee Lady, Amazon Belle, Ganges Gal, Nile Princess, Mekong Maiden, and

TREASURE & TRIVIA

Cast members refer to the large island close to the boarding area as Manhattan and the island farther away as Catalina.

Irrawaddi *Woman.* The fleet has grown to include Ucayaali Una, Hondo Hattie, Orinoco Adventures, Zammbesi Miss, Magdalena Maiden, and Yanngtze Lotus. In 1967, one of the boats was rechristened as The Kissimmee Kate. It's a cute pun, but the name has a symbolic value as well. Named after the Kissimmee River in Florida, it offered a clue to Disney's plans for what would later become Walt Disney World in Florida.

The original boats were made of fiberglass and wood. They measure 27 feet in length and can carry between 30 and 36 passengers. When empty, they weigh almost two tons and are powered by Gray Marine engines that burn natural gas. When the Indiana Jones attraction opened, the boats were reconceived with weathered styling, rust color metalwork, fishnet awnings, and dangling lamps to blend with the 1930s motif of the attraction.

HIDDEN MICKEY

About 12-15 ft. from the dock, look right through the base of the staircase. You might see a Hidden Mickey.

TREASURE & TRIVIA

There is a window dedication across from the entrance of Jungle Cruise: *Oriental Tattooing by Prof. Harper Goff, Banjo Lessons.* This dedication window, although not on Main Street U.S.A., is perfectly situated on the back of the Golden Horseshoe building. Harper was the set designer for *African Queen* and *Calamity Jane.* The film *African Queen* served as inspiration for the Jungle Cruise and *Calamity Jane* served as inspiration for the Golden Horseshoe. Ironically, the film *Calamity Jane* was not Disney's. Read more about it under Golden Horseshoe in Frontierland.

In 1951, Harper met Walt Disney in London at the Bassett-Lowke Ltd. Shop. Both Walt and Harper were trying to buy the same model train. The two men struck up a friendship

and Harper soon after joined Disney as an illustrator. He designed many of the buildings for Main Street U.S.A. using his hometown of Fort Collins, Colo., for inspiration. The City Hall and Train Station on Main Street resemble the former Courthouse in Fort Collins. Harper saw some early renditions of some of the windows and quickly made known his interest in the Tattoo Parlor, which was a fitting tribute for an artist. His window also notes Banjo Lessons; Harper was the banjo player in The Firehouse Five Plus Two Dixieland Jazz Band with Ward Kimball and Frank Thomas. Harper died in 1993 and was named a Disney Legend the same year.

In 1962, Disney added landscapes and in 1964 more Audio-Animatronic animals, including the elephant bathing pool, the African Veldt (lions with a zebra), and Lost Safari (men on a pole with a rhino). In 1976, more than 30 new animals were added, including a gorilla, crocodiles, tiger, lions, a python, baboons, water buffalo, hornbills, and a cobra.

Notice the large-leafed upright tree in the Cambodian ruins section. It is a *Ficus religiosa*, the same species of tree under which Buddha received enlightenment in India many centuries ago.

Look around in the two-story

boathouse. You'll see a lot of inside references and props to entertain you while you are waiting in line for this popular attraction.

During the first few years of the attraction, the Jungle Cruise captains recited facts about animals and nature and described the dangers of traveling in the jungle. By the mid-60s, the guides were permitted to add humor and were given a list of suitable puns.

Indiana Jones and the Temple of the Forbidden Eye

This attraction was a 1995 collaboration between George Lucas and Disneyland. The concept came from Lucas' film, *Indiana Jones and the Temple of Doom*. The attraction takes you back to 1935 and Indiana Jones' discovery of the Temple of the Forbidden Eye. Here a powerful god rewards visitors with a special gift, the Fountain of Eternal Youth, Chamber of Earthly Riches, or Observatory of the Future. But if anyone looks into the eye of Mara, the entire truck plunges into eternal doom. Choose your fellow passengers wisely, or you may be in for a long journey.

The Chamber of Earthly Riches is encrusted with solid gold, priceless treasures that seem to flow mysteriously out of the bowl continuously.

The Observatory of the Future has an amulet offering visions of the future when you stare into it. Indiana Jones himself stared into the amulet only to see himself carrying the Arc of the Covenant. (Perhaps this was wishful thinking.)

The Fountain of Eternal Youth is a room with jugs that pour water so pure people claim to grow younger.

Interaction is key to enjoying this ride. You begin in the queue. Imagineers were challenged to make 12 passengers interact while they traveled at 13.6 mph through the ride. The idea of asking guests to do something was replaced instead with asking them *not* to do something. The chances are one person is always bound to do the forbidden. Guests are constantly warned inside the queue *not* to look into the eyes of Mara. Someone usually does!

Imagineers developed many different variables to the attraction. There are nearly 160,000 journey combinations. The attraction features booby traps, swarms of snakes, bugs, and rats, poison darts, and a five-ton rolling boulder.

Among the variables of this ride are the different comments heard from Indiana Jones, including:

"Tourists, why did it have to be tourists?"

"That wasn't so bad."

"Next time you're on your own."

"I ask for help, but they send me tourists."

"I have a bad feeling about this." (Harrison Ford, who starred as Indiana, said this line in the George Lucas film *Star Wars*.)

Indiana Jones and the Temple of the Forbidden Eye is sponsored by a generous financial contribution from AT&T that made it possible to design, plan, and build the attraction.

TREASURE & TRIVIA

Before you enter the building, look on the outside of the Mara Temple. Do you see the small wooden bucket on the roof? Nearby, made of stone, is an unmistakable copy of the sorcerer's hat Mickey Mouse wore in *Fantasia*.

TREASURE & TRIVIA

The Indiana Jones attraction was built over the old Eeyore section of the parking lot. Someone left a parking sign there. It is carefully hidden away, but you can see it behind you, above the slide projector as you exit the film room.

TREASURE & TRIVIA

Outside the Indiana Jones Adventure is one of the German patrol trucks used in the 1981 film, *Raiders of the Lost Ark*. The side of the German patrol truck says "Lost Delta Archeological Expeditions." Notice the handlebars with golf balls on the top of the front bumper. These handlebars were put there specifically for a car chase stunt in the film.

Photo by Dave Hawkins

This is a movie prop from the Raiders of the Lost Ark.

TREASURE & TRIVIA

If you are squeamish, don't look in the holes in the wall along the queue. Skeletons are hiding in them!

HIDDEN MICKEY

As you walk through the queue, look in the office. A 1939 copy of *Life* Magazine lies on the desk, with Mickey Mouse on the cover.

TREASURE & TRIVIA

The office wall is made of crates, one of which says, "Deliver to Obi Wan." This is a tribute to the *Star Wars* character. George Lucas helped Disney develop both Star Tours and the Indiana Jones attractions.

TREASURE & TRIVIA

Another crate is printed with the name "M. Brode." Marcus Brode was a character in the Indiana Jones films.

TREASURE & TRIVIA

All props are authentic antiques or movie props from the Indiana Jones series.

HIDDEN MICKEY

In the hall of promise, look straight at Mara holding out her hands. Her nostrils form the ears and the indention above her lip forms a Hidden Mickey. Better yet, just take my word for it, *Don't* look at Mara!

HIDDEN MICKEY

There's a hidden Mousekeeter hat on one of the skeletons. When the Truck travels down what feels like stairs and turns to the left, look over your left shoulder at the back wall. Three skeletons are standing up; one of them is wearing the hat backwards. Facing you will be the word "Bones," but you'll be moving too fast to read it.

Most Disney attractions move along a stationary track, but the Indy car is a moving base, a new design for any Disney attraction. The moving base was later used in EPCOT and Animal Kingdom in Florida.

Mara Fonts: Thousands of AT&T Mara Font Decoder Cards were handed out when the attraction opened. Most of the wall messages are deciphered here, but feel free to use the photo (right) to translate.

Tombstone at entrance: *If you dare to look into the eyes of Mara you shall be. . . .*

Photo by Dave Hawkins

As you enter the building: *Beware the Eye of Mara.*

As you walk into the second tiny room: *It is forbidden to pass beyond this chamber without a servant of Mara to guide your path. Heed this warning of risk incurring the wrath of Mara for doom awaits the unbeliever in the darkest beyond.*

HIDDEN MICKEY

In the Flooded Maze area in Mara Font, about three feet from the floor in lighter print is a Hidden Mickey. On a plain column right after you go through a doorway, on the left side waist high, as you're looking directly at the two drinking fountains, you'll find the initials MM in Mara Font.

A copy of the Mara Font card sponsored by AT&T and Disney. Use it to decipher wall writings.

Above the plaque to the right of skeletons in the wall: *Only the blind shall see.*

Above a statue: *Earthly riches.*

Above the fountain: *Only one spring can restore youth and vigor. Choose wisely.*

Right of fountain: *Drink deeply the water of life.*

On the side of the wheel: *The gates of doom are ever open.*

Just before you walk into the circular queue room (painted not carved): *True rewards await those who choose wisely.* This code is a tribute to the attraction's sponsor AT&T.

At the front of the film room: *Beware the eyes of Mara. Future-Riches-Youth.*

In the hallway after Indiana's office: *Only the pure of heart shall gain admittance to the chamber of destiny.*

As you walk over the bridge just before you descend to the loading area: *Mara shall guide you through the doorway of your most secret desire in the chamber of destiny.*

TREASURE & TRIVIA

The mine car just outside the exit is also a movie prop from the film, *Indiana Jones and the Temple of Doom*, the second film of the trilogy.

This mine car appeared in the film Indiana Jones and the Temple of Doom.

Photo by Dave Hawkins

As you exit either side of the attraction and deboarding areas: *Beware the eyes of Mara. One look will lead through the tunnel of torment to the gates of doom.*

Tarzan's Treehouse

This attraction was built in 1962 and redesigned in 1999. Edgar Rice Burroughs wrote *Tarzan of the Apes* in 1912, the story of a man raised by apes. Disney animated it in 1999. One day after the film was released, the attraction opened. The 70-foot tree is a *Disney-dendron semperflorens grandis*, or "large, ever-blooming Disney tree." The tree weighs 150 tons, features 450 branches, and is anchored 42 feet into the ground. The tree is entirely man-made, with concrete roots, steel limbs covered with concrete, and 6,000 vinyl leaves that were attached by hand. The original cost of the tree was $254,900, with $40,000 budgeted for leaves.

This tree is one of four original manmade trees; the others are Tom Sawyer Island Treehouse, Tahitian Terrace, and the ever-twilit Blue Bayou Restaurant tree.

The play area at the base of the tree was designed around the scientific equipment that the characters Jane and her father brought to the jungle in the novel and the movie.

From 1962 to 1999, this attraction was known as the *Swiss Family Treehouse*. It was inspired by the Disney live-action film, *Swiss*

Family Robinson, released in 1960, but based on Johann Wyss' novel of 1813. John Mills, who starred in the film, and daughter Hayley were on hand for the dedication ceremony, along with Walt and his five grandchildren. For years, Buddy Baker's song, "Swiskapolka," played from the tree. Currently, you may hear the soundtrack from *Tarzan* written by Phil Collins.

TREASURE & TRIVIA

Notice the teapot and cup in the play station. You may have seen each in *Tarzan*; you may also recognize the China pattern as Mrs. Potts and Chip from the Disney animated film, *Beauty & the Beast.*

HIDDEN MICKEY

Opposite where Jane is drawing Tarzan, you'll see a Hidden Mickey made of rope curtain rods hanging on the wall.

Photo by Dave Hawkins

Tarzan's Treehouse

The architecture goes to great lengths to replicate the flavor of New Orleans.

Chapter 5

TREASURE HUNTING IN
New Orleans Square

New Orleans Square is the only area of Disneyland to be designed after a real city — New Orleans, La., circa the 1850s and 1860s. Lilly Disney wanted a place to enjoy with her guests. The three acres with intimate shops, fine dining, graceful wrought iron balconies, and Dixieland music recreate the deep South. Mayor Victor H. Schiro and Chief Administrative Officer Thomas Heier of New Orleans along with Walt Disney opened and dedicated New Orleans Square in 1966. Sadly, Walt passed away five months later and never saw the completed project.

You'll enjoy a casual stroll down the cobblestone streets, admiring the shops, architecture, and artwork. The music will draw you in to enjoy the southern hospitality. The area was meticulously researched to resemble the French Quarter prior to the Civil War, down to the buildings, streets, wrought iron, ornaments, and artifacts of the "Crescent City." Notice the details. The ornate spikes on the poles keep people from climbing to the second floors. Fire station plaques hang above the doors in an authentic recreation of fire insurance. Some of the Mardi Gras ornaments were acquired directly from New Orleans before the square was open. The area was the first new

LESSON TO LEARN

The small flags representing France, Spain, and United States are flown because New Orleans has been a part of all three countries in its long history. Toward the back of New Orleans, the Louisiana state flag proudly hangs from the top of the buildings.

Illustration by Karl Yamauchi

land added to Disneyland and cost $18 million dollars, which was more than the original price tag to open the entire park.

Music is a very important part of New Orleans Square. Many different jazz bands play in this area, perhaps this is why New Orleans Square is a great resting place in the park. You can read more about these bands in the "Entertainers" chapter of this book (see page 181).

Pirates of the Caribbean

This attraction has been open since 1967 and is still a park favorite. Riders board a boat at Laffite's Landing and discover pirate treasures, narrowly escape the lair, and find New Orleans being plundered by drunken pirates. The attraction was built with a light-hearted comic spirit.

In the early 1960s, Walt asked Marc Davis to sketch some light-hearted pirate gags. Pirates of the Caribbean became one of Marc's favorite projects. His characters are at the heart of this attraction. Marc drew every scene and worked with the sculptors and the machine shop to follow its progress.

Disney costumer, Alice Davis, Marc's wife, was challenged to dress the pirates, whose feet and knees were often bolted to the floor or cannons. Her costumes are made with a lot of Velcro®. Unlike the costumes of the human cast members, these costumes wear out from the inside because of the oil and machine movement. Alice was concerned that the machinery would rip the costumes and force the attraction to be shut down, so she asked if she

LESSON TO LEARN

Laffite's landing is appropriately named for a real pirate who hid his headquarters in the Louisiana swamps. The French-born Jean Laffite terrorized the Gulf of Mexico in the 1800s. He was notorious in New Orleans as a successful smuggler, yet he was able to hire the best lawyers to get an acquittal on the piracy charge. He served against the British under Andrew Jackson during the battle of New Orleans. He then became a spy for the Spanish who wanted to put a stop to the Caribbean piracy that was disrupting trade with America. His reputation grew during his years of smuggling in Barataria Bay and socializing in New Orleans. Laffite spent much of his later years in Europe as a political philosopher. Many people from Galveston, Texas, still search for his buried treasure along the beaches of the Gulf of Mexico.

could make two sets of costumes. When she was told no, she ordered twice as much fabric, made a second costume for each character, and hid the costumes away. About two months after the attraction opened, a fire destroyed several costumes. When Disney asked Alice for another set of costumes, she revealed her wardrobe treasure. Thanks to her forethought, three sets of costumes are now made for every character.

Space was limited in this part of the park. Marc had drawn so many good ideas for the attraction that Disney made an expensive decision. They invested $15 million dollars (almost as much as Disneyland itself) into New Orleans square so that Pirates of the Caribbean could be built underground. The attraction actually goes outside the park berm and under the train tracks. The first tunnel under the railroad is the cave just before the ship attacks the fort; the second is the burning area before the pirate shoot-out scene. The 46 bateaux (Creole for small boat) carry 22 people each, resulting in a capacity of 3,400 guests per hour. There are 750,000 gallons of water in the attraction.

Borrowing new technology from the New York World's Fair, the Audio-Animatronics from Great Moments with Mr. Lincoln, and the moving boats system from It's A Small World, Disney turned Pirates of the Caribbean into one of his most elaborate undertakings. There are over 64 human figures and 55 animals in the attraction. In addition to the Audio-Animatronics, special effects worth noting in this attraction include fireflies, moving clouds, lightning, and the bullets ricocheting off the armor.

Walt never saw the completion of this project. He died in December of 1966; the attraction opened three months later.

X. Atencio, who wrote the dialog for all the character scenes and the lyrics for the song "Yo Ho, A Pirate's Life For Me," is the voice of the talking skull at the first down ramp. In fact, X's voice can be heard often in the attraction uttering key phrases such as: "There be squalls ahead, and Davy Jones be waitin' for them that don't obey!" and "Dead Men Tell No Tales."

HIDDEN MICKEY
When you see the skeleton of the captain in bed reading a map, look for a chair between the bed and the harpsichord. There's a Hidden Mickey on top of the back of the chair.

HIDDEN MICKEY
When the "Wicked Wench" ship bombs the Spanish fort, look for a Hidden Mickey from the cannon balls in the pit impacts on the fort.

TREASURE & TRIVIA

Before you get off the boats, you'll see a treasure map with lights that introduce the attraction. Look carefully when all the lights go out for the skull and crossbones in the map.

As the ride was being built, the Imagineers built a mock up of the auction scene in one of the Disney warehouses. They rigged up a dolly with a chair and pushed Walt through the prototype at about the speed of the boats. X apologized that the multiple voices and music made it difficult to understand what all the characters were saying. Walt, however, was pleased. He said, "It's like a cocktail party. You tune into one conversation and then into another. Each time guests go through, they'll hear something new and different."

In a 1997 renovation, a number of new lighting techniques enhanced the show. New illusions such as a skull and crossbones in the clouds, lightning streaks, and a silhouetted sword fight freshened the attraction. Other changes include the synchronization of the Audio-Animatronics so that each of the pirates has his own voice and mouth movements fittingly appropriate for the song. Even the flute player's fingering is accurate. Most of the upgrades were overshadowed by the politically correct changes that were made. For example, instead of men chasing women, the women now chase the pirates who are carrying stolen food.

Local residents may recognize the two trees in the outside queue. Each of the 10-ton giants was transplanted from Pershing Square in Los Angeles.

Laffite's Anchor: Near the water's edge is an old anchor supposedly from one of Jean Laffite's ships. Dorothy Lamour broke a bottle of Mississippi River water over the anchor to give it a Disneyland christening.

Disney Gallery: This location was originally intended to be Walt and Roy's 3,000-sq.-ft. private apartment to replace the one above the firehouse on Main Street.

Photo by Dave Hawkins

The WD for Walt Disney (shown here) was subtle decoration for the intended apartments for the family.

TREASURE & TRIVIA

The oak leaf and acorn ironworks are patterned after the La Branche House in the French Quarter of New Orleans. The romantic balcony has become a trademark of New Orleans. The La Branche House has been located on the corner of Royal and St. Peter Street since 1832.

Unfortunately, Walt died before the apartment was finished, and Roy decided afterwards not to use it. At first, it became a VIP lounge and offices for the planning of Tokyo Disneyland. Later, Disney Imagineer Tony Baxter redesigned the queue area for Pirates of the Caribbean and added the curved stairways to the second floor. The Gallery, which opened in July 1987, was a long-awaited place where guests could find vintage memorabilia and models of future attractions. The artwork changes from time to time, and regular signing of books and prints take place here. The opening exhibit, "The Art of Disneyland 1953-1986," featured artwork that was part of the planning and design of Disneyland.

The parlor fits the theme of New Orleans Square with its damask wallpapers, classic columns, and moldings, all set off by period furnishings on parquet floors. Notice the wrought iron on the balcony by the right stairway; can you spot the WD (Walt Disney) and RD (Roy Disney) hidden in the ornate railing?

Imagineers wanted the gallery to be special, since it had been designed as Walt's apartment. The artwork demonstrates what goes on behind the scenes to create the park attractions. The interior patio is a quiet, comfortable place for guests to rest. Walt planned to do a lot of entertaining there, so it has year-round climate control.

HIDDEN MICKEY
Check out the fireplace in the display room against the eastern wall. Under the marble shelf is a carved Hidden Mickey.

Royal Street Veranda (Under the Disney Gallery): The bread bowl filled with delicious clam chowder or gumbo is one of the favorite meals at the park.

Blue Bayou Restaurant: This is one of the most attractive dining areas of Disneyland. Diners watch as guests board the boats for their pirate adventure. The theme of a night sky, fireflies, and bayou sound effects provides a welcome respite on a hot summer day. The Monte Cristo Sandwich is a lunchtime favorite at the park. This is one of the two waitered restaurants in the park; the other is Carnation Corner on Main Street U.S.A.

Street Side: For a nominal fee, you can have your child's portrait drawn in chalk. The picture emerges before your eyes. New Orleans Square also offers face painting, cookie decorating, street performers, and artists, all of which make the experience unique.

Club 33: Since 1967, Club 33 has been an exclusive, private membership restaurant located upstairs in New Orleans Square. Walt wanted a special place to entertain visiting dignitaries and other high-profile guests. This is the only place in the park where alcohol is served. The club opened in June of 1967, but it was rarely used in the early years. Lucky guests dining at Club 33 will see how Walt and Lilly decorated the club with help from Emile Kuri and Dorthea Redmond. Eventually, membership in Club 33 was offered to the public. If you want to join today, though, you'll have to put your name on a lengthy waiting list.

Those who know how the club got its name aren't telling. Some believe that the 33 stands for the 33 companies that were lessees when the park opened, or that it is limited to only 33 members, or that it is named after the 33 charter members of the club. John Hench and Bill Martin, the designers of New Orleans Square, say that 33 refers to the club's street address on Royal

TREASURE & TRIVIA

Dorthea Redmond was well known to the Imagineers as a painter and illustrator. After she earned her degree from the University of Southern California, she went to work for David O. Selznick, where she contributed to the set designs for movie classics *Gone with the Wind, Rebecca, The Road to Bali,* and *Rear Window.* She joined the Disney staff in 1964.

Street. Like many street addresses in New Orleans, buildings are often numbered with two digits. A street address was necessary to obtain a California liquor license, but the address is obviously not the same as Disneyland Park.

Cristal D'Orleans: Similar to the store on Main Street, the Arribas Brothers sell glasses, decanters, and trinkets with engraving. If you look toward the ceiling on a crystal plate you may find the one and only "Hidden Walt."

Jewel of Orleans: The jewelry store offers fine estate jewelry. It is owned by a local jeweler, Dianne's Estate Jewelery, LLC, which is known for quality and interesting pieces. The cozy corner shop was once Mlle. Antoinette's Perfumeries and is still decorated with feminine touches. The floors are done in exacting parquet, while the woodwork is a pale green overglazed with silver leaf. Walt Disney purchased the antique chandelier on one of his trips to Louisiana.

The beautifully decorated mirrors, eight in all, are one of only two works of art in the park with an authorized artist's signature. Commissioned especially for the shop by Disney, these priceless, irreplaceable mirrors were designed by Dorthea Redmond. The project was a two-year undertaking and is believed to be the largest of its type ever created. It exemplifies a Chinese art made popular in 16th-century Europe. The largest panel is 1-ft. wide and almost 7 ft. high. They were produced by a painstaking technique known as the reverse painted method. Artists painted directly on the blown glass because plate glass was expensive in the 1770s. The elaborate details were painted first. Then the background was painted around the detailed birds, bouquets, and butterflies. This process is the opposite of putting oils on canvas in which the background is painted first and the detail work later. The last step after the entire piece is painted is the silvering, which makes the glass reflective.

Café Orleans: You may sit inside or outside at this buffet-style restaurant. The tables outside overlook Tom Sawyer Island and the many

activities on Rivers of America where New Orleans Square and Frontierland meet. Open for lunch or dinner, the menu changes from time to time, serving primarily southern food.

French Market Restaurant:

The largest food facility in New Orleans Square is the French Market sponsored by Stouffer's. This outdoor dining area with lively jazz music is situated near the New Orleans Square Depot. The buffet-style restaurant takes pride in its food, music, and atmosphere. Cajun chicken breast, jambalaya and thick clam chowder served in a bread bowl are some of the house specialties. The desserts are a good excuse to sit and listen to the Dixieland music played live by one of the bands that appear periodically throughout the day.

Mint Julep Bar:

This tiny window-service counter is tucked behind the seating for the French Market. Here a non-alcoholic mint julep and New Orleans beignet with jam will transport your taste buds to the Crescent City. A mint julep is similar to a mint-flavored lemonade and beignets or fritters are similar to donuts.

New Orleans/Frontierland Railroad Station:

In 1962, the railroad station was moved across the track to make room for New Orleans Square. However, the station name remained Frontierland station until 1996, and now bears the name of both lands.

The station is a Victorian-era wooden building designed by Ward Kimball for the 1949 Disney motion picture, *So Dear to My Heart*. Originally, Walt wanted to use the three-sided set piece from the motion picture, but he had already promised it to Ward Kimball for his own backyard railroad. Walt designed a new station using the same blueprints, but made the depot much larger (206-feet long) than the original. The working set of weighing scales, express wagon, vintage trunks, and crates were all added outside the station. One of the crates is addressed to Earl Cox in Merger, Mo., an uncle of Walt's.

A functioning, wooden water tower stands at the north end of the station. This tower provides water for the locomotive tenders. At the south end of the station is a genuine train-order signal donated by William White, chairman of the board of the Delaware & Hudson & Lackawanna Railroad. The signal had been used to tell engineers if there were messages or mail to be picked up.

The telegraph continually clicking at the New Orleans Square Railroad Station actually sends out Walt's Disneyland opening-day dedication speech. This is not in Morse code, but its predecessor called landline telegraphy.

Railroad telegraphers communicated with train dispatchers and telegraphers at other stations with telegraphy. Lilly Disney had once trained as a telegraph operator in her hometown of Lewiston, Idaho. With her help, they were able to change the telegraph message to Walt's opening day address instead of the previous adult-oriented commentary:

To all who come to this happy place, welcome. Disneyland is your land. Here, age relives fond memories of the past, and here, youth may savor the challenge and promise of the future. Disneyland is dedicated to the ideals, the dreams, and the hard facts that have created America, with the hope that it will be a source of joy and inspiration to all the world.

When you ride the Disneyland Railroad from New Orleans Square to ToonTown, keep a sharp eye out for a doghouse with Indiana printed on it. The tribute is two-fold. In the movie *Indiana Jones and the Last Crusade*, the audience learns that Henry Jr., the movie's hero, takes his nickname from his dog. The second and lesser-known bit of trivia is that George Lucas also had a dog named Indiana and borrowed the name for the character in the films.

Haunted Mansion: The exterior of the building was finished as early as 1963, but the attraction didn't open until 1969, leaving guests with six years to speculate about the horrors to come. Actually, Walt and the Imagineers were working on the World's Fair attractions and left the house sitting empty until they got back. For a while, a sign on the empty building informed guests that Walt was out recruiting ghosts.

Like any "haunted house" in any city in America, this attraction has many rumors and speculations about its history and its inhabitation by the undead. One variation of the Disney myth is shown on the following page.

Look for clues that give away the story of this house: a skeleton hanging from the ceiling, a picture of a sailor with a bloody ax in one hand and a noose in the other, a bride in the attic with a glowing

Director George Lucas had a dog named Indiana. He used the name for one of his famous movie characters.

Photo by Dave Hawkins

The Haunting of the Mansion

In 1810, a wealthy sailor, Captain Bartholomew Gore, built this Southern-style house for his young bride, Priscilla. Just before the wedding ceremony, the groom left to sail the sea and asked his bride to move into the mansion and wait for him. His one request was that she never enter the attic.

Many months passed. Fearing that her lover had died, Priscilla decided to learn his secret. She entered the attic and opened some old trunks. There she discovered that he was a bloodthirsty pirate. Just as she closed the trunks, Bartholomew appeared behind her. In a rage, he cut his fiancée's head off with an ax. Realizing that he had killed the woman he loved, he hanged himself from the rafter's in the attic.

Priscilla's ghost still haunts the mansion, her glowing heart a symbol of her enduring love. Over the years, other ghosts have come to stay at the mansion, some taunting the bride by popping out of unexpected places and screaming "I do." Eventually, many other spirits have come to "live" in the house: "999 Happy Haunts . . . but there's room for one more."

heart. From the exterior, a sailing ship's weather vane stands atop the house, and other nautical clues embellish the second floor.

Disney rrban legend: Outside the mansion is an antique white hearse with a ghost horse. Legend states that this hearse carried the body of Brigham Young to his burial place in 1877. However, the director of The Church of Jesus Christ of Latter-day Saints Museum of Church History and Art reports that no wheeled vehicle was used to carry Brigham Young, who was borne on a platform carried by clerks and employees, as he had requested in his will. The hearse may be from Utah, but it bears no manufacturing plate or documentation about its origin. Speculating about the history of the carriage is fun, though, and will continue to keep guests wondering who might have taken their last ride in such a fanciful cart.

Imagineers designed three different facades for the Haunted Mansion to let Walt choose between. The Imagineers favored a scarier, dilapidated version, but Walt preferred the Southern mansion. He wanted everything at Disneyland to be clean and attractive. He once said, "Let the ghosts have the inside."

The Haunted Mansion was the first ride built and opened without Walt Disney's guidance. There are two distinct ways to enact the haunting of a house. One is to let visitors see the ghosts; the other is to make them invisible. Scenery specialist Claude Coats developed the first section with hallways and rooms and translucent ghosts. Marc Davis, who is known for character development, created the second half of the attraction with the ballroom and graveyard scenes bursting with ghost characters.

Fortunately, during the delay while they directed their attention toward the New York World's Fair in 1964-1965, the Imagineers came up with some new and different ideas for the Haunted Mansion. A variation to the ride design developed for "The Magic Skyway," an attraction for Ford Motor Company at the World's Fair, improved the original walk-through idea. These black "Doom Buggies" can accommo-date 1,200 guests per hour in the Haunted Mansion.

One idea that didn't come to full realization is a narrating raven. Partially inspired by Edgar Allen

Photo by Debbie Smith

Poe's story, *The Raven*, the idea seemed a little too creepy. The raven, however, still exists. Look for it in the séance room on the back of the chair, and again on the coffin in the conservatory, on the balcony against the rear wall in the ballroom, on the rooftop as you enter the graveyard, and overhead as you exit the crypt.

The séance was an innovation of Ub Iwerks, Walt's longtime partner

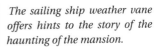

Photo by Dave Hawkins

The sailing ship weather vane offers hints to the story of the haunting of the mansion.

and artist of the first Mickey Mouse. He tested the idea of projecting a film of a talking human face onto a wig stand. Don Iwerks, Yale Gracey, and Ub Iwerks refined the idea and used it again in the graveyard scene with the singing busts. (Read more about Ub Iwerks in the ToonTown chapter (see page 154).

TREASURE & TRIVIA

Yale Gracey (1910-1983) started his career in 1939 as a layout artist on *Pinocchio* and *Fantasia*. In 1961, he joined WED as a special effects and lighting expert. He made a number of contributions to the Haunted Mansion and Pirates of the Caribbean before he retired in 1975.

Yale Gracey, a special effects guru. The current Haunted Mansion movie refers to the house as Gracey Mansion.

HIDDEN MICKEY

Look carefully at the 4-in. circles on the wallpaper across from the portraits in the walking gallery. They form the head of Hidden Mickeys.

HIDDEN MICKEY

In the walking gallery, watch the lower left sail of the sailing ship as it changes from new to old. A Hidden Mickey will appear in the bottom left corner.

TREASURE & TRIVIA

In the ballroom, the pipe organ (without the pipes) is the movie prop Captain Nemo played in the movie *20,000 Leagues Under the Sea.*

HIDDEN MICKEY

One set of dishes are arranged in the shape of Mickey Mouse in the ballroom scene.

TREASURE & TRIVIA

Current Disney Animators enjoy referring to Disney classic moments. One example is in the animated film, *Hercules.* As the character Megara sings her song, "I won't say (I'm in Love)," the muses reprise the singing busts from the Haunted Mansion.

TREASURE & TRIVIA:

Look for a decorative plaque up the stairway in the Court of Angels, it reads:

Plaque Musique Des Anges Music Lessons Vocal Instructions, Mme. Sally McWhirter, Instructor. Sally began her career with Disney in the Disney Stores Inc. in Indiana. Sally was promoted to District Manager before coming to work in Disneyland. Here she was named director of store operations in 1995 until her untimely death in 1997. She died at age 40 as a result of non-Hodgkins lymphoma. Sally sang with her church choir, which explains the plaque reference to music of angels and vocal lessons. Her tribute is thoughtfully near this heavenly stairway, in the Court of Angels.

In the graveyard scene, the voice and face of the fallen bust is that of Thurl Ravenscroft. Thurl may be equally well known as the voice of Tony the Tiger and the singer of "You're A Mean One, Mr. Grinch."

A week after the Haunted Mansion opened, the park set a single day's attendance record of 82,516. The record was not surpassed for nearly 15 years. Because of the multiple Hidden Mickeys, speculations about the story of the house, and the wonderful special effects, this attraction is still one of the most talked about and visited attractions.

Overall, New Orleans Square is a beautiful, musical, delicious part of your day in Disneyland. The two main attractions in this small area are favorites among most visitors. The Magic Kingdom in Florida opted for Liberty Square instead of New Orleans Square, which is a significant difference between the two parks.

As a result of the addition of Splash Mountain, Disneyland changed the name of this land from Bear Country to Critter Country.

Chapter 6

CLUES IN
Critter Country

Imagine a world run by animals that walk, talk and think like people. Critter County is a glimpse of just such a humorous wilderness where endearing critters exist solely to entertain. This area opened in 1972 and was originally called Bear Country. In 1988, the area was renamed Critter Country to include the Splash Mountain characters. Although it was built long after Walt was gone, the area was modeled after his idea to open a ski resort in Northern California.

The area's Northern California feel is made possible in part by the tall, shady trees. The different varieties of trees include aleppo, Canary Island, Monterey, Italian stone pines, redwood, locusts white birch, and evergreen elms. The beautifully carved benches and rustic buildings provide a natural and quiet setting. Critter Country is not the 100 Acre Wood, but it's still a great environment to meet Winnie the Pooh and Friends.

Splash Mountain

Imagineer Tony Baxter wanted to develop a log ride while Disney was looking for something to do with the Audio-Animatronic characters from the closed attraction, America Sings. An inspiration hit Tony Baxter. He would develop a log ride in Bear Country after the 1946 film *Song of the South*, which was based on Joel Chandler Harris' *Adventures of Uncle Remus' and Brer Rabbit*. The ride opened in 1989.

Many of the Audio-Animatronic characters from the America Sings attraction were recast in Splash Mountain. Marc Davis had the unique opportunity to work as an animator on the *Song of the South* film and an Imagineer to create the characters for the America Sings attraction. Among the characters lucky enough to find a new home in Splash Mountain were frogs and alligators with hats, a porcupine, a raccoon with a harmonica, foxes, hanging possums, chickens, and a vulture. There are 103 characters in Splash Mountain, almost as many as Pirates of the Caribbean, which has 119.

The theme song "Zip-a-Dee-Doo-Dah" received an Oscar for Best Song in 1947. Among one of the greatest songs in Disney history, this bouncy upbeat melody has become the anthem for happiness. It was written by Allie Wrubel and Ray Gilbert.

Nick Stewart gave Brer Bear his voice for the film and 43 years later Splash Mountain.

The top of the mountain, Chickapin Hill, stands at 87'. The drop is one of the tallest and sharpest of any attraction in the world—52 ft. at a 45° angle. You can almost always expect an extra thrill when you get wet. The little log is the fastest moving ride in the park, built to attain a speed of 40 mph. Planning and construction of Splash Mountain cost five times the as much as the original Disneyland Park, but most visitors agree it was worth every penny.

England had read about Pooh, that the film would be divided into three separate featurettes. Walt's intuition proved right as the public learned to love *Winnie the Pooh and the Honey Tree* when it released in 1966. Then two years later *Winnie the Pooh and the Blustery Day* won the Oscar for best animated short film. Finally, in 1974 *Winnie the Pooh and Tigger Too* was released. In 1977, all three were combined with a little extra footage added in and retitled *The Many Adventures of Winnie the Pooh.* Over 20 years later, Tigger and Piglet would come to have their own full-length films.

While waiting in line at the Pooh attraction, you'll hear original music from the films, arranged by Buddy Baker and written by the Sherman Brothers. Try to identify and sing along to "Winnie The Pooh," "The Wonderful Thing About Tiggers," "Heffalumps and Woozles," "Rumbly in My Tumbly," "A Rather Blustery Day," "Little

The Many Adventures of Winnie The Pooh opened in April 2003.

The attraction shares its name with Disney's 22nd full-length animated film. Both the film and ride are inspired by the English childhood classics written by A.A. Milne.

In 1965, the Sherman Brothers had written about two-thirds of the songs for the film when Walt surprised people by announcing that since not many children outside of

HIDDEN MICKEY
There are a lot of incomplete Hidden Mickeys in the honey, but you can really find one in the heffalumps and woozles room. On the right side there is a purple heffalump, toward the bottom. Look near the trunk and you'll see an upside down honey drop in perfect proportion.

TREASURE & TRIVIA

The Country Bears were the previous tenants in the building where you'll find the Pooh attraction. Although the bears are hibernating, your fellow Country Bear fans, Buff (the buffalo), Max (the deer) and Mel (the moose), whose heads could be seen hanging on the wall, are hidden in the Pooh attraction. To see them, pay attention as the honey heaven sequence ends, as you enter the next room look directly up and the vehicles pass right under them.

independent of each other. There are 22 beehicles, each with a name of a Pooh character or story word. This is the first attraction built in Disneyland where wheelchair-bound guests don't need to leave their chair to ride. Two special beehicles, Winnie and Woozle, are made for the wheelchairs, although during the flood sequence the cars are unable to have the floating effect.

In line you'll see Eeyore's house (stick lean-to) and Rabbit's garden. In the attraction you'll see Piglet's house marked "Trespassers Will" named for his grandfather Trespassers William, but what name appears on Pooh's house?

Answer: Mr. Sanders, it also says "Rnig also."

Black Rain Cloud," and "When The Rain Rain Rain Came Down."

The queue also has a small footbridge that on a slower day is fun to play Pooh sticks. Have each person take a small stick and toss into the water on one side of the bridge and go to the other side to see which stick floats under the bridge first.

This dark ride through the 100 Acre Wood was built in the old Country Bear Theater. The existing walls, columns and high ceiling had to be used, but the floor had to be flattened in order to accommodate the Beehive vehicles, or "Beehicles." Most of the "beehicles" have three rows that can accommodate about 2-3 people. The cars run on a track, but are

TREASURE & TRIVIA

Tigger is very computer savvy as he inspired the code TTFN as Ta Ta For Now.

Winnie the Pooh is known as a bear with very little brain, and this would explain the multiple ways to spell honey. The trick is to find it spelled correctly in the attraction.

In one of the main rooms you'll see Pooh riding in a hot air balloon. He floats up and down, which is possible thanks to Country Bear Teddi Bara and her swing that once descended from the ceiling.

Thotful Spot

This area resembles the 100 Acre Wood where live the popular characters from the A.A. Milne stories. Pooh Bear, Piglet, Tigger, and Eeyore anxiously await guests for a photo opportunity.

TREASURE & TRIVIA

Paul Winchell, who supplied the voice of Tigger in Disney's Winnie the Pooh cartoons, started in show business at the age of 14. He was a ventriloquist on the Major Bowes Amateur Hour radio program. By 1937, Winchell and his dummy had a television program, The Paul Winchell-Jerry Mahoney Show. During the 1950s, Winchell witnessed thoracic surgeries performed by Dr. Henry Heimlich (who later developed the Heimlich maneuver). Paul Winchell's observations inspired him to learn more about the human heart. He later earned worldwide recognition as the co-inventor of the world's first artificial heart valve.

Paul Winchell recorded the voice for the lovable Tigger.

Winnie the Pooh gets a hug and a voice from Sterling Holloway.

Sterling Holloway had a velvet-like voice that was popular with the Disney animators. Sterling's voice was first used as the stork in the film *Dumbo*. He narrated *Peter and the Wolf*, and his voice credits include such memorable characters as adult Flower in *Bambi*, the Cheshire Cat in *Alice in Wonderland*, Kaa the snake in *Jungle Book*, Roquefort in *Aristocats*, and of course Winnie the Pooh in the *Pooh* series. Sterling was named a Disney Legend in 1991 and died a year later.

Davy Crockett's Explorer Canoes

This attraction opened in 1956 as the Indian War Canoes. It was renamed in 1971. The 35-foot fiberglass canoes do not run on a track. Although the helmsman and stern man are strong, guests contribute to the 2,400' trip around the island. The loading dock has been moved several times as Rivers of America has evolved.

Old Town Canoe Company of Old Town, Maine, made the first canoes of varnished wood. They are covered with canvas for a textured birch bark appearance. Disney artists added the warlike markings on each end. The first six boats were 30 ft. long, carrying 18 passengers in addition to a "native" Indian guide. Later, Arrow Development made canoes of wood and fiberglass and painted them to resemble birch. Today, there are nine boats with portable pumps and a flotation tank to make them virtually unsinkable.

The canoes share the river with the Mark Twain, Columbia Sailing Ship, and Tom Sawyer Rafts. Canoes must yield the right of way to all the other watercraft.

The guides are dressed like Davy Crockett, replete with 'coon skin caps. The "bowman" faces the "crew" and teaches guests how to

TREASURE & TRIVIA

Walt needed a little "throw away tune" to bridge the time gaps in the story of Davy Crockett he was making for television. He asked for a song to carry the story from one sequence to another. "The Ballad of Davy Crockett," with words by Tom Blackburn and music by George Bruns, took the country by storm. Seven million copies of the song were sold in the first six months, making it the fastest-selling record ever up to that time. It reached *Billboard* charts on the pop, country/western, and children's categories. Several versions of the song were recorded; the most popular was by Bill Hayes. Among the singers who have also recorded the tune are Fess Parker, Tennessee Ernie Ford, Mac Wiseman, Vincent Lopez, Walter Schumann, Eddie Arnold, Fred Waring, The Sons of the Pioneers, Steve Allen, Mitch Miller, Rusty Draper, Burl Ives, Stephen Bishop, and Tim Curry.

TREASURE & TRIVIA

Since 1964, Disneyland has hosted the Canoe Racers of the World "C.R.O.W." race. It's a cast-member canoe competition, including crew members from Walt Disney World. The Disneyland team has a strong winning tradition, owing part of their success to heavy canoes. The Florida canoes are much lighter than the California ones, giving the California crew a slight advantage.

paddle. The "stern man" in the back steers the canoe for its quick 10-minute trip around Rivers of America.

Disney made a series of television shows starting in 1955 on the life of Davy Crockett. Actor Fess Parker played Davy, while Buddy Ebsen played Crockett's sidekick, George Russel. Ebsen actually spent some of his earlier years on the development of Audio-Animatronics. He was named a Disney Legend in 1993.

LESSON TO LEARN

Davy Crockett is truly an American hero. He lived from 1786 until his death at the Alamo in 1836. Davy was an expert hunter, scout, and soldier. He was elected to the U.S. Congress three times from his home state of Tennessee. He served with Andrew Jackson (the future president) in the campaign against the Creek Tribe in 1813. He partially wrote two autobiographies *Sketches and Eccentricities of Colonel David Crockett of West Tennessee* (1833), and *A Narrative of Life of David Crockett of the State of Tennessee* (1834). Several publishers printed *Crockett Almanacs*. These were very popular between 1835 and 1856. They recounted tall tales and oral legends that established Davy as a permanent figure of American folklore.

Kids of all ages love the interaction of paddling in the Davy Crockett canoes.

This is an old movie prop from the film Hot Lead and Cold Feet.

Chapter 7

Frontierland

FACT FINDING

Walt Disney once said "Frontierland is a tribute to the faith, courage and ingenuity of the pioneers who blazed the trails across America." Inspired by the cowboys and pioneers of the 1870s, the wooden buildings and sidewalks give a TV western feel. Frontierland is a voyage to the days of the wild west of the popular imagination during the 1950s. The success of the television shows "Davy Crockett" inspired a pop culture wave for Westerns in the 1950s.

Westward Ho Trading Co.

Formerly the Frontier Trading Post, this shop opened in 1987. The elk and deer horns on the roof give the shop an authentic touch. It was a common practice in the old west to place elk horns on the general store so that horseback riders coming into town knew where they could restock supplies.

Frontierland Shootin' Arcade/Exposition

The gallery is set in an 1850s town in the Southwest Territory. Eighteen genuine Hawkins 54-calibre rifles have been modified to shoot infrared beams. The backdrop, a small mining town called Boothill, is complete with bank, jail, hotel, and stables. Amusing things happen whenever you hit a target. If you hit the jail door, for example, the cell door opens. When you hit the Boothill sign, it changes its message to

TREASURE & TRIVIA

Westward Ho the Wagons is the 1956 Disney film about a wagon train of immigrant families from Missouri to the Pacific Northwest. Fess Parker starred with several cast members of the Mickey Mouse Club, including Tommy, Karen, David, Cubby, and Doreen.

TREASURE & TRIVIA

Sam McKim is one of the original Imagineers and a Disney Legend. In childhood, he had a lengthy career as a motion picture actor "Sammy McKim" in B-westerns and serials with Gene Autry, Hoot Gibson, John Wayne, Three Musketeers, and others. In 1954, he joined WED as a conceptual artist designing a lot of Main Street and Frontierland. Sam McKim is most known for the Disneyland souvenir maps from 1958-1964. When "Great Moments with Mr. Lincoln" was brought from the 1964-65 New York World's Fair to Disneyland, Sam painted 35 paintings of "The Life of Lincoln" as a prelude to guests going into the main theater to see and hear the Audio-Animatronic Lincoln. Other works include Haunted Mansion, Carousel of Progress, shooting galleries & arcades (such as the Pirate Arcade as well as a full-colored map of the Pirates of the Caribbean). He retired in 1987, but has come out of retirement to design for Disney (for example: the large souvenir map for "Disneyland Paris.")

Sam McKim came out of retirement to design the large souvenir map of Disneyland Paris.

"For sale". The shooting gallery costs 50 cents for 20 shots. George Whitney, was one of the designers of the original shooting gallery, and an avid gun collector. He has a window on Main Street.

Golden Horseshoe Revue was one of the opening attractions at Disneyland. It's difficult to tell, but if you look carefully you'll see that the building is in the shape of a horseshoe. The bar, inspired by Paul Bunyan, was originally the "longest little bar in the world" and served real beer (root beer). When Pepsi signed on, it became the "Tallest soda in the West."

When Walt asked Harper Goff to create the design for the saloon, he mentioned the 1953 Doris Day musical, *Calamity Jane*. Walt did not know that Harper had been employed by Warner Brothers in 1953 as the set designer for *Calamity Jane*. He made a copy of the blueprints, scaled them down to Disneyland size, and turned the Golden Horseshoe into one of the quickest attractions ever built at Disneyland.

Inside the theatre, Walt wanted an 1871 wild west vaudeville show. The dress rehearsal was timed to

Mark Twain Riverboat was an opening day attraction.

celebrate Walt and Lilly's wedding anniversary, just a few days before the park opened. The opening day show, "Slue Foot Sue," ran from July 1955 until October 1986, putting it into Guinness' *Book of World Records*. Walt loved the show and watched it frequently from his box next to the stage—stage left. Roy preferred front row center.

The three primary roles in the show were the silver-toned tenor, Slue Foot Sue, and the comedian, travelling salesman. Donald Novis, Judy Marsh, and Wally Boag were the original cast. Soon thereafter, Fulton Burley became the silver-toned tenor and Betty Taylor became Slue Foot Sue. This cast remained intact for several years.

In September 1962, the Golden Horseshoe Revue was televised to celebrate its 10,000[th] performance. Betty Taylor, Wally Boag, Mouse-keteer Annette Funicello, Gene Sheldon, and Ed Wynn appeared with them on television that night. The show remained unchanged for many years, including the four can-can dancers and small live orchestra. Wally Boag later earned a window on Main Street for his work.

Mark Twain

The Disneyland Publicity Department claims that the Mark Twain was the first paddle wheeler built in the United States in 50 years. The Mark Twain Riverboat weighs 150 tons and stands 28-ft. high and 105-ft.-long. The ship is an authentic, steam-powered vessel with a diesel boiler. It runs on an underwater guide 2,450 feet long. Roger Broggie, Dick Bagley, and Roland Peterson designed the Mark Twain using historic riverboats *The Little Rufus* and *The Natchez* for inspiration. The ship's hull was built in one piece in San Pedro, Calif. The structure was constructed in Burbank at Disney Studios and then trucked down Interstate 5 to Disneyland, one deck at a time. Final assembly was done at Fowler's Harbor. The Mark Twain is one of the most accurate, authentic, and beautiful riverboats ever built.

LESSON TO LEARN

Mark Twain is the pen name of Samuel Clemens. Most American children are familiar with his classics: *The Adventures of Tom Sawyer*, *The Adventures of Huck Finn*, and *The Prince and the Pauper*.

The graceful ship carries 300 passengers, a captain, engineer, and deckhand on a 15-minute ride. The superstructure from bow to stern is spoon shaped, or slightly slanted inward on both sides. The first floor is called the Main Deck. The second floor, the Promenade Deck, has a small non-commissioned bar. The third deck is the Texas Deck, which is smaller than

LESSON TO LEARN

The term *Texas Deck* comes from the riverboats on the Rio Grande. Texas passengers often congregated on the uppermost deck to get a better view of the North Shore of Texas.

the Main Deck to give the ship a graceful appearance.

Above the Texas Deck is the wheelhouse where the Captain steers, watches the river ahead, rings the bell, and blows the whistle. The whistle always blows one long and two short blasts.

Walt and Lillian celebrated their 30th wedding anniversary on the maiden voyage of the Mark Twain Riverboat, four days before the park opened. The party began on the boat and continued with a reception at the Golden Horseshoe. Actress Irene Dunne officially dedicated the ship on opening day.

The Mark Twain travels around Tom Sawyer Island, passing scenes of a Native American village and assorted wildlife, all brought to life by Disney Imagineers. The music on the riverboat is "Come Back Sweet Papa," "Milanbury Joys," and "Western Saloon." The song "Milanbury Joys" is performed by the Firehouse Five Plus Two.

The Mark Twain has much in common with the Jungle Cruise in Adventureland. Each attraction uses Audio-Animatronic figures to create natural environments. Both were created to be educational yet entertaining. The themes and live narrations are the only critical differences.

HIDDEN MICKEY

Another Hidden Mickey can be seen on the island from the Mark Twain. After you pass the mill, look on the rocks over a cave opening. You'll see a slight indention and discoloration in the shape of Mickey.

Disney's True Life Adventure Series inspired the scenes along the river's edge. There are three kinds of animal movement along the river. The first group of animals is motionless. These are probably some of the original characters in the attraction. The second group is stationary, but makes small movements, such as an ear twitching or tail wagging. The final group is composed of showcase figures that perform in some manner. The Chief is one such showcase figure. He wears a full headdress and sits on a painted horse while he waves to the guests on the Mark Twain and turns to wave at the passengers on the train. This figure is known by two names, Chief Big Thunder and Chief Waves A Lot.

HIDDEN MICKEY

Check out the building on the water's edge to the right of the Mark Twain boarding area. A large mural says "River Excursions." Look closely at the passengers on the Main Deck for a Hidden Mickey.

Sailing Ship Columbia
(Built in 1958)

The Columbia is exclusive to Disneyland and operates only when attendance warrants or when the Mark Twain is out for maintenance. Modeled after the first United States sailing ship to circumnavigate the world, she is 84-ft. tall and 110-ft. long. Columbia has three masts, 10-guns, and is a fully rigged replica at full scale of the

TREASURE & TRIVIA

The last of the 1956 Rainbow Caverns Mine Trains can be seen from the Mark Twain along the banks of Rivers of America. Engine No. 3 appears to have been abandoned by all, but some prairie dogs after it hit a rock slide. The Rainbow Caverns Mine Train once operated where Big Thunder Mountain Railroad exists today. The rainbow effect can still be seen on Big Thunder Mountain.

The Rainbow Caverns Mine Train once took Disneyland guests for rides. Today it's home to some Audio-Animatronic friends.

Photo by Dave Hawkins

1787 commercial shipping vessel known as "Gem of the Ocean." The Disneyland Columbia was named "Gem of the Kingdom." The maritime museum below deck recreates the quarters and lifestyle of 18th-century seaman. The ship's hull was built in Long Beach, but the body was built at Disneyland.

LESSON TO LEARN

The original *Columbia* was built in Plymouth, Mass., and christened *Columbia Redivivia* (freedom reborn). She took three years to travel around the world. She also explored the mouth of the river in Oregon that took the same name.

TREASURE & TRIVIA

In the Captain's Quarters there is a fish on a plaque. The fish is an artifact from the ship Bounty and was also used in the film, *The Bounty.*

Petrified Tree Stump

Added to the park in 1957, this stump weighs five tons, is 10-ft. high, and measures almost 8-ft. around at the base. When it was alive, the tree may have stood 200-ft. tall. The 75-million-year-old stump is the oldest

The sailing ship Columbia is docked at Harbor Fowler. The ship is a floating museum.

attraction at Disneyland. It was a 31st wedding anniversary present to Lillian Disney from Walt. Lilly donated it to the park after it arrived from Pike's Peak, Colorado Springs, Colo., a year later, on their 32nd wedding anniversary.

Fowler's Harbor, the mooring place of the Columbia, was named for Disney Legend, Rear Admiral Joseph Fowler (1894–1993). In 1954, Walt asked Admiral Fowler to help build Disneyland. He was in charge of construction of both Disneyland and Walt Disney World. He retired in 1972 and was made a Disney Legend in 1990.

Admiral Fowler once ran the San Francisco Navy Yard, where he became known as "Admiral Can-Do." He was instrumental in finding an appropriate engine for the submarine ride and others. After 32 years with the U.S. Navy, he took a temporary construction assignment and ended up working for Disney for another 18 years. He started as vice-president of Disneyland Operations, then moved to Florida and became vice-president of engineering and construction, WED Enterprises chairman of the board, and director of construction for Buena Vista Construction Company. He died at the age of 99 in 1993. In Florida, one of the two stern-wheel steamboats in the Magic Kingdom is named for him.

Admiral Joe Fowler

Tom Sawyer Island

The rafts to Tom Sawyer Island were inspired by the story *Adventures of Tom Sawyer.* The dock for the rafts have been moved many times since the ride opened in June 1956.

The small rafts are named for characters in the *Tom Sawyer* book.

Photo by Dave Hawkins

Tom Sawyer Island as seen from the balcony of the Disney Gallery.

They take people across the river to Tom Sawyer Island.

Rivers of America captures the essence of the mighty Mississippi and Missouri Rivers, much as "Rivers of the World" reproduces the marvels of the world's river on the Jungle Cruise. Rivers of America is about 100' wide and almost a mile long with a maximum depth of 5 ft. The first time water filled Rivers of America, Walt and Imagineers watched the water seep quickly away into the soft orchard soil. The entire river bed had to be encased with nonporous clay to hold the water, causing added expense and delay before the attraction could be finished. Along the banks you'll hear chirping birds throughout the day. Imagineers change the night-

time noise to chirping crickets and croaking frogs.

Tom Sawyer Island was built in 1956. The island was inspired by

The island is a cool, shady, and sometimes quiet oasis.

the American classic *Adventures of Tom Sawyer*, by Mark Twain.

Walt Disney personally oversaw the design of Tom Sawyer Island. He wanted guests to wander and play over the suspension bridge, Barrel Bridge, Injun Joe's Caves, Castle Rock Ridge, Tom and Huck's Treehouse, teeter-totter rock, and Fort Wilderness.

At the southernmost tip of Tom Sawyer Island is Harper's Cider mill, which is used as a backdrop for *Fantasmic!* Disney's nighttime show, (please refer to the entertainer's chapter-page 182). It was built to reproduce an area where Walt used to

Walt Disney personally designed Tom Sawyer Island after his childhood play areas.

TREASURE & TRIVIA

The graves behind Fort Wilderness are fictitious except for two that salute Disney cast members, W. Pierre Feignoux, and Lt. Laurence Clemming. Raoul Wallace "Wally" Feignoux joined the company in 1936 after meeting Roy and Walt through a mutual friend. He was responsible for a staff of 10 and supervised the RKO's distribution of Disney films throughout Europe. When Hitler seized Paris three years later, Wally took all the Disney film prints and buried them to keep them out of Nazi hands. After the war was over, Wally returned the films. He managed to keep the Disney office open during the cccupation and took great personal risk. After 35 years with the company, Wally retired in 1971. His grave is a tribute to the heroic actions he took early in his career. This grave may just be another trick on the Nazis. Wally died in 1981, and posthumously named a European Disney Legend in 1997.

Larry Clemmons, a.k.a. Lt. Laurence Clemming, was a television writer/story-man that worked for Bing Crosby for many years before Disney hired him in 1932. He worked on stories for many of the Disney animated films, beginning in 1941 with *The Reluctant Dragon*. He retired in 1978 and died 10 years later.

The graves behind Fort Wilderness provide more Disney credits.

Photo by Dave Hawkins

Wally Feignoux, a Disney hero, with a secret in the grave.

Burbank, disassembled, trucked to Frontierland, floated across *Rivers of America*, and reassembled. Wander behind Fort Wilderness; many of the "graves" there are dated around 1812.

Big Thunder Mountain Railroad

The landscape of this 1979 ride was inspired by the gold rush era in Utah's Bryce Canyon. The name comes from an old Indian legend about a sacred mountain in Wyoming that thundered whenever white men tried to mine its gold.

The miniature town above the queue is left over from the Rainbow Caverns Mine Train, which was built in 1956. The town, Rainbow Ridge, was a favorite of Walt and Lilly. You can hear a local barmaid flirting with a miner to the accompaniment of "Red River Valley" or "Listen to the Mockingbird." The little town is also referred to as the International Village. Rainbow Caverns were incorporated into the track of Big

play as a kid. Inside is a flour mill. No one knows what's in the bag marked "May Flour."

Fort Wilderness

At the northernmost tip of the Island is Fort Wilderness. The fort was built entirely backstage in

Photo by Debbie Smith

Big Thunder Mountain Railroad boasts it's "the wildest ride in the wilderness."

Legend of Big Thunder

I n 1849, a young inventor living in a small gold-rush town devised a drilling machine that could bore into the very heart of Big Thunder Mountain. There, the veins of gold ran so deep, it was rumored, that they came from a mother lode large enough to bring a man the wealth of a hundred lifetimes.

Then a cave-in on Big Thunder buried 26 miners alive. They would have drawn their last breath had it not been for the inventor and his laughable drilling machine. He burrowed into the Earth's core and rescued the miners from certain death. It should have been a moment of joy and celebration, but as the men scrambled to safety, a massive earthquake shook the ground, opening up a cavern that swallowed the inventor and his machine.

The miners and the citizens of the village struggled day and night against the mountain, trying to dig the young man from his living tomb. They never saw him or another nugget of gold again. Big Thunder had taken its vengeance, not only on the miners, but on their wealth as well. The mountain had gone bust, and it became just a matter of time before only ghosts resided there.

Years later, an old miner named Sam was prospecting inside the mine by himself when he fell into an ore car. The car took off into the mine, rolling through a cave of bats and rainbow pools, past stalactites and stalagmites, past the powder house, and finally ending in front of Big Thunder Town. Old Sam never went near the ghost town or mine again, but he did retell the story to an Imagineer who recreated the adventure and made it safe for guests to share.

Thunder Mountain Railroad.

Other props reused from the Mine Train include the rockwork buttes at the start of Balancing Rock Canyon, the mine tunnels on both sides of Cascade Peak, and part of the dinosaur.

Big Thunder Mountain took five years to plan and two years to build at a cost $16 million. This attraction was initially developed for Walt Disney World in Florida, where it

TREASURE & TRIVIA

A crate in the queue is marked "Burke Assay Office." This crate is an Imagineer credit for Pat Burke, who traveled the country looking for the mining equipment to display in the queues of the Big Thunder Mountain Railroad.

TREASURE & TRIVIA

The steam engine you pass while you are in line is a prop from the 1978 film, *Hot Lead and Cold Feet*. The film is about twin brothers, both played by Jim Dale, in a contest for a town. The good brother, Eli, rides Engine No. 11. Another steam engine from the movie can be found as you exit Frontierland en route toward Fantasyland.

HIDDEN MICKEY

An upside down Hidden Mickey can be found while riding the attraction. First you travel through a cave, then a tunnel. After you exit the tunnel, and begin to climb the hill, look on your left for three gears, making the famous icon.

TREASURE & TRIVIA

A crate next to the left exit is marked "Sedona Mining Company." The attraction has the look of Sedona, Ariz., to which this crate is a tribute.

was so popular that a replica was developed for Disneyland. Imagineers faced an unusual problem. In Orlando, the attraction was built on the west side of Orlando's

Photo by Dave Hawkins

TREASURE & TRIVIA

A horseshoe hangs on railroad ties framing the entrance to the mine. It is turned to the superstitious upright position, which supposedly makes it "full of luck." Elsewhere, at the opening to a cave with railroad ties framing the entrance, the horseshoe is turned upside down. It means you have "run out of luck." This is the cave with the avalanche.

Rivers of America; it didn't fit on the east side of Rivers of America. To solve the problem, the blueprints were flipped. The ride fit perfectly.

The three-minute, 2,780-ft. ride is known as the "Wildest Ride in the Wilderness." Big Thunder was the inspiration for a famous climactic scene in *Indiana Jones and the Temple of Doom*. Some of the mine car sound effects heard in the film are actual recordings of the *Big Thunder Mountain* Railroad.

The authentic mining props include a 10-ft.-tall, 1880 mill stamp, a hand-powered drill press,

TREASURE & TRIVIA

Just before climbing the stairs under Thunder Ridge Depot. you'll see a crate labeled "Baxter Boring Company." This is a credit to Imagineer Tony Baxter, one of today's outstanding Disney Imagineers. He began his career in 1965 scooping ice cream on Main Street at Disneyland. His innovative ideas eventually won him a position at WED Enterprises. There, he worked his way through the ranks to become executive vice president in charge of design for Disney parks. He designed Big Thunder Mountain Railroad, Splash Mountain, and Indiana Jones among other park favorites. The

Fantasyland and Tomorrowland renovations were put under his watchful care.

The highly creative, talented and respected Tony Baxter.

Photo used with permission of Tony Baxter.

and a 1,200-lb. cogwheel used to break down ore. Imagineers visited auctions, ghost towns, swap meets, and abandoned mines throughout the western United States to find the props.

The brown stone walls near the loading area were created from 100 tons of real gold ore from the former mining town of Rosamond, Calif. The 10'-tall stamp mill named "Big Thunder Mine 1880" also came from Rosamond. The names of the trains are another example of the Imagineers' creative humor: U.R. Daring, I.M. Brave, I.M. Fearless, I.B. Hearty, U.B. Bold, and U.R. Courageous.

Conestoga Fries

McDonald's hosts the little covered wagon that features only french fries. There is a clever tribute to the number of fries served in the Old West of Frontierland.

Bonanza Outfitters

Window: *Texas Glenn Honey Bee Farms "Our Bees are Real Hummers" Glenn Hicks Proprietor.* According to Disney Archives, Glenn is the retired director of New Orleans

> ### 🔍 HIDDEN MICKEY
> Sometimes the park uses a wooden cart for stocking and selling tamales. Look at the axle underneath the platform. It bears scrollwork in the shape of a Hidden Mickey.

Square, Bear Country, Adventureland, and Frontierland. He also coached the winning company baseball team for years.

FLAGS OF FRONTIERLAND

At first, Frontierland was physically and thematically too similar to Main Street, so designers created a bridge to make a distinct transition. Flags were traditionally flown outside the gates of forts to identify the counties, colonies, divisions, and regiments of the soldiers inside. Originally there were 13 flags on the Frontierland fort, but the flags haven't always been replaced as they have worn out. Be a Disneyland Detective and see how many flags you can find, and learn their origins.

All flag illustrations by Karl Yamauchi

FLAG 1- Bedford Flag

This flag flew over the Battle of Concord on April 19, 1775, carried by Bedford Minuteman, led by Nathaniel Page. The original hangs in the Bedford Town Library in Massachusetts. The arm from the clouds represents the arm of God. The Latin inscription "Vince Aut Morire" means "Conquer or Die."

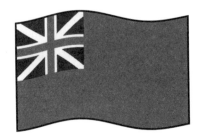

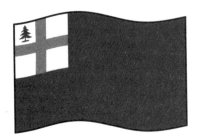

FLAG 2- British Red Ensign:

This flag has many names including "Colonial Red Ensign," "Meteor Flag," and "Queen Anne's" flag. This colony flag (without the words Liberty and Union) was created in 1707 for use on ships. It was used in the colonies until "the shot heard round the world." Indignant townspeople in Taunton, Mass., gathered on the Village Green on October 21, 1774, and hoisted the flag with the added words, "Liberty and Union."

FLAG 4-Bunker Hill

The Battle of Bunker Hill (June 17, 1775) was the first large battle of the American Revolution. Colonel William Prescott led 1,200 American troops with the famous order "Don't one of you fire until you see the whites of their eyes." The British had to charge the hill three times to claim it, suffering 1,000 wounded and casualties. American losses totaled 440. The battle strengthened the spirit of resistance throughout the colonies, especially since many men were volunteer militia who ached to hold their own against the British.

FLAG 3- Gadsden Flag

This flag was named for Colonel Christopher Gadsden of South Carolina in 1776. Gadsden was the Commander in Chief of the Continental Navy. The snake was a very popular revolutionary symbol of vigilance with deadly striking power.

FLAG 5-Continental Flag

This flag is also known as the "New England" flag and sometimes the Bunker Hill Flag. It is also believed to have been carried at the Battle of Bunker Hill. Under the tree memorialized on the flag, the Sons of Liberty met and planned the Boston Tea Party.

**FLAG 6- John Cabot Flag,
or the Cross of Saint George**

John Cabot flew this flag in 1497 during his voyages from England to New Foundland and North America. Sir Walter Raleigh's men later flew it over the colony in Roanoke, Va., in 1585. It is believed to have flown over the Mayflower when the ship landed on Plymouth Rock in 1620.

This flag also appears above the dock of the Mark Twain and Columbia. The plaque reads: "The first flag flown over the America mainland in 1607, it bears England's red cross of Saint George." Disneyland refers to this English flag as the John Cabot Flag, although it's recognized as the cross of Saint George. The flag dates back to the crusades of 1277 and is considered the first emblem of England. In 1497, John Cabot brought it from England during his voyages. Although the Union Jack had already been adopted, the St. George flag was still flown on English ships, including the Mayflower.

LESSON TO LEARN

John Cabot (1450-1499) was an English navigator and explorer who sought a direct route to Asia. In 1497, shortly after Christopher Columbus returned from his expedition, Cabot explored the coasts of Labrador, Newfoundland, and New England with a crew of 18 aboard the ship *Matthew*. Here is an interesting minor mistake on Disneyland's part: John Cabot did fly this flag over North America when he landed in 1497, but he died in 1499. The plaque refers to the year 1607, the year when the first colony was settled in Virginia.

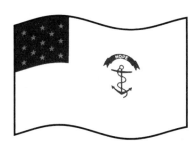

FLAG 7-Rhode Island Regiment

The flag was carried by the Rhode Island troops after 1776 and is believed to have flown at Trenton, Brandywine, and Yorkstown. The flag is predominately white because Rhode Island soldiers wore white uniforms during the revolutionary war. Native Rhode Islanders were among the first to join the minutemen outside of Boston. The anchor was a symbol of both the seafaring activities of Rhode Island and hope. There are 13 stars representing each of the original colonies. The original flag is preserved in the State House in Providence.

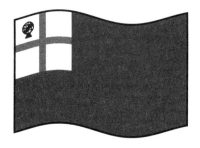

FLAG 8-New England

Very little can be found about this flag other than that it was flown to represent New England. New England is composed of six states: Maine, New Hampshire, Vermont, Massachusetts, Rhode Island and Connecticut. The globe replaced the tree most likely because the artist couldn't decipher what design he was copying.

FLAG 9- Fort Moultrie

In June 1776, two militia regiments in Charleston, S.C., gathered to defend the harbor. Led by Colonel William Moultrie (1731-1805), they successfully defended Sullivan's Island. William Moultrie was promoted to General and later served as

the Governor of South Carolina. Sullivan's Island was renamed Fort Moultrie. The flag is blue because the South Carolina soldiers wore blue uniforms and cap badges. The crest represents Liberty. Even today, the state flag of South Carolina bears a crescent moon on a field of blue.

FLAG 10-Culpepper

The 100 military men of Culpepper County, Va., adopted this flag with its popular rattlesnake emblem and the immortal words of Patrick Henry. The Revolutionaries of Culpepper County named themselves Minutemen because they could prepare for battle at a minute's notice. In October and November 1775, 300 men gathered under Col. Edward Stevens at the Culpepper Court House. From there they marched to Williamsburg, catching the attention of all they passed in their unusual attire. The breasts of their hunting shirts were emblazoned with the words, "LIBERTY OR DEATH." Buck tails hung from their hats and belts. They carried tomahawks and scalping knives.

Star Spangled Banner

The center of the entrance is standard location for the flagpole of a fort, but here it also helps the flow of traffic by forcing people to choose one side of the street or the other. This flag has only 15 stars and 15 stripes, unlike the current flag with 50 stars and 13 stripes. A flag like this one, only much larger, flew above Fort McHenry in Baltimore during the British bombardment of the War of 1812. Upon seeing the flag still flying the day after the assault, Francis Scott Key wrote the poem that became the American National Anthem more than a century later by an Act of Congress in 1931. Look for this flag in three places in Frontierland.

Rivers of America Boat Dock

More historic flags fly above the landing where the Mark Twain River Boat docks. All the flags at one time represented North America. In addition to ones named previously, you might find these flags.

King's Colors Flag

When King James VI of Scotland ascended to the English throne, the national flags of England and Scotland merged. Saint George's cross was superimposed on Scotland's white cross of Saint Andrew over a blue background. This flag, also known as the Union

Jack, was adopted in 1606.

Pine Tree Flag

Also known as the "Liberty Tree Flag" and "Washington Cruisers," the tree is modeled after an old elm in Boston's Hanover Square. Under this tree, the Sons of Liberty met and planned the Boston Tea Party. Because manufacturing of the flag was often inexact, the tree often looked like a pine. In the fall of 1775, the flag flew above the fledgling American Navy at Charles River as they attacked the

LESSON TO LEARN

Grand Union Flag

George Washington (1732-1799), a general in the American Revolutionary War and first president of the United States, laid siege to Cambridge, Mass., without any fighting. He captured 50 heavy cannons from the British Fort Ticonderoga in New York and dragged them to Boston. Seeing the mounted cannons on Dorchester Heights, Sir William Howe of the British forces knew his position was vulnerable and fled to Nova Scotia to wait for reinforcements, thus removing British troops from Massachusetts.

This flag was first raised by George Washington in Cambridge Mass., in 1776 to commission the Continental Army. It has 13 red and white stripes that represent the original colonies. The British Union Jack in the upper corner indicated a continued loyalty to England. This was the first national flag of the united colonies; it was used from late 1775 to 1777.

British troops in Boston. When the Navy flew this flag on the Delaware River while defending Philadelphia, it became the first Naval Ensign. Some people wanted to make it the national flag, but it was too closely associated with Massachusetts and New England to be widely accepted throughout the first states.

Betsy Ross Flag

Adopted by the Continental Congress in 1777, it has the same 13 red and white strips as the Grand Union Flag, but in the upper corner, a circle of 13 stars shine on a blue field.

Betsy Ross (1752-1836) was a Philadelphia seamstress who was asked to design and make a national flag. George Washington and Colonel George Ross, her late hus-

band's uncle, commissioned her in secrecy.

The 13 stripes and stars represent the original colonies that ratified the constitution.

Old Glory

With 13 red and white stripes and 24 stars, this flag was adopted in 1818 and given its nickname by a sea captain in 1831. The stripes symbolize the 13 original colonies and the stars represent the states in the union. In 1846 during the Mexican War, the flag only had 29 stars. At the beginning of the Civil War in 1861, the flag had 34 stars, including the seceding states. During the Spanish-American war in 1898 the flag had 45 stars.

TREASURE & TRIVIA

How many stars were on the U.S. flag when Disneyland opened in 1955? Answer: The flag had only 48 stars until Alaska and Hawaii joined in 1959.

Notice the spire on the far left of this photo. It is the only one not to have gold plating. This is a symbol that Disneyland will never be finished as long as there is imagination left in the world.

Chapter 8

A NEW SPIN ON
Fantasyland

> "Fantasyland is dedicated to the young and young at heart. To those who believe that when you wish upon a star, your dreams come true."
>
> —*Original Fantasyland dedication plaque read aloud at the opening of Disneyland, but never installed.*

Fantasy touches all of us. Walt Disney, as much as anyone, understood that fantasy was one of humanity's few universal pleasures. "Fantasy," he said, if it's really convincing, can't become dated for the simple reason that it represents a flight beyond the reach of time." Most of the fairytales we grew up on were European, so Walt made sure that you would enter his land of fantasy through a courtyard inspired by the Old World architecture of Germany, Great Britain, and France.

From the day the park opened, Fantasyland has been the heart of Disneyland. More attractions in Fantasyland were available on opening day than in any other land in the park. Because so many of these attractions were inspired by Disney's familiar animated films, visitors recognized them immediately. Popular rides, such as Dumbo, The Mad Tea Party, and Sleeping Beauty Castle, became instant icons representing not just Fantasyland, but all of Disneyland.

Some years later, Fantasyland was remodeled at a cost of $55.5 million. It took two years to complete. Fantasyland reopened in 1983, although it wasn't until spring of the following year that it was finished. Many of the attractions were moved and given elaborate facades while several new attractions were added.

Triton Garden and Ariel's Grotto

When you enter Triton's Garden, you'll see tidepools, landscaped walkways, and jets of water that leap from rocks over a bridge. When you go at night, the lights, colors, and fountain spray

Photo by Debbie Smith

transform the garden into a place of romance. At one time, the all-plastic Monsanto House of the Future stood here, so this may be the only flower garden with electrical and plumbing hookups. Look here for Ariel, the Little Mermaid. You'll find her in the grotto signing autographs and posing for pictures.

Snow White Grotto

The centerpiece of the grotto is the wishing well, one of the most romantic sites in the entire park. Are you thinking about proposing marriage? This is the place to do it! Listen carefully you may hear the original voice of Snow White, Adriana Caselotti, singing "I'm Wishing." This timeless recording was made in 1937 for Disney's Oscar-winning film. It still sounds like it belongs here.

Over by the waterfall you'll see white marble statues of Snow White and the seven dwarves. These were anonymous gifts, sculpted in Italy and shipped to Walt Disney's studio. Their shapes were inspired by a set of soaps that were all created the same height to fit into a box. The marble statue of Snow White is the same size as the dwarves, an error no Imagineer would make. Walt used "forced perspective" to trick your eye into thinking that Snow White is the right size. By placing Snow White at the top of the waterfall and the dwarves below her, Walt created the illusion that Snow White is actually larger than the dwarves. Imagineers added other animals in

various sizes to enhance the illusion. The trick was so successful that when plans were drawn up for the Tokyo Disneyland, the Japanese sponsors insisted that their Snow White Grotto be identical to the original.

Sleeping Beauty's Castle

The castle is the quintessential symbol of Disneyland. During construction of the park, Walt insisted the castle be built first to provide the inspiration and vision for everything else. It continues to symbolize the Disney mystique. Even today, you'll see an animated

The figures from Snow White Grotto were an anonymous gift from Italy.

version of the castle whenever you go to the movies and see a film distributed by "Buena Vista Distribution Company," owned by the Disney Corporation.

During the 1950s, millions of viewers watched Tinker Bell open The Wonderful World of Disney on television by waving her wand and sprinkling fairy dust as she flew above the Disneyland Castle. Why not Mickey Mouse, the character almost everyone identified with Disney? Walt's executives were afraid to identify Mickey Mouse with the park in case Disneyland wasn't a success. They chose other, secondary characters—like Tinker Bell—to represent the park. As a result, Tinker Bell has become very collectible and the real symbol of both the television series and the park.

Sleeping Beauty Castle looks very much like Neuschwanstein castle in Bavaria (although a number of medieval European castles were also used as models). The castle looks larger than it really is, because the smaller faux building stones at the top and larger ones at the bottom create another illusion of size. The castle itself rises only 77 ft. above the moat. Walt explained that tyrants in Europe built huge, imposing castles in order to intimidate the people. He wanted his castle to be friendly, so he built it on a smaller scale.

The castle's fiberglass turrets were built in the studio and shipped to Anaheim. The tallest tower was originally supposed to contain a periscope-type devise that visitors could use to view the

Sleeping Beauty Castle.

Photo by Debbie Smith

entire park from its highest point. Unfortunately, it was too difficult to make the periscope work, so the idea was set aside.

TREASURE & TRIVIA

Look for the gold nail in the floor of the hallway, near the back entrance of the castle. It was placed there in 1955 to mark the center of Disneyland. With the later addition of Toon Town, New Orleans Square and Critter Country, the nail is now a tribute to the early days of Disneyland, for it is no longer the center of the park.

The interior of the castle opened in April 1957. Shirley Temple was there to greet the first guests and escort them up the stairway to see the three-dimensional dioramas that recreate Disney's *Sleeping Beauty* film. Though it was already in production, the animated feature wouldn't be finished for another two years, so some of the scenes in the diorama bear no resemblance to the film.

The castle drawbridge has been lowered only twice. The first was on opening day when Mickey Mouse welcomed children during the dedication ceremonies. When Fantasyland was remodeled in 1983, the drawbridge was lowered again for the new dedication. This time the children of the original

kids who had crossed the drawbridge were invited to be the first to enjoy the rides.

If you stand near the Partner's Statue, you will be facing the back of the castle. Sleeping Beauty Castle was originally designed to face the other way. The Imagineers built a scale model of the castle to show to Walt. As they disassembled the model, Walt asked to see it again. They accidentally placed the castle backwards. Walt liked it better that way because he could see more spires than he could from the front. Turning the castle around also gave it a different look from the Neuschwanstein original.

With one exception, the castle spires never need to be polished—they are plated in 22-karat gold leaf. When they were being built, Roy Disney objected to the gold leafing. It was too expensive, he said. Then one day he left town and Walt took charge of the checkbook. When Roy returned, the money for the gold had been spent. That was the last time Roy gave Walt control of the checkbook. One spire was left unplated to be a symbol of Walt's intended idea "Disneyland will never be complete as long as there is imagination left in the world."

Swans grace the moat. They may remind visitors of the last Silly Symphony in Disney's 1939 feature, *The Ugly Duckling*. At first, the swans ate all the foliage about the castle, so the gardeners had to find plants that swans wouldn't touch.

That's why you'll see a lot of juniper planted around the water's edge. Not even swans like the taste of Juniper.

TREASURE & TRIVIA

The coat of arms you see above the archway entrance of the castle is that of the Disney clan. The three lions on the shield represent three times courage and strength.

The Disney Family Heraldry.

Snow White's Scary Adventures

This was one of the opening day attractions. Walt Disney's first, full-length, animated feature was *Snow White*, which was based on a fairy tale by the Grimm Brothers'

TREASURE & TRIVIA

An inscription in the front courtyard of the castle says: "When you wish upon a star your dreams come true." This quote is from the song, "When You Wish Upon A Star," that Jiminy Cricket sang in Disney's film, *Pinocchio*. Over the years, the inscription has become the Disney mantra and an inspiration to people everywhere.

released in December of 1937. The music you hear during the ride is taken from rare recordings used in the original soundtrack, and the vehicles you ride in are named after the seven dwarves. These dwarves never had names at all until Disney's animated feature. The staff took two years to choose seven names out of more than 50 that were originally proposed. Except for Doc, the dwarves are named for emotions or common states of being. (There are times we are all a little Happy, Bashful, Grumpy, Sleepy, Sneezy, or Dopey, even at Disneyland!)

The Snow White ride is one of the three original "dark" rides. (The others are Mr. Toad and Peter Pan.) These attractions are set in buildings with no windows. They use ultraviolet black lights with specially painted sets that glow in the dark. Ken Anderson, who worked on many of the original animated films and was one of the developers of the dark rides. He understood that visitors who were distracted by bouncing around in the cars would have no opportunity to appreciate the subtleties of character and plot so central to the animated movies. Rather than to try to tell a linear story, he built these rides around the emotions of the environments where the stories took place.

At first the main characters were not even seen in the rides because riders were supposed to become the main characters as if they stepped right into the story themselves. Some years later, though, Disneyland added the characters to the rides, because Walt discovered that people still wanted to see the real stars of the stories. The dark rides were so popular that in the 1983 remodel of Fantasyland, 25 percent more tracks were added to each of the dark attractions.

TREASURE & TRIVIA

The apple the old hag offers in the ride was one of the most frequently stolen items at Disneyland, especially at Grad Night. Imagineers solved this problem by replacing the "real" apple with a holographic one. It hasn't been stolen yet.

When you arrive at the cottage, you'll see the dwarf band. That's Grumpy on the organ, Sleepy on the fiddle; Bashful on the guitar, Happy on the accordion, Doc on the mandolin and Dopey on Sneezy's shoulders. One trick to remember all seven dwarves' names is to think of 2 S's (Sleepy & Sneezy), 2 D's (Dopey & Doc), and a Big, Happy Grin (Bashful, Happy and Grumpy).

This attraction was remodeled extensively in 1983 and again in 1994, when Snow White finally became part of the attraction.

TREASURE & TRIVIA

Look above the castle door. Every few moments the evil Queen opens the curtains to gaze out of the beautiful gothic window at you and the other guests below. When he was preparing the animated picture, Walt asked the artists to think of the Queen as part Lady MacBeth and part Big Bad Wolf. Artists Albert Hurter, Gustaf Tenggren, and Joe Grant developed the elegantly evil queen as one of the most memorable villains in Disney history. Silent Screen Star and Stage Actress Lucille LaVerne was the voice of both the queen and the witch. She managed the cold, commanding voice of a regal queen perfectly. Then she removed her dentures to master the cackling voice of the old crone.

TREASURE & TRIVIA

A wicked voice may advise you to touch the golden (actually, it's brass) apple outside the entrance of the Snow White attraction. The apple is next to the golden book. Find out what happens when you touch it.

Pinocchio's Daring Journey

This attraction was not built until Fantasyland's 1983 renovation. When the park opened in 1955, this building was the Mickey Mouse Club Theatre. It was the park's headquarters for Jimmy Dodd, Roy Williams, and the Mousekeeters until 1963, when they moved to the Opera House. Mickey Mouse films and Disney cartoons were shown here. In 1964, the building became Fantasyland Theatre where short films could be viewed in air-conditioned comfort. Movie-cast members often viewed recent Disney films after hours here.

This attraction actually opened in Tokyo Disneyland one month before it opened in California. Collodi's (Carlo Lorenzini) story of *Pinocchio* first appeared in a children's magazine in 1881). Disney's 1940 animated feature *Pinocchio* was his second full-length cartoon. The film won an Oscar for "Best Song" for "When You Wish Upon a Star." This classic Disney song was written by Leigh Harline, and Ned Washington.

Pinocchio's Daring Journey is the most recent dark ride and a complement to Snow White's Scary Adventures. People usually remember only two things: the things that make them laugh and the things that give them a real scare. Overcoming fear gives people a sense of confidence and accomplishment. Pinocchio's Daring Journey was designed by Tony Baxter and does a fair job of telling the full story. The attraction uses a lot of fiber optics, holograms, and special effects. Pinocchio is the first dark ride to have a happy ending.

The weathervanes on top of the attraction are actually models of Monstro the Whale and other characters from the animated movie. Disney and the Imagineers seldom missed opportunities to build a motif out of material they found in Disney's features.

King Arthur Carrousel

This was an opening-day attraction. It is an old 1875 Dentzel merry-go-round from Sunnyside Park, a Toronto, Canada, amusement park. When Ross Davis found and purchased it, the ride animals, including a giraffe, deer, and cats, were arranged in rows of three. Arrow Development, an outside vendor, engineered a new crankshaft for a fourth row of animals, all of which move up and down. Eventually all the other animals were replaced by horses Disney obtained from Coney Island Pier and Whitney's Playland in

San Mateo. Some of the old animals were stored, but you can see a number of them at the Casey Jr. Circus.

Why is this a "carousel" and not a "merry-go-round?" Purists insist that carousels have only horses while merry-go-rounds have other animals. Carousels rotate counter-clockwise, while merry-go-rounds move clockwise. By either measure, Disney's Carousel is a true carousel.

Most of the horses were carved in 19th-century Germany. Each is uniquely shaped and painted with lots of gold, silver, and copper leaf ornamentation. It takes workers six hours every night to polish just the 182 brass poles.

There are 17 rows of four horses each. Disneyland keeps another 17 horses in storage. All of them are maintained constantly. They are all "outside quality," which means that any of the horses could be placed on outside row of the carousel. The horses are more decorative on the right (or visible) side. Because only the most beautiful of them actually end up on the outside row,

Jingles, the lead horse on King Arthur's Carrousel, has a Hidden Mickey.

the carousel is always a visual treat. The park interchanges the horses four at a time, so they may appear in different locations throughout the year.

Carousels usually have several types of horses, and Disney's is no exception. The most ornate horse is called the lead horse. "Jingles" is the lead horse. It has carved flowers in its mane and forelock and straps of silver and gold bells that give it a truly distinguished look. All of the horses have been given names. You can get a complete list at City Hall.

HIDDEN MICKEY

There is a Hidden Mickey made of gems on the front of Jingles.

During the early 1970s, the horses were black, tan, gray, or brownish red. In 1975, John Hench and Kim Irvine decided that the horses should be white. They paid attention to the lines of visitors. In the beginning, when there was only a single white horse, guests would wait and wait to ride it. Perhaps the white horse was popular because King Arthur rode a white horse or because Prince Charming rescued his lady on a white horse. Whatever the reason, today all the horses are white.

The faces of the Jester, Lady Liberty, and Cherub on the carousel are covered with 23-karat

Photo by Dave Hawkins

TREASURE & TRIVIA

There are several other kinds of carousel horses. All of Disney's animals are "jumpers" because they have all four legs in the air. A horse with one ear forward and one ear back is a "Listener." A horse with its head back and eyes up is a "Star Gazer." A horse with a heavy forelock blowing straight up is a "Top Knot Pony." Because Disney wanted all the horses to leap and move, any standing horses on the carousel were recast into jumping configurations.

in 1982, the carousel was moved back several feet to open up the courtyard and give guests a better view of the carousel. It now sits where the Teacup platform used to sit. Moving the carousel also allowed an expansion to the Mr. Toad's Wild Ride and the Peter Pan attractions.

The carousel bell is actually a recording made by the band organ behind the Dumbo ride. When it rings once, workers perform a safety check to make sure that all children are safely aboard. When the bell sounds twice, the two-minute ride is about to start. Hold on tight and enjoy the 4.4-mph ride.

gold leaf. These are parts of the original carousel. A high-peak canopy diverts your attention away from the ornamentation and instead invites you to focus on the horses. The carousel was so ornate that Ross Davis was afraid that Walt would want to remove all the ornamentation. The canopy distracts the eye away from all of the decoration. This was an Imagineer tactic to preserve the carousel from those who might have thought it too gaudy. On top of the carousel's inner main face are nine hand-painted scenes from *Sleeping Beauty*. The romance of the Middle Ages is central to the story of Sleeping Beauty, so Disney made sure it was part of the activities in the courtyard and castle as well.

When Fantasyland was remodeled

LESSON TO LEARN

Did King Arthur really exist or is he merely part of folk legend? Some scholars believe he is a composite of several British kings, while others insist he really lived during the fifth century. Legend or truth, his adventures are inspiration. Raised as an orphan, he grew up to become King of England by pulling the sword Excalibur from the Stone. He was known for his leadership, valor, swordsmanship, and most of all for bringing together the Knights of the Round Table, named after a table that Arthur received as part of his dowry when he married Queen Guinevere.

Notice the shields on the lances that support the big overhead canopy on the carousel. They are inspired by the heraldry of the Knights of the Round Table. Start with the shield to the left of The Sword in the Stone and move counterclockwise:

crass and rude behavior. Eventually Kaye betrayed Arthur and was reduced to a steward.

The Chevron is common in heraldry (not pictured here). It is not exclusive to the Knights of the Round Table.

Illustration by Karl Yamauchi

The shield for Sir Kaye, King Arthur's seneschal.

Illustration by Karl Yamauchi

Sir Gareth was a good friend of Sir Lancelot and trained under him.

The first shield belonged to Sir Kaye, Arthur's foster brother. According to legend, when Kaye lost his own sword, Arthur went in search of a replacement and found one in a stone in a churchyard. The sword, of course, was Excalibur, and when he pulled it from the stone, Arthur earned the right to the throne of England. Arthur promoted Kaye to seneschal, an official in medieval times that took care of the castles domestic needs. Sir Kaye's shield has keys because he was the keeper of the keys. Sir Kaye was known for his

The next shield belonged to Sir Gareth, the youngest brother of Sir Gawain. At first Gareth took a kitchen position in order to enter King Arthur's Court. Treated poorly by Sir Kaye, he was befriended by Sir Lancelot who trained and knighted him. When his brothers acted unchivalrously, an angry Gareth disappeared for a while. Years later, Sir Lancelot blindly killed him in a battle to rescue Queen Guinevere. This turned Gawain against Lancelot and was the beginning of Sir Mordred's takeover.

Illustration by Karl Yamauchi

Illustration by Karl Yamauchi

Sir Lancelot was the most famous Knight of the Round Table. He was a close friend to King Arthur and Guinevere.

Sir Tristan was the Sorrowful Knight.

Next comes Sir Lancelot's shield. Lancelot was the first knight of the Round Table and the greatest swordsman and fighter at the court. Known for his courtesy, courage, gentleness, and willingness to serve others, he also possessed great pride. Lancelot was the father of Sir Galahad, the perfect knight. He went on the quest for the Holy Grail, but because of his pride, he was unable to see it. Queen Guinevere favored Lancelot because he rescued her several times. Their love affair caused the destruction of the Round Table. Following King Arthur's death in battle, Guinevere became a nun and Lancelot spent the rest of his life in penitence.

The fourth shield belonged to Sir Tristan (Tristram), who was known as both the Knight of song and music and the "Sorrowful Knight." As a young man, he took up service with his uncle King Mark of Cornwall. Tristan fought a duel that allowed Mark to make a truce with Ireland. Tristan was then appointed to deliver the beautiful Iseult (Yseult) for marriage to King Mark. Tristan and Iseult fell in love and fled from Mark to live as fugitives. King Mark learned of their love and killed them both in a fit of rage. He later felt remorse and buried them together in the same grave. The non-Disney film *Shrek* is loosely based on the story of Sir Tristan.

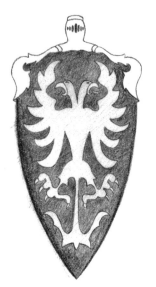

Illustration by Karl Yamauchi

Illustration by Karl Yamauchi

Sir Mordred was the son and rival to King Arthur. Though he was not a knight, his shield was made part of this exhibit.

Sir Galahad was the Perfect Knight who found and protected the Holy Grail.

The next shield belonged to Sir Mordred, who was not a knight of the Round Table, but a treacherous rival. Unknown to Arthur, Mordred was his son with the witch, Morgan le Faye. In his fight to take over Camelot, Mordred kidnapped Queen Guinevere. Arthur eventually learned of his identity and, in a final battle, both Arthur and Mordred delivered mortal blows to each other.

The son of Lancelot, Sir Galahad was the purest and most religious of the knights. Galahad was raised in a nunnery, hence the cross on his shield. He set out on the Quest for the Holy Grail and assumed the responsibility of protecting it. He was known as the "perfect knight" because he sat at the "perilous" seat at the Round Table. This was the one seat at the round table that was usually vacant as a reminder of Judas at the final supper. Only the hero of the Grail quest was allowed to sit there.

50th
Anniversary
UPDATE

Photo by Debbie Smith

Special Section

Buzz Lightyear Astro Blasters

The Buzz Lightyear Astro Blasters officially opened in Tomorrowland March 17, 2005, as part of the Happiest Celebration on Earth to celebrate Disneyland's 50th anniversary. The attraction is based off of the Buzz Lightyear concept from the Disney Pixar film *Toy Story* (1995), the sequel *Toy Story 2* (1999), and the weekly animated television series (2000-2001). This attraction appeals to all ages because it is created as a slow moving, interactive dark ride. The continual movement allows for high guest capacity in a short amount of time.

The building originally housed the *Circarama*, and later *Circle-Vision 360* with such films created especially for the attraction as *A Tour of the West*, (1955-1960) *America the Beautiful* (1960-1984), *American Journeys* (1984-1996)

TREASURE & TRIVIA

Back in 1998, Walt Disney World Florida's Magic Kingdom Park opened a similar attraction in Tomorrowland based on the film *Toy Story* called Buzz Lightyear's *Space Ranger Spin*. Tokyo Disneyland opened *The Buzz Lightyear Astro Blaster* attraction in 2004.

and *Wonders of China* (1986-1996.) The building also served as the pre-show for *Rocket Rods*.

The Astro Blaster attraction enlists guests to help Buzz Lightyear defeat the evil Emperor Zurg by climbing aboard a toy Space Cruiser and firing laser beams on targets. The more targets guests hit, the more points guests accumulate. The more points guests accumulate, the

Disney Myth

Evil Emperor Zurg has unleashed himself upon our galaxy. Equipped with his Dreadnought Spaceship and rapid-fire-sponge ball gun, he is set out to rule the universe. Zurg is building a secret weapon that requires excessive batteries. To get the batteries he has recruited an army of toy robots to steal the batteries from toys everywhere. His first target is the Green Planet, home of the Little Green Men, and second is Buzz Lightyear's own Star Command.

Since the Space Rangers have been robbed of their "power cells," you've been asked to help thwart Zurg and his robotic forces. Climbing aboard the XP-40s armed with Astro Blasters your mission is to find Zurg's army and secret weapon and blast them!

TREASURE & TRIVIA

Pixar used some famous voices for its cast in the film *Toy Story*. You might recognize comedian Tim Allen as Buzz Lightyear, in both the film and the attraction. But in the film you might also hear Tom Hanks as Woody, Don Rickles as Mr. Potato Head, John Ratzenberger as Hamm, Annie Potts as Bo Peep, Jim Varney as Slinky Dog and Wallace Shawn as Rex. Toy Story was the first animated feature completely generated by computer. John Lasseter directed the film and won a special Academy Award for "the development and inspired application of techniques that have made possible the first feature-length, computer-animated film."

higher the rank of Buzz Lightyear's elite regiment guests earn.

Entering the building, the staging is as if you just become one of the toys. The queue has a toy-like feeling to it, just as you've stepped into Star Command. There is an oversized official Buzz Lightyear walkie-talkie informing you Star Command is under attack.

Since most Americans don't like to read instructions, the poster explaining the targets often gets passed over. Bright orange targets with a "Z" are placed strategically throughout the attraction. (The letter Z is Zurg's logo.) When targets are hit, scores are recorded and special effects and movements are set off. Just so you know which targets are most valuable:

Circle targets are worth 100 or 500 points when lit.
Square targets are worth 5,000 or 10,000 points when lit.
Diamond targets are worth 10,000 or 20,000 points when lit.
Triangle targets are worth 20,000 or 50,000 points when lit.

Tip: There is a black diamond target in Hyperspace worth 50,000 points although it doesn't light up for extra points.

The highlight of the queue line is the life-size Buzz Lightyear in the briefing room. He is an Audio Animatronic figure with moving face animation. To his left is a giant Etch A Sketch that illustrates Buzz Lightyear's instructions.

HIDDEN MICKEY

In the queue of Buzz Lightyear, you'll enter the second room with a mural of the "Planets of the Galactic Alliance" on the right hand side. Look carefully at Sector Two at the planet "Ska-Densii." The landmass makes up a profile of Hidden Mickey. You'll see the same planet throughout the queue, ride and exit.

The Space Cruiser is named the XP-40 and utilizes Disney's Omnimover system. The X stands for unknown capabilities of the cruiser and the P signifies protection for Star Command and the Universe. The batteries on the Space Cruiser XP-40 and throughout the attraction are "Crystolic Fusion" which is taken from the *Toy Story* film when Buzz mentions his main power source as "crystolic fusion."

Scoring:

L7 Score 999,999+
Galactic Hero
L6 Score 600,000-999,999
Cosmic Commando
L5 Score 300,001 – 600,000
Ranger 1st Class
L4 Score 100,001 – 300,000
Space Scout
L3 Score 10,001 – 100,000
Planetary Pilot
L2 Score 1,001 – 10,000
Space Ace
L1 Score 0-1000
Star Cadet

HIDDEN MICKEY

As you exit the first room with targets, on the lower left side you might see a reverse Hidden Mickey. Since the room is dark, this Hidden Mickey will be made of three white hollow circles that glow in the dark on a block of wood.

TREASURE & TRIVIA

The first Space Cruisers in the Buzz Lightyear attraction in Walt Disney World Florida were the XP-37, the second Buzz attraction in Tokyo were the XP-38s, the Space Cruisers in Hong Kong are the XP-39s, although they opened later than the Disneyland XP-40s.

The Space Cruisers are designed to look like toys and can be maneuvered by a joystick. Equipped with two Astro blaster ray guns, the XP-40 cars have the ray guns attached to a cord, rather than stationary to the car. Another upgrade of the XP-40 is evident when a target is hit; a vibrating response lets you know.

After earning your highest score, as you exit the attraction there is a set of stations so you can e-mail your photo and score to family and friends.

UPDATE:

Window Dedication on Main Street (Refer to map on page 36, between windows #24 and #25):

The window reads: **New Century Character Company Custom Character Design and Parade Illuminations Bill Justice Master Delineator.** Bill was born in Dayton, Ohio, February 9, 1914. He attended the John Herron Art

Photo by Debbie Smith

On May 5, 2005, Sleeping Beauty Castle donned special decorations to celebrate Disneyland's 50th anniversary. Kim Irvine created the designs.

worked on among others *Fantasia, Bambi, Alice in Wonderland* and *Peter Pan*. In total his career touched 19 features, and 57 featurettes. He is well known for animating Thumper from *Bambi* and Donald Duck's antagonists Chip and Dale. By the 1950s, Bill was asked to direct the animation for the Mickey Mouse March for a new television series called *The Mickey Mouse Club*.

Bill joined WED Enterprises in 1965 and helped program the audio-animatronics. He gave life to Great Moments with Mr. Lincoln, Pirates of the Caribbean, Haunted Mansion, Country Bears and more attractions in Walt Disney World Florida. He designed character costumes for parades, and the first

Institute in Indianapolis, which is now the Indiana University. He graduated with a degree in art in 1935. He began his career in 1937 at the Walt Disney Company where he

Photo by Debbie Smith

Photo by Debbie Smith

Disneyland Christmas Parade floats. The floats for the Main Street Electrical Parade were also designs of Bill Justice. After 42 years with Disney, Bill retired in 1979 and was named a Disney Legend in 1996. His autobiography *Justice for Disney* is rare and coveted by Disney collectors. In fact Bill is well known and loved by the Disney collectors as it was common to have him draw a character for you on a restaurant linen napkin. Bill and his wife Kim started the Bill Justice Foundation, a non-profit organization to create grants for Bill's alma mater, the Herron School of Art. A building there has been named in his honor. Bill was finally awarded his much-deserved window October 29, 2004.

UPDATE:

Window Dedication in Frontierland: The window reads: **Davy Crockett Coonskin Cap Supply Co. Fess Parker Proprietor.** Walt Disney had a television agreement with ABC to create a few television shows to supplement the funding for Disneyland. One of the most famous series was "Davy Crockett Indian Fighter" which aired on December 15, 1954. The television show with its western appeal and American hero was an instant success. The following episodes, "Davy Crockett Goes to Congress," and "Davy Crockett at the Alamo," catapulted its star Fess Parker into orbit. Children began wearing coon skin caps and singing the theme song, "The Ballad of Davy Crockett,"

BRIAN McKIM '05

immediately signed him to a contract at the Disney Studios. After filming the Davy Crockett series, he went on to appear in such Disney films as: "Westward Ho the Wagons," (1956). "The Great Locomotive Chase,"(1956) "Old Yeller"(1957) and "The Light in the Forest." (1958). In the 1960s, he not only starred in a television series about Daniel Boone, but also co-produced and directed a few episodes. His career continued working in the movie industry for Disney, Warner Brothers, and Paramount while laying the ground work for a future in real estate development. Fess Parker was named a Disney Legend in 1991 and he owns The Fess Parker Winery and Vineyard with a resort spa in Los Olivos, Calif. For more information about the winery go to www.fessparker.com.

turning the song into a gold record for multiple artists. Fess Parker instantly became famous and will forever be associated with the legendary hero. On the 50th anniversary of the television premier, Fess Parker was honored with a Disneyland window in Frontierland.

Fess Parker was born August 16, 1924, in Fort Worth, Texas. He grew up in San Angela Texas and graduated from University of Texas in 1950 with a degree in history. Following graduation he moved to Los Angeles to pursue a career in acting. He earned a master's degree in drama at the University of Southern California and landed his first film role in "Untamed Frontier" (1952) with Shelley Winters. In 1954, the 6'6" Fess appeared in another film, "Them!" where Walt Disney saw him and

Photo by Debbie Smith

Illustration by Karl Yamauchi

Sir Gawain fought the Green Knight.

Illustration by Karl Yamauchi

Sir Bors De Ganis witnessed the quest for the Holy Grail.

Sir Gawain/Gauen was Arthur's nephew and a loyal supporter of his uncle. He was half brother to the evil Mordred. In his most important adventure, Gawain fought a battle with the Green Knight. After Sir Lancelot killed Gawain's brothers and son in his overzealous rescue of Guinevere. Gawain's desire for revenge broke up the Round Table. Sir Lancelot mortally wounded Sir Gawain who languished on his deathbed for days. Before he died, Sir Gawain forgave Lancelot. He was buried in Dover Castle.

The final shield belonged to Sir Bors De Ganis, a cousin of Sir Lancelot who supported him in his battle against Arthur. Bors was a knight of great courage, one of the three peerless knights. He witnessed the Quest of the Holy Grail by Sir Galahad, but was denied its powers of eternal life and truth. After Galahad's death, Bors returned to Arthur and gave an account of the circumstances surrounding the discovery of the Grail. He was faithful and loyal and died fighting to maintain the principals of knighthood.

Casey Jr. Circus Train

One attraction that has not been redesigned since 1955 is the Casey Jr. Circus Train. It is one of the original rides, even though it was not quite ready on opening day because of mechanical problems. It was inspired by a three-minute clip from the 1941 animated feature, *Dumbo.* Imagineers stayed a little too faithful to Ward Kimball's original design for the little engine. Three days before the park opened, they realized the design wasn't well suited for good balance. As the train approached the half-way mark of its first steep hill, it began to tip until it reached the crest of the hill, where it turned a somersault backwards. Disney Legend Roger Broggie spent opening day engineering the little train so no one would be hurt. He added lead weights to the engine, smoothed out the track, and advised the engineer not to lean back. That fixed the problems for Black Sunday, and the train was reworked and had an official opening two weeks later. It later had a mechanical overhaul and has been working flawlessly ever since.

Pay careful attention to the sounds of Casey Jr. Circus Train. The engine begins by saying "I think I can, I think I can," and finishes by saying "I knew I could, I knew I could." You can also hear the voice of the ringmaster from the *Dumbo* film as you enjoy your ride on the circus train.

This attraction is unique to Disneyland. Its ornate benches were recycled from King Arthur's Carrousel. The train depot was the original ticket booth. Two other ticket booths still exist, the lighthouse in Storybook Land and the Mushroom in Alice in Wonderland.

Photo by Debbie Smith

The Casey Jr. Circus Train

Dumbo Flying Elephants

This ride was built in August 1955, shortly after the park opened. The story of a circus elephant born with huge ears was first part of a comic strip that appeared on a cereal box. The other elephants and the kids visiting the circus humiliated the baby elephant and his mother. After he drank a barrel of water spiked with champagne, Dumbo discovered he could fly.

Released in 1941, this animated feature won the Academy Award for Best Score. Oliver Wallace wrote the music for the film, including the songs "Baby Mine," "Pink Elephants on Parade," and "When I See an Elephant Fly." The lyrics from "When I See an Elephant Fly" were written by Ned Washington, who was also the lyricist for "When You Wish Upon A Star." "When I See an Elephant Fly" includes some of the most clever puns found in Disney music. Ned Washington was named a Disney Legend in 2001.

Dumbo had been scheduled for the cover of *Time* magazine at the time of its general release in 1941, but world events got in the way. Following the invasion of Pearl Harbor, *Dumbo* was replaced on the cover by Admiral Yamamoto.

Children often ask, "Why are there 16 Dumbos flying around?" Like Mickey and Goofy, there is and can be only one Dumbo. The

TREASURE & TRIVIA

Timothy Mouse, Dumbo's manager and friend, sits on top of the organ holding a magic feather. Years ago, he held a trainer's whip. Ed Brophy gave Timothy a voice and a Brooklyn accent. Dumbo has no voice, which makes him more endearing.

original artwork for the ride called for 10 Pink Elephants on Parade, inspired by the nightmarish scene where Dumbo is intoxicated. Walt objected—he'd rather have everyone riding Dumbo, not an alcohol-induced hallucination. So the pink elephants became gray and the one and only Dumbo became 10 Dumbos. After Fantasyland was remodeled in the 1980s, there were 16 Dumbos.

The music you hear comes from the vintage band organ nearby. Its brass pipes spew water from the base. The 1,500-lb. organ, built in 1915, has plenty of oomph; you can hear its music over a mile away. The organ is adorned with the stacking pachyderms from the film.

Photo by Dave Hawkins

The band organ plays music that can be heard over a mile away.

TREASURE & TRIVIA

In 1957, President Harry Truman refused to ride Dumbo the Flying Elephant because he was a democrat and elephants are the Republican Party symbols.

TREASURE & TRIVIA

At the Disneyana convention in 1992, an original Dumbo vehicle from the ride sold for $16,000.

Storybook Land Canal Boats

This attraction was built in 1956, a year after the park opened. Riders take a seven-minute cruise past miniature scenes from Disney movies past the homes of the Three Pigs, the Dwarfs' Diamond Mine, Aladdin's city of Agrabah, and Geppetto's Village. Above, on the hill, is Cinderella's Castle, with a pumpkin coach traveling up the winding road to the castle. The patchwork quilt of flowers was inspired by the 1933 animated short "Lullaby Land."

This attraction is exclusive to Disneyland. It was one of Walt's personal favorites. Originally, he wanted to build a whole land devoted to miniatures and call it Lilliputian land. Even though the ride was scaled back, model makers still labored over six months to develop the miniatures. Everything you can see from the Storybook Land Canal Boats is created at $1/12^{th}$ scale down to the smallest detail. The living shrubs, flowers, and trees were selected to maintain exact scale. There is even a 150-year old miniature pine tree. Growth retardant keeps all the trees and shrubs from growing more than an inch per year. To truly appreciate the detail, look at the toys in Gepetto's toyshop and the goods in the peddler's kiosk in the town of Agrabah.

A lesser-recognized scene is the three windmills that were inspired by the film, *The Old Mill,* a Silly Symphony cartoon released November 5, 1937. In this cartoon, frightened birds, mice, owls, and other creatures in an old mill try to stay safe and dry during a terrifying nighttime storm. This film was significant because it was the first to use the multi-plane camera, for which it won an Oscar. In addition to his Academy Award for Best Cartoon, Walt Disney also received a Scientific and Technical Class II plaque for the design and application of this multi-plane camera.

Outside the queue is a red and white striped lighthouse. The building was once the ticket booth for this attraction. Disney aficionados may recall that this ride cost you a "B" ticket.

Mad Tea Party

Also one of the opening day attractions. This spinning teacup attraction was modeled after the 1951 animated film, *Alice in Wonderland*, which was inspired by Lewis Carroll's 1865 fantasy. Carroll was the pen name of Charles Lutwidge Dodgson, a minister, mathematician, photographer, and author.

In *Alice's Adventures in Wonderland* (1865) and its sequel, *Through the Looking Glass and What Alice Found There* (1872), Alice falls down a rabbit hole and meets a host of unusual characters.

The animated film released in 1954 modified the Mad Hatter sequence to an "unbirthday" tea party. Since everyone has only one birthday, this mad host decided to celebrate the 364 unbirthdays in a year. That was the idea behind the film's "Unbirthday" song written by Mack David, Jerry Livingston, and Al Hoffman. The *Alice in Wonderland* score featured 14 original songs, more than any other Disney animated feature.

The bright, festive look of the Mad Tea Party attraction comes from those colorful Japanese lanterns hanging above the table. The ride operation booth is designed after the movie home of the March Hare. Notice that the crooked smokestacks resemble rabbit ears.

Photo by Dave Hawkins

LESSON TO LEARN

Walt found many of his song-writers on Tin Pan Alley, the name given to 28th Street in New York City. At the turn of the 20th century, many of the largest song publishers in the United States collected along 28th Street. In the summer days before air conditioning, the songwriters in their small offices would open their windows to get relief from the heat. The sound of all the pianos echoing through the street sounded a lot like banging on tin pans, hence the name. Disney turned to Tin Pan Alley when he needed scores for both *Alice in Wonderland* and *Cinderella.*

TREASURE & TRIVIA

The Mad Tea Party was one of the inspirations for Roger Rabbit's Cartoon Spin. Imagine taking a teacup for a "spin" on Mr. Toad's Wild Ride and you'll have the Roger Rabbit attraction.

Alice in Wonderland

Built in 1958, this dark ride is based on the Lewis Carroll story. A curious Alice dreams of adventures while following a white rabbit. The attraction was remodeled at a cost of $8 million in 1984. Among the additional three-dimensional scenes added were singing flowers, strange birds, Tulgey woods, and the tea party. You will see 24 sculpted figures in the attraction, some of which are reused from a Florida attraction, the 1971 Mickey Mouse Review. These include the Flower Garden Heads and the Mad Hatter, March Hare, and Alice figures. It is the only dark ride to travel to multiple levels in Disneyland.

Kathryn Beaumont voiced the character of Alice and recreated the voice for the attraction in 1984. The fuzzy voice of Sterling Holloway can be heard as the Cheshire Cat.

That large yellow mushroom outside the queue was once the ticket booth for this attraction.

Claude Coats drew the designs for the cars, although he claims they were Walt's idea. The studio insisted Claude be given the patent and asked him to sign it over to Disney for $10. The cars run on a one hp electric motor. Arrow Development builds the gearing for the cars that run on a 764-ft. track. The caterpillar cars are the slowest as they run on the lowest gear ratio to move the heavy cars up the incline.

Mad Hatter Store

The Mad Hatter store is modeled after the White Rabbit's house. On one side of the thatched roofed cottage is a doorway that says, "White Rabbit, Esq." The building was designed from the scene where Alice eats some of the mushroom and grows to the size of the White Rabbit's house. Stripped telephone wire was used for roofing material to look like hair.

TREASURE & TRIVIA

Behind the counter in the shop is a mirror with a Cheshire Cat that disappears and reappears.

Mr. Toad's Wild Ride

This attraction was based on Kenneth Grahame's classic tale, *The Wind in the Willows*. It was one of the opening day attractions. Disney's adaptation begins in a library where Basil Rathbone tells the story of J. Thaddeus Toad, Squire of Toad Hall, a lover of transportation vehicles. With his friends, Rat, Mole, and MacBadger, Toad's adventures lead them all across the English countryside. Eventually, Toad loses the deed to Toad Hall and is charged with car theft. Toad escapes from jail and learns that Winkie, the tavern keeper, and his buddies, the weasels, have taken over Toad Hall. With the help of his friends, Toad recovers his good name and the deed to his estate. Toad promises to reform . . . until he sees a 1908 biplane. The ride is inspired more by "The Merrily Song" from the movie than the actual plot of *Wind in the Willows*.

Mr. Toad's Wild Ride is one of the original three "dark rides." Of these, it has the most humor and excitement. When it first opened, all the scenery was flat. The dimensional scenery was added later. In 1961, Disney added gags, track movement, animation, and breakaway doors activated by electronic triggers in the track. In 1983, the cars began crashing through the fireplace and into Winky's Pub, the Courtroom, and the Green Dragon Inn with the statue of Cyril with Toad.

TREASURE & TRIVIA

Isn't that Melvin the Moose from Country Bear Jamboree hanging on the wall of Winky's tavern?

HIDDEN MICKEY

As you burst through the leaded-glass window in Toad Hall, there is a tiny shadow near the center of the window, close to the sill. It's a Hidden Mickey!

Arrow Development supplied the cars. Originally, there were nine, but when the track was expanded in 1983 the ride was enlarged to 12 cars (with three more in reserve). The cars are made of fiberglass and sheet metal. They weigh about 200 lbs.

TREASURE & TRIVIA

In the town square, there is a silhouette of Sherlock Holmes in a second floor window.

TREASURE & TRIVIA

Next to Holmes is a painting of "Blind Justice." The blindfold is supposed to represent an impartial judgment, but look carefully. She's peeking!

and run on electric motors. The attraction can accommodate about 700 people per hour on an adventure that lasts a little over a minute and a half.

Each of the vehicles is named for a character in the story. There is

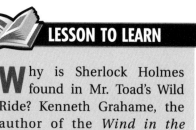

LESSON TO LEARN

Why is Sherlock Holmes found in Mr. Toad's Wild Ride? Kenneth Grahame, the author of the *Wind in the Willows*, was a good friend of Sir Arthur Conan Doyle, the creator of the Sherlock Holmes stories. Both Grahame and Conan Doyle were born in Edinburgh, Scotland, in 1859. Mr. Rat in *The Wind in the Willows* was based on the character of Sherlock Holmes.

one Mr. Toad car, one MacBadger, one Moley, one Ratty, and two each of Toady, Cyril, Winky, and Weasel. Incidentally, the Weasel characters are the same team that appeared in *Who Framed Roger Rabbit?* and again in *Roger Rabbit's Cartoon Spin*.

The shield outside the manor says "Toadi Acceleratio Semper Absurda." This translates roughly as "Speeding with Toad is always absurd."

TREASURE & TRIVIA

The attraction features a lot of gags, from the books in the library to the signs along the route. The ride is so fast that that you can't catch all the gags unless you ride it over and over again . . . something many visitors to Disneyland have been known to do.

TREASURE & TRIVIA

In the top right corner of the mural in the loading area, you'll see a train with a very recognizable conductor. Here's a hint: the train is named the "WED Railroad."

Peter Pan's Flight

Another one of the opening day attractions, it was patterned after the animated feature *Peter Pan* that Disney released in 1953. Adapted from the novel and play by Sir James M. Barrie, *Peter Pan* is the story of a boy who refuses to grow up and brings Wendy, John, and Michael Darling to Neverland where Peter Pan lived in perpetual childhood.

In 1960, the attraction was refurbished with improved tracks. In 1982, the teacups, carousel, and Dumbo attractions were moved to allow more room for Peter Pan and the other dark rides. The ride's mural was given an "old world" appearance and the track system was again upgraded, even though the length, descents, and ascents were not changed. At the same time, Audio-Animatronic figures were added.

Each fiberglass boat carries two to three passengers through Peter Pan's adventures. A half-foot wider and longer than the original boats, the current boats measures 7.5-ft. long and 5-ft. wide and run on a one-hp. motor. You are at the highest point of the attraction, almost seven feet from the floor, when you fly around the replica of London's Big Ben.

The twinkling London scene is based on an authentic map of the city. The three-dimensional Tower Bridge, Thames River, and St. Paul's Cathedral are easily recognized. More than 175 miles of fiber optic lighting illuminate this ride.

Sammy Fain was the primary composer partnered with Sammy Cahn to write most of the music for Peter Pan including the attraction's theme song "You Can Fly! You Can Fly! You Can Fly!" Sammy Fain won an Oscar for Best Song in 1953, the same year *Peter Pan* released. His Oscar was not for *Peter Pan*, but for "Secret Love" from the movie *Calamity Jane**. (For *Calamity Jane*, please refer to Golden Horseshoe.)

TREASURE & TRIVIA

Look carefully at the blocks on the floor of the nursery. The blocks spell secret messages, sometimes Disney, (DIZNEY) and other times Peter Pan.

Matterhorn Bobsleds

It was built in 1959 as an original "E" ticket attraction. The ride was based on James Ramsey Ullman's *Banner in the Sky*, the 1959 Disney film made from it (*Third Man on the Mountain)* and, of course, Switzerland's majestic peak itself.

At 147-ft. high, the Matterhorn is the largest and tallest structure in Disneyland. It is actually a 1/100-scale model of the actual peak, which is 14,692-ft. high. Disney's forced perspective makes the model look larger. Notice the trees on the side of the mountain: they become progressively smaller as they ascend the model.

The cottage-like queue is adorned with shields. The largest is modeled after the Swiss Flag. The rest represent the 23 cantons (states) and the three subdivided cantons.

The Matterhorn ride was the first tubular steel coaster ever built. Previously, all roller coasters were built on a wooden frame. It was also the first ride to have multiple cars running on one track at the same time. Early in the ride's history, bales of hay were put at the bottom to stop the ride. Walt liked the effect so much that the added a splash at the end of the ride. The small body of water was named Alpine Lake.

If you are looking for a bigger thrill, the track closest to Tomorrowland is shorter and faster. For a longer ride, take the track closest to the castle; it is longer by about 30 seconds. The ice cavern, glowing crystals, and the Abominable Snowman were added to the ride in 1978.

The shields on the Matterhorn represent the cantons of Switzerland.

Photo by Dave Hawkins

When the Abominable Snowman was added, Imagineers wanted a sound for the large creature. They decided to hold a 'growl off' contest. Anyone interested could try out. The winner was so loud during his first take that his growl came out distorted. Nevertheless, it was the best take, so that's the sound you'll hear.

In one of the icy caverns, you'll see an ice ax, snowshoes, and trunk marked "Wells Expedition." This is a tribute to the late Frank Wells, former president and chief operating officer of the Walt Disney Company who died in a helicopter accident in 1994. In true Disney fashion, Frank's tribute is in the Matterhorn because Wells had a passion for mountain climbing. He also has a window dedicated to him on Main Street.

Occasionally you'll see Mickey, Goofy, and other cast members climbing the Matterhorn. They use the same equipment mountain

The shield for Valais, the canton where the Matterhorn is found.

TREASURE & TRIVIA

Frank Wells co-wrote a book about his mountain climbing experiences. In *Seven Summits*, he describes climbing the tallest mountain on each continent.

climbers' use when they climb real mountains. There are about 30 routes on the mountain above the bobsled ride—about 50 if the bobsleds aren't running. (The toughest routes on the Matterhorn are rated 5.12, according to the climb rating system. A rating of 5.0 is the easiest and 5.14 the toughest of the scale.) From the summit you can see Catalina on a clear day and sometimes even the Hollywood sign. Stand with your back to Autopia and look above the waterfall and to the left. You'll see a round window called an eiger; Climbers crawl out of this eiger to scale the mountain.

It's A Small World

This show was moved in 1966 from the World's Fair that was held in New York during 1964 and 1965. It is often referred to as the "happiest cruise that ever sailed." In February 1963, Pepsi-Cola asked Disney Studios to prepare a pavilion for the United Nations Children's Education Fund. Marc Davis developed the details of the ride, including the trio of Dutch geese that quack in time to the music and the five-year-old Cleopatra. Claude

Coats laid out the path of the river so that the boats would pass 302 Audio-Animatronic children and 257 moving toys representing every country in the world.

The dolls, with their snub noses, big heads, and tiny features, were taken directly from two series of Hallmark note cards designed by Mary Blair under the Walt Disney label in the 1940s. One set of cards employed country themes tied to the release of *So Dear to My Heart* in 1949. The other set of cards was inspired by places Mary Blair and Walt visited during their Latin American junket to create *The Three Caballeros*. Her drawings were used for the "La Pinata" sequence in the film. Mary Blair had once been a color stylist and designer at Disney Studios in the 1940s. She became a famous illustrator of children's books, but Walt invited her back to develop the attraction.

Illustration by Brian McKim

Mary Blair, creator of It's a Small World Designs.

The dolls in their national costumes dance in dreamlike settings with symbols to identify their places of origin. Whether they are placed in front of an igloo or a pyramid, you'll see the same smiling figures. They all look alike, possibly to emphasize the similarities rather than the differences in the human race.

Originally, the dolls were to sing their national anthems, but the sound was simply terrible. Imagine a room full of people all singing a different anthem and you can imagine what the ride would have sounded like. Disney asked his staff writers, the brothers Richard M. and Robert B. Sherman (see sidebar on page 68), to write a tune that could be repeated while being sung in different languages. Walt wanted a tune that had the spirit of brotherly love and goodwill. The song "It's A Small World" became one of the best-known Disney tunes of all times. You'll even hear the song in the Disney animated film, *The Lion King*, which was made 30 years after the ride opened. The Shermans became Disney Legends in 1990 for their numerous memorable tunes.

The river in the ride is known as "The Seven Seaways." At the opening of It's a Small World in Disneyland, children from different countries pour a liter of water from each ocean into the seaways.

The centerpiece of the façade, which was designed by Mary Blair, is a clock that rings every 15 minutes and marks the passage of time with 24 dancing dolls, one for each hour of the day. During construction of the attraction in Disneyland, Walt suggested adding a clock outside the entrance, so Rolly Crump designed a huge clock tower featuring a parade of stylized animated toys that march around as the clock strikes the time. A mechanical hammer strikes a wooden block to create the "tick-tock" of the clock, while a microphone broadcasts the sound from the façade of the tower. The parade of dolls worked so well for the theme that it was duplicated in Tokyo and Paris.

TREASURE & TRIVIA

The dolls representing China were added in 1970, about the time when Richard Nixon became the first American president to visit China.

Images of the Eiffel Tower, the Leaning Tower of Pisa, Big Ben, and the Taj Mahal now adorn the façade, which also features spires and finials covered in 22-karat gold leafing. It took all the gold leaf available in the United States to decorate the façade.

Rolly Crump first started his career at Walt Disney Company in 1952. Off and on for 24 years he worked for the Disney Company, first as an animator, then Imagineer, artist, sculptor and eventually art director. During his career he worked on films such as *Lady and the Tramp, Sleeping Beauty* and *101 Dalmatians*. At Imagineering, he worked on illusions for Haunted Mansion, sculptures and Tiki gods for the Enchanted Tiki Room. He is most recognized for the Tower of the Four Winds that stood in front of the It's a Small World attraction at the 1964–1965 New York World's Fair. He also designed the magnificent façade for It's a Small World in California, inspired by the work of Mary Blair. He created a lot of the toys and dolls for the attraction as well. As art director, he designed the floats, stages, props, and costumes for Disneyland events and parades. Later, he returned to help with EPCOT as a Project Designer, involved with the Life/Health

Rolly Crump

Photo by Kendra Trahan

and Land pavilions and Communicore. Rolly has had an important impact on Disney, as he learned from Walt Disney himself. Inspired and taught by many of the Disney legends, Rolly Crump evolved to have a style all his own.

Photo by Dave Hawkins

Ever since the winter of 1997, the attraction has featured a holiday rendition where traditions of different nations are displayed and the holiday caroling includes such favorites as "Deck the Halls" and "Jingle Bells."

The topiaries at the entrance and exit are living plants. Giraffes, elephants, rhinos, lions, horses, and other wonderful creatures have graced Disneyland since 1960. The park also has a famous collection of topiaries of Disney characters. Each character requires three to five years of constant care to become a topiary at Disneyland.

Fantasyland Theatre

Built in June 1995, sponsored by Nestlé Ice Cream, it features daily stage shows, special events, and elaborate musical productions with Disney characters. The open-air theatre hosts the special Christmas Candlelight Ceremony and Processional during the Holidays. Staged by a live orchestra and 800 voices, the ceremony features a celebrity guest who narrates a Christmas story. By tradition, cast members make up the choir and stand in the formation of a Christmas tree.

Camera Kiosk

Kodak hosts the gazebo offering film, batteries, and anything the visiting photographer may need to recapture the day at Disneyland. Kodak also sponsors many photo spots around the park to offer variety to the future photo album.

Troubadour Treats

Ice cream is a favorite snack at the park. Nestlé is all too happy to provide opportunities to buy frozen treats.

Even the landscape has a sense of Fantasy.

Roger Rabbit greets guests on the top of this clever fountain in front of the Cartoon Spin.

Chapter 9

WHO FRAMED
Mickey's ToonTown?

Mickey's ToonTown opened in 1993, the first new land to open at Disneyland in 20 years. According to Disney myth, although the public was invited in 1993, Mickey says the three-acre lot opened exclusively for toons back in the 1930s. Legend has it back in 1952 when Walt was looking for land to build Disneyland, Mickey suggested the property next door to ToonTown.

The public was introduced to ToonTown in the 1988 film, *Who Framed Roger Rabbit?* where cartoons live in a crazy cartoon world of their own. The movie was based on Gary K. Wolf's 1981 book, *Who Censored Roger Rabbit?* ToonTown was intended as a temporary exhibit, but it proved so popular that it was turned into a permanent addition. Here you can tour the homes of Mickey, Minnie, Goofy, and meet one-on-one the Mouse that started it all. Not surprising, the homes resemble the owners in this entirely interactive town. You can visit the firehouse, post office, and dog pound, and even detonate cartoon explosives at the *Fireworks Factory*. Everything in ToonTown is created for touching, pushing, and jumping on.

The designers and workers had to improvise a lot of on-the-spot solutions. Art director Joe Lanzisero carried models to the work site in Plexiglas® boxes so that the unusual angles and shapes could be studied in three-dimension by the framers and plasterers who were struggling to duplicate the plans. There are almost no straight lines or right angles. All the buildings are exaggerated, inflated, and composed of colorful three-dimensional cartoon elements.

Lift the receiver of the police phone outside the Power House; you may hear a voice over the toon police car announcing "Someone put mail in the box, and the box doesn't like it. Please respond post haste." Or step on a mousehole cover near the Post Office; and you could hear "How's the weather up there?" or "Is it time to come out now?"

Jolly Trolley

Board the Jolly Trolley for a trip from one end of ToonTown to the other. The Jolly Trolley is a giant wind-up toy with a large gold key on the top that makes a figure eight path through the town. You can board at Mickey's House or Roger Rabbit's Cartoon Spin. Imagineers arranged for the wheel size to vary so the trolley jiggles and sways, adding a comic effect. This attraction is exclusive to Disneyland.

Roger Rabbit's Car Toon Spin

This attraction was added in January 1994, you can take a tour of ToonTown courtesy of ToonTown Cab Company.

The queue reveals the dangers of "dip" and the villainous weasels from *Mr. Toad's Wild Ride*. The weasels are on the loose at ToonTown and ready to use "dip." Dip is the one thing that can destroy a toon, since dropping pianos, safes, and other heavy objects never seems to work. Dip is made of one part benzene, one part acetone, and one part turpentine. Lenny, the taxicab, drives guests through the three-dimensional cartoon adventure.

TREASURE & TRIVIA

David L. Lander, more commonly known as "Squiggy" from the television show Laverne and Shirley, is the voice of the weasels.

During your ride, the steering wheel remains rigid until you skid into some "dip." Then the attraction becomes a hybrid of the Mad Tea Party and Mr. Toad's Wild Ride. You'll see or hear some of the best all-time cartoon gags here, from being punched by a boxing glove, to dropping a safe, piano, and elephant. There are the classic cream pies in the face and spins through the "Bullina" China Shop. The attraction features 16 Audio-Animatronics, 59 animated props, and 20 different special effects. The comical music featured in the attraction is Franz Liszt's *Hungarian Rhapsody no. 2.*

TREASURE & TRIVIA

In one warehouse scene, two Imagineers appear as jack-in-the-box characters. In this case it is a Joe Lanzisero-in-the-box with the letter "J" on the box and Marcello Vignali-in-the-box with an "M" on the front. Marcello drew the scene for the gag warehouse.

The gags while waiting in line, are part of the attraction, from the wallpaper in Baby's Herman's room to his favorite brand of cigars, El Cheapo. The calendar is a tribute to 1930s movie legend Betty Grable. You'll also see a giant paintbrush with a half-painted wall. Below the brush is a can of multi-colored paint that allows color to go to the right place with one coat, reminiscent of the opening to *Walt Disney True Life Adventures* films. Some of the buildings in the alleys appear to be watching you while weasels pop up everywhere. The license plates entering the garage are the ones you would expect Disney characters to have.

City Hall

Toon residents emerge from this building and proceed to the band-stand out front to greet guests. When a character is about to arrive, the colorful "Clockenspiel" above City Hall comes to life; mallets ring bells, gloved toon hands pull whistles, and figures of Roger Rabbit and Mickey Mouse pop out of cannons, blowing shiny horns. Out of the horns, bouquets of flowers pop out.

For window watchers, the name above the library is Walt Disney's. Since he was the only human allowed in ToonTown prior to 1993, he has an honorary window. It says, *Laugh-O-Gram Films Inc., W.E. Disney Directing Animator.* His window is the only human credit in ToonTown.

Goofy's Gas

Only cartoon vehicles can refill at this station, but the restrooms and telephones are for

LESSON TO LEARN

Laugh-O-Gram Films was Walt's Kansas City Company in 1922. He made a series of six modernized versions of fairy tales: *The Four Musicians, of Bremen, Little Red Riding Hood, Puss in Boots, Jack and the Beanstalk, Goldie Locks and the Three Bears,* and *Cinderella.* The company filed bankruptcy after its distributor defaulted on payments.

human characters. The water fountain beside the station dispenses colorful water.

Minnie Mouse House

Minnie's House is the interactive home of Mickey's sweetheart, Minnie Mouse. The top window, weather vane, and welcome mat are all shaped like sweethearts. When

TREASURE & TRIVIA

Minnie Mouse made her movie debut in *Steamboat Willie* on November 18, 1928. She is Mickey's girlfriend and appeared in 73 cartoons with Mickey and Pluto. Her first voice was courtesy of Marcellite Garner, an Ink and Paint Department employee from the Disney Studios. Many others succeeded her, although Russie Taylor gives Minnie her current voice.

LESSON TO LEARN

Ub Iwerks (1901- 1971). Since we just mentioned Laugh-O-Gram Films, it seems fitting to talk about Ub Iwerks. Ub doesn't have a window in ToonTown or Main Street, although since he was an original partner in the company, he probably should. At the age of 19, Ub met Walt Disney in Kansas City. Soon after that, they went into business together, calling the company Iwerks-Disney Studio. The venture lasted about a month. Then Walt founded Laugh-O-Gram Films in 1922, with Ub as the chief animator. Laugh-O-Gram Films also went bankrupt. When Walt moved to California, he recruited Ub, who designed Mickey Mouse and animated him for his first three cartoons, *Plane Crazy, The Gallopin' Gaucho,* and *Steamboat Willie.* Ub left the studio in 1930 to start his own venture, but he returned to Disney Studios in 1940. Ub's interest in cameras and special effects created some of the most memorable Disney scenes. He invented a multihead optical printer and modified the Xerox process in animation. He won two Academy Awards for special effects (1965) and for collaborating on the perfection of color travelling matte photography (1966). He contributed to It's a Small World, Great Moments with Mr. Lincoln, Haunted Mansion, and Circle Vision 360. Ub was the first Disney legend in 1989 (posthumously) along with the Disney's Nine Old Men. His sons Don and Dave were also longtime Disney employees. For more information about Ub Iwerks, see *The Hand Behind the Mouse, An Intimate Biography of Ub Iwerks, the Man Walt Disney Called 'The Greatest Animator in the World.'* The book was written by his granddaughter, Leslie Iwerks, and John Kenworthy.

you visit Minnie's house, you may hear messages from Mickey on her answering machine. You can also create new fashions for her on her dressing room computer.

Minnie's kitchen has a cake in the oven that rises when a knob is turned, spoons that clatter, and pots and pans that clank out a melody when the stove is switched on. The dishwasher churns when a button is pushed. Check out the diet cookies on her kitchen table. As you leave her house, don't be surprised if the wishing well offers you a few parting thoughts. Minnie Mouse is often at home to meet guests and take photos.

Mickey Mouse House & Movie Barn

In the Mickey Mouse House and Movie Barn you can walk through, viewing Mickey's living quarters along with memorabilia from his long career. The letters on the table inside the house identify Mickey's address as 1 Neighborhood Lane, Mickey's ToonTown. His living room has a player piano and a curio cabinet filled with memorabilia, including Mickey's baby shoes and a picture of him with Walt Disney. Pluto has some treasure there too, including a half-eaten shoe and a huge bone. The washing machine chugs away with the interesting cleansing agents in the laundry room. The greenhouse leads you to the backyard and garden. Look for the disappearing carrots. If you wait long enough, you may be able to see the thief.

Mickey's barn is a working studio. The movie barn stores props from his famous cartoons. You may hear Goofy and Donald in the screening room, projecting clips from remakes of Mickey's finest film moments including *Steamboat Willie, The Band Concert, Thru the Mirror,* and *The Sorcerer's Apprentice.* You may catch Mickey on the set of any one of these films. When he's not viewing movie clips, Mickey Mouse receives guests in his dressing room.

HIDDEN MICKEY
Look for a Hidden Mickey in the driveway in the exposed stone.

The design for Mickey's house was heavily researched from his earlier cartoons. Meeting Mickey at home is one sure way to get a photo with him.

Photo by Dave Hawkins

TREASURE & TRIVIA

Mickey Mouse made his movie debut in *Steamboat Willie* on November 18, 1928, at the Colony Theater in New York. He appeared in over 120 cartoons and the *Mickey Mouse Club* television show in the 1950s. Walt Disney gave Mickey his first voice, although Jim Macdonald took over in 1946. Wayne Allwine gives Mickey his current voice. These three men have been the only voices of Mickey Mouse. Wayne Allwine is married in real life to the current voice of Minnie Mouse, Russie Taylor.

TREASURE & TRIVIA

Pluto, Mickey's faithful dog, made his debut in 1930 in the cartoon short *The Chain Gang*. He appeared in 48 cartoons of his own. He got his name from headlines of the time as a new planet had been discovered.

Chip 'N Dale Treehouse

Next door to Mickey is the Redwood home of Chip and Dale. This high-rise can accommodate kids, but not adults. A spiral staircase leads to a lofty perch, where the windows provide a great view of ToonTown.

LESSON TO LEARN

Clyde Tombaugh discovered the planet Pluto in 1930 at the Lowell Observatory. The temperature on the planet is –390° Fahrenheit. Pluto is the smallest planet in the solar system and the ninth planet from the sun. It takes Pluto 248 Earth years to go around the sun one time.

TREASURE & TRIVIA

You can tell the Chipmunks apart if you remember that Chip has a dark nose, like a chocolate chip. Together, the two chipmunks appeared in 24 cartoons as Donald Duck's nemeses. In 1989, they appeared in their own television series *Chip 'n Dale's Rescue Rangers*.

Gadget Go-Coaster

The Go-Coaster is the workshop of *Chip 'n Dale's Rescue Rangers* costar, Gadget. The Go-Coaster is a miniature roller coaster made of recycled oversized toys. The coaster is true to Gadget's size and resourceful personality.

Giant toy blocks are support beams for the tracks, hollowed-out acorns are the cars, and bridges are built from oversize combs, pencils, paper clips, rubber bands, and anything else Gadget can find.

HIDDEN MICKEY

In the stone wall of the queue to Gadget's Go-Coaster study the Hidden Mickey made of three stones near the curve of the wall.

"The Miss Daisy"

Donald's Boat, is docked at Toon Lake, though Donald lives in the nearby town, Duckburg. The "Miss Daisy" is named for Donald's lifelong sweetheart. This houseboat has a rope ladder to climb and a spiral staircase to the pilothouse. Here your kids can steer the wheel that turns the compass or toot the boat's whistle. "The houses actually look, in a very subliminal way, like their inhabitants," says Joe Lanzisero, WDI Senior Concept Designer. "The top of the wheelhouse is literally Donald's cap. The bow is painted like his shirt, and the whole ship looks like a duckbill. If you just walk by and glance at it, it's a cartoon boat, but if you stop and study it, it's Donald."

Goofy Bounce House

To enter the Bounce House children must be *under* the posted height limit. Kids have to remove their shoes before they leap into the inflatable balloon house, where they can bounce off the walls, furniture, and even the fireplace while

TREASURE & TRIVIA

Donald Duck is an honorary alumnus of the University of Oregon. In 1947, the University's first athletic director, Leo Harris, struck a handshake agreement with Walt Disney to use Donald as the mascot for the "webfoot state." It wasn't until 1973 that the first written contract was signed with Disney representatives. Donald remained the only collegiate or professional duck mascot until 1993, when the Anaheim Mighty Ducks were founded. The Mighty Ducks are a National Hockey League Team owned by Disney Corporation.

TREASURE & TRIVIA

Donald Fauntleroy Duck is one of the most popular Disney characters. He made his debut June 9, 1934, in the Silly Symphony short, *The Wise Little Hen,* and appeared in more than 128 cartoons. Donald Duck's feet are imprinted at Grauman's Chinese Theatre in Hollywood. Clarence "Ducky" Nash provided the voice for Donald for over 50 years. Tony Anselmo succeeded Clarence in giving Donald his sometimes-incomprehensible voice.

parents watch the craziness inside through the netted windows.

Check out Goofy's garden. You'll see some unusual things growing such as "Bell" peppers, stalks of popcorn, spinning flowers, watery watermelons, jack-o'-lanterns, and squished squash.

TREASURE & TRIVIA

Goofy made his first appearance in the cartoon Mickey's Revue in 1932 as a member of the audience. In 1938, his name was changed from Dippy Dawg to Goofy. Goofy appeared in more than 48 cartoons, the most famous of which are the "How To" series of the 1950s. In the 1990s he had his own television series, Goof Troop, and a spin-off movie. Pinto Colvig, a Disney story man, musician and former circus clown, gave Goofy his voice and raucous laugh. George Johnson, Bob Jackman, and Bill Farmer have also provided voices for Goofy.

Photo by Dave Hawkins

Goofy's house looks as though he built it himself.

Chapter 10

Tomorrowland
PREDICTIONS

In the fall of 1954, during construction of the park, money and time were running short. Walt was persuaded to open Disneyland without Tomorrowland. He planned to open Tomorrowland after the park had some revenue coming in. It was a major disappointment for Walt, but it freed up the designers and builders to concentrate on the endless construction problems surrounding Main Street U.S.A., Adventureland, Frontierland, and Fantasyland. But Walt had second thoughts. He believed that the success of the park relied on his total concept. So, with six months left until opening day, construction resumed at breakneck speed to prepare Tomorrowland for opening day. Dressed up with balloons and flowers to hide the lack of attractions. Tomorrowland did open July 17th on time and has received much attention in the years since.

The dedication for Tomorrowland addressed dreams of the future, technology, and space exploration. Walt despaired of

LESSON TO LEARN

Halley's Comet was named for the British astronomer, Edmund Halley (1656-1742). He proved that the comet of 1607 was identical to the comet of 1531, and he successfully predicted the same comet's return in 1759. The earliest records of Halley's Comet date back to 240 BC. It has returned every 76 years since then. Halley's Comet should return again in the year 2062.

all the doomsday approaches to the future and wanted Tomorrowland to be positive and inspiring. It was Walt's vision that Tomorrowland be set in the year 1986 when Halley's comet was scheduled to return.

The biggest challenge facing Tomorrowland has been to stay ahead of the times. Disney has constantly renovated and updated the five acres of entertainment. In 1959, a $6 million investment brought the Monorail, Submarine Voyage, and the Matterhorn to Tomorrowland. Seven years later, another major renovation cost $23 million and added People Movers, Adventure Thru Inner Space, Circle Vision, and, straight from the New York World's Fair, the Carousel of Progress.

Major attractions have been added every few years—Space Mountain in 1977 and Star Tours and Captain EO in the late 1980s. A new renovation in 1998 tied everything together, requiring a major remodel and rededication. This time, in an effort to stay in tune with the future, Imagineers looked to the past. Tomorrowland took on a timeless look that is fantasy-like. The visionaries Jules Verne, H.G. Wells, and Leonardo da Vinci inspired the new Tomorrowland

LESSON TO LEARN

Leonardo da Vinci (1452-1519) was an Italian painter, sculptor, scientist, engineer, and architect. He is a master of the Renaissance era. His most famous paintings are "The Last Supper" (1495-1497) and "Mona Lisa" (1503-1506).

look. To celebrate the new opening, Buzz Lightyear partnered with one of the first men to set foot on the moon, Buzz Aldrin.

One of the most interesting recent changes to Tomorrowland is that every living tree, plant, bush, and flower is edible. Crops are rotated with the seasons. They include corn, cabbage, kale, and kumquats. The terrain and palette of colors used in the area are warm and earthy, not

LESSON TO LEARN

The French author Jules Verne (1828-1905) is considered the father of science fiction. In his books, he predicted some of the technology available today, including helicopters, air conditioning, motion pictures, aircraft, spacecraft, and guided missiles. His works include *Journey to the Center of the Earth*, (1864), *Twenty Thousand Leagues Under the Sea*, (1870), and *Around the World in Eighty Days* (1873).

The 1998 Tomorrowland renovation was not the first time Disney took inspiration from Jules Verne. Walt considered Verne to be one of his favorite writers. He produced *20,000 Leagues Under the Sea* in 1954, *Captain Grant's Children* in 1962, and the *Island at the Top of the World* in 1974. Like Verne, Walt believed that travel to the Moon was possible. Walt died more than two years before Neil Armstrong proved him right.

sterile or otherworldly. Futuristic boulders and architecture sit next to apple, orange, lemon, and pomegranate trees.

Astro Orbitor

Built in Bavaria in 1956, this attraction has circled in Tomorrowland for more than 40 years. Astro Orbitor probably has had more names than any other Disneyland ride. It started as Astro Jets and later became Tomorrowland Jets, Rocket Jets, and finally Astro Orbitor. The same attraction in Florida is named StarJets.

Here pilots raise and lower their spaceship while they enjoy the beautiful view. This attraction is

LESSON TO LEARN

H.G. Wells (1866-1946) was an English author and political philosopher. He wrote more than 80 novels, including many science fiction books: *The Time Machine* (1895), *War of the Worlds* (1898), and *The Invisible Man* (1897). In 1938, Orson Wells' radio dramatization of *War of the Worlds* caused unintended public panic.

even more spectacular at night. For a time, this attraction sat atop the People Mover loading area and gave an even better view of

Photo by Dave Hawkins

Tomorrowland—if you could tolerate the spinning.

The planet motif was modeled on a drawing made by Leonardo da Vinci five centuries ago. The Zodiac signs dress up the ride giving it a yet another connection to the stars.

The American Space Experience

This temporary exhibit built in 1998 celebrates 50 years of American Space exploration. Authentic NASA artifacts, Hubble photos, and Mars Pathfinder discoveries are on display along with a moon rock gathered by the crew of Apollo 16. You can spend a lot of time on the interactive exhibits here.

Radio Disney

Although Radio Disney hit the airwaves in November of 1996, the Disneyland broadcast began in 1999. This is the first 24-hour, kid-oriented radio programming. On-air personalities present hit music, guests appearances, Disneyland visitors, games, kid friendly news, sports, and other features targeted to an under 12 audience. In his autobiography, *Work in Progress*, Michael Eisner admits he enjoys listening to Radio Disney from time to time. "The radio network just for kids" airs live from Disneyland Sunday through Wednesday from 1–5 p.m. P.S.T. While you are in the Los Angeles area, you can listen to Radio Disney at 1110 on the AM dial.

Atop the Radio Disney is the Observatron. This colorful, highly kinetic art sculpture announces the quarter hour with a light and music display.

Disneyland Monorail

This original "E" ticket attraction was built in 1959. Walt's passion for both trains and the future made the Monorail special. The Monorail only appeared to be futuristic transportation. In reality, it dates back to 1878. The early monorails used in Germany were suspended from the track. Lilly Disney suffered from motion sickness, and the swaying motion often made her ill. She once asked "Why can't they run the cars on top of the track?" Finally, while they were traveling in Cologne, Germany, the Disneys discovered a monorail that did ride on top of the track. The Alweg monorail had been developed by Dr. Axel WennerGren, a Swedish businessman who was prohibited, at the end of World War II, from taking his investment profits out of Germany. Instead, he put the money toward the first monorail that ran on top of the tracks. It made its first trip in 1949.

Walt was so impressed by the Alweg Monorail, he thought it would be appropriate for Tomorrowland. He sent Imagineers Joe Fowler and Roger Broggie to Cologne to see it. Soon after they returned, Walt built his Monorail with the help of the Alweg consultants, advisors, and prints. That's why early Monorails had "Disneyland-Alweg Monorail System" printed on the side of the futuristic cars designed by Bob Gurr. Disneyland's Monorail was the first passenger-carrying monorail in the Western Hemisphere to operate daily. Airports in Seattle, Orlando, Las Vegas, and elsewhere around the country now use a monorail system.

On June 14, 1959, the World Premiere of the Monorail was televised. Vice President Richard Nixon cut the ribbon during the ceremonies. About an hour before the event, Walt invited Nixon to take a test ride. As they pulled away, chaos broke out at the loading dock. It took a minute for Walt to realize he had left the Secret Service behind and had technically kidnapped the Vice President. As they coasted back to the station, Secret Service men jumped on top of the Monorail cars while they were still moving. Walt and Nixon got off the train and looked back at the Secret Service men who were still on top of the cars and heading for another trip around Tomorrowland.

Monorail Red was the first train, followed by Monorail Blue a month later. The first trains carried 82 guests until an extra car was added to increase capacity. New trains were added in 1968 and again in the late 1980s. The current trains have five-cars.

The original track was a closed circle in Tomorrowland spanning 8/10ths of a mile. The elevated track is about 20 inches wide and 35 inches in depth and climbs to a height of 31 feet. A bar beneath each beam electrically powers the monorail. The Monorail track was remodeled in 1961 when a Monorail station was added at the Disneyland Hotel, extending the trip to over two-and-a half miles. The Disneyland Hotel station was remodeled, but not moved when Downtown Disney opened in 2001. The Monorail does travel through Disney's California Adventure, but it does not stop there.

The Monorail glides quietly on the concrete beam way at a top speed of 70-80 miles mph. In the park, though, it travels at 20 mph. It makes the round trip in nine minutes. The Monorail belonged to Retlaw, Walt's personal company, until 1981, when it was sold to the Disney Company. Walt leased the right of way for tracks and stations from Disneyland. In December of 1986, Disney's Monorail System was recognized as a National Historic Mechanical Engineering Landmark.

Tomorrowland Autopia

This is one of the last opening day attractions left in Tomorrowland. Walt's daughters, Sharon and Diane, reportedly inspired the ride. The story goes that they learned to drive on the studio lot on weekends. The first time Diane put the car in reverse, she backed the car over a curb at the end of the parking lot and broke a water pipe. With

TREASURE & TRIVIA

Years ago, Fantasyland had a Junior Autopia for smaller Disneyland drivers. In 1966, Junior Autopia was donated to the children of Walt's boyhood hometown of Marceline, Mo. It's the only gift of its kind and the only attraction to leave Disneyland and be reassembled outside of Disney property. The unique gift was a kick off to another of Walt's dreams: The Marceline Project. On the corner of his desk Walt kept preliminary plans for this project.

This was to be a fully operational, turn-of-the-century farm located in the small Missouri town. Walt recognized that technology was changing rapidly and children would not long continue to understand how people survived early in the century. To launch the project, Walt and Roy Disney donated the entire Junior Autopia attraction. Admiral Fowler was sent to oversee the construction. Walt was sick and couldn't fly out for the dedication ceremony. Sadly, no one realized just how sick Walt was, because he died just a few weeks later. The residents of Marceline still have the Junior Autopia and plans to continue the Marceline Project.

The new Autopia driver's licenses are sponsored by Chevron.

Photo by Dave Hawkins

the rear wheels hanging over Riverside Drive and water gushing high into the air, Walt thought of *Autopia* as a place where children can practice driving. Years later, Walt gave Diane's two oldest children red Autopia prototype cars

From 1955 till about 1970, Atlantic Richfield Fuel Company, handed out free driver's licenses to kids on the ride. When Richfield dropped its association with Disneyland, the driver's licenses became collector's items. In 2000, when the remodeled Autopia opened, its new sponsor, Chevron, again issued driver's licenses. For a small fee your picture can be added to the Autopia license.

The original prototype cars were modeled after the Porsche 550 Spider and a one-of-a-kind custom Ferrari. The cars today are seventh-generation vehicles that were introduced in 1967. They've logged millions of miles since then. They each weigh about 1,000 lbs. and reach a maximum speed of seven mph. Each car cost about $5,500, which was more than a real automobile in 1967. The ride has remained popular from the beginning for all ages.

The track travels a mile along a single street that is two cars wide with room to pass. The first cars were roadsters, sports cars, grand prix cars, two police cars, and one Walt parade car. They ran on 7.5–hp., single-cylinder engines capable of 25 mph, but were restrained to 11 mph. Although the body styles changed in the year 2000, the engines are the same type as in the 1967 cars.

The three new vehicle styles have distinctive personalities. "Dusty" is a rugged sports utility vehicle, "Suzy" a cute coupe, and "Sparky" a freewheeling sports car. Many sight gags were added during the latest remodel, even an opportunity to drive "off road."

Innoventions

Built in 1968 and reopened in 1998, the 200-foot diameter Innoventions is the largest attraction in Tomorrowland. This two-level pavilion was once known as the Carousel Theater. The attraction closed in 1973 and moved to Walt Disney World Florida. In 1976, a

TREASURE & TRIVIA

One of the original Junior Autopia cars was collected from Marceline, Mo., as a monument in the Car Park.

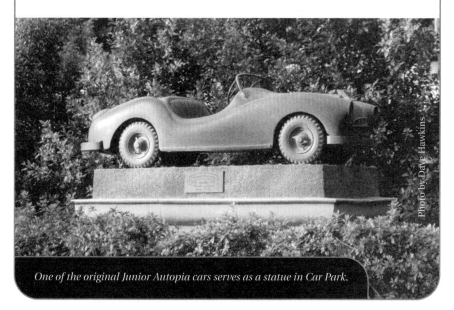

One of the original Junior Autopia cars serves as a statue in Car Park.

Photo by Dave Hawkins

TREASURE & TRIVIA

A statue of an old Mr. Toad's car is also found along the roadways of the new Autopia attraction.

Photo by Dave Hawkins

Another monument to the cars of Disneyland is the statue of Mr. Toad's car.

Bicentennial program, "America Sings," opened in the former theatre with 114 Audio-Animatronics characters. The bicentennial show closed in 1988, and the building sat empty until 1999. Almost the entire Audio-Animatronic cast was recast in the Splash Mountain attraction in Critter Country.

The Innoventions building rotates and has a lot of interactive computer activities.

Innoventions restored Walt's idea of showing the future in a way that people could become excited about it. There are five "stations": Home, Transportation, Entertainment, Work & School, and Sports & Fitness. Each station has a demonstration of products for the near future; some are already on the market, but all are on the cutting edge of technology. Items such as high-definition television, voice-activated computers, and electric cars are showcased. The attraction is part science museum, part arcade, and part trade show integrating technology and interactivity.

The song, "There's A Great Big Beautiful Tomorrow" was written by Robert B. and Richard M. Sherman for the Carousel of Progress attraction that came directly from the 1964–1965 World's Fair. When the *Innoventions* attraction opened, the Sherman Brothers wrote five new sets of lyrics for the song, so a new generation of Disney guests can hear a song familiar to guests of Disneyland 35 years earlier.

The host of Innoventions is the wise-cracking Audio-Animatronic, Tom Morrow (voiced by Nathan Lane). Tom Morrow was the chief scientist in the old Flight to the Moon attraction who interacted with Disney cast members.

Following the demonstrations,

you are welcome to explore other areas and test new products supplied by Compaq, Kaiser Permanente, AT&T, General Motors, and the German firm, SAP.

Space Mountain

Walt wanted a flagship attraction for Tomorrowland. He held a series of meetings to develop a Space Port as early as

Look for a Hidden Mickey on the mural of the Innoventions building as it spins.

1964. His goal was to transport guests through space. Planets, comets, other galaxies and shooting stars swirl around this roller coaster in the dark. In June of 1966, this concept was named Space Mountain, but waited another 11 years to be built.

The attraction opened first in Florida in January 1975. Six months later, construction began at Disneyland. In Florida, where there is more room, riders can sit side by side on one of two tracks. In California, guests sit one behind another. The Florida ride is so large that if the California attraction were built to the same size, it would tower above everything on Main Street and destroy the illusion of scale. California's Space Mountain was reduced to a height of 118 feet with a single track and a foundation built 15 to 20 feet below the ground. Space Mountain is 200 feet in diameter compared to Florida's 300 feet in diameter. It is built of 1,000 tons of steel. The 3,500 feet of track is longer than either of Florida's tracks and can accommodate 12 two-car rockets shooting through space at 32 mph, just a little slower than the speed of light. More than 2,000 passengers can ride Space Mountain each hour. You'll see shooting stars, meteor showers, and far-away galaxies before you experience Disney's version of "reentry" back into the atmosphere.

Originally, Space Mountain was to be sponsored by DASA, Disney Aeronautics and Space Administration; but RCA put up $10 million for funding. In honor of Disneyland's 50th anniversary, Space Mountain received a complete refurbishment.

Walt Disney was slow to add roller coasters to Disneyland because they usually don't have a theme. Both the Matterhorn and Space Mountain are dressed up with architecture, landscape, and costumes.

The film *2001: A Space Odyssey* inspired the loading area. The noses of the passenger cars are red, because real rockets turn red from the friction caused when they are fired into space at the speed of bullets. In 1996, a state-of-the-art sound system was built into each car to provide synchronized music and sound effects. The musician is Dick Dale, "The king of surf music," who is playing Camille Saint-Saens' composition, "Aquarium."

Honey I Shrunk the Audience

The 575-seat theatre that opened in 1998 hosts an 18-minute 3D movie with Rick Moranis, Marcia Strassman, and Eric Idle. The 1989 film, *Honey I Shrunk the Kids*, inspired the attraction. As you enter the laboratory of Imagination Institute, you and the audience become the accidental victims of Professor Szalinski's famed shrink

LESSON TO LEARN

The six surviving astronauts of Project Mercury were there to celebrate the grand opening of Space Mountain. Project Mercury was the United States' first man-in-space program. It was begun in 1958 and was completed in 1963.

The six astronauts on the maiden voyage of Space Mountain were Alan Shepard, Jr., John Glenn, Jr., Walter Schirra, Jr., Scott Carpenter, L., Gordon Cooper, Jr., and Donald "Deke" Slayton. The only astronaut missing from the opening ceremonies was Virgil "Gus" Grissom, who died in the Apollo 1 accident; instead his widow joined the other astronauts. John Glenn's Mercury mission earned him the distinction of the first American to orbit the earth. The Project Mercury astronauts inspired the book and film *The Right Stuff.*

ing machine. Watch out for that giant python, the gigantic five year old, and all those multiplying mice.

Eric Idle, the former Monty Python member, wasn't the original head of Imagination Institute. One day while sitting in a bar with Eric, Marcia Strassman mentioned that the actor had fallen ill. Teasing he said, "Well, I'm not doing anything tomorrow." He received a phone call the next day and was asked to join the show. He began working with another python, this time a 10-ft. snake.

This attraction is sponsored by a generous gift from Kodak. Unlike traditional movie theaters, this theatre requires special platforms for the seats. Each seat is also custom-made to enhance the interplay between the film and the audience.

Starcade

There are at least 200 games in this two-level arcade simulating motorcycles, race cars, skateboards, snowboards, bicycles, jet skis, horses, spacecraft, and tanks. Certainly noteworthy is the R360, a turbulent, 360° pilot game. Local teenagers often come to play the wide assortment of games and nothing else.

Star Tours

In collaboration with George Lucas, Star Tours was built in 1987. Inspired by the *Star Wars* films, this attraction takes place years after the *Return of the Jedi.* Rebel forces who want to rebuild their world in peace have decided that an influx of adventurous tourists and potential homesteaders is just what they need to revitalize the galaxy. Star Tours invites potential immigrants from Earth to travel to the planets of Tatooine and the Moon of Endor on a Star Speeder 3000. Do you see a pink bunny traveling tirelessly to other planets? Guess who hosts this attraction! Energizer.

Star Tours was the first Disney attraction to use aerospace simulators. Simulators have now become a staple at theme parks across America.

A page for "Tom Morrow" is not only a play-on-words, but also a salute to the scientist from the former Mission to Mars attraction. The aliens who scan guests for weapons as they walk through the first queue was an idea originally considered for Space Mountain.

TREASURE & TRIVIA

While standing in line, listen for George Lucas to be paged. They'll say his name backwards:"Egroeg Sacul." George Lucas, creator of the *Star Wars* movies, worked with Imagineering to develop the Star Tours attraction.

Attraction designers' initials and telephone extensions decorate the pipes on the walls near the entrance. Others who worked on the ride can find their initials and birthdates marked in the overhead

TREASURE & TRIVIA

The R2D2 and C3PO units that service the fleet of Star Speeders in the pre-show area are original props from the *Star Wars* movie.

C3PO (gold robot) and R2D2 (droid in Star Speeder) are the original units from the film Star Wars.

Photo by Dave Hawkins

baskets in the line area. Much of the "space junk" was actually found in junkyards, but some of it was found in the "bone yard" where former Disneyland attractions are stored. The General Electric tags on a few of the Disneyland "bone yard" pieces suggests that many items may have come from the G.E. Carousel of Progress.

In the pre-boarding film passengers aboard the Star Speeder Cabin are Imagineers, family members, and *Star Wars* characters.

Other droids in the pre-show area have been recycled from the America Sings attraction. They were once Audio-Animatronic geese. They may not have feathery skins, but they still have webbed feet.

The building for Star Tours is the former Monsanto's Adventure Through Inner Space attraction. During Star Tours, when RX-24 accidentally turns a wrong corner and the Star Speeder soars down into a warehouse, look for the Inner Space microscope from the original attraction.

After exiting the attraction, you'll see a Star Wars theme shop with models of Darth Vader, and a Storm Trooper. The items are for sale, but they aren't costumes. Darth Vader and the Storm Trooper are limited editions priced at $6,500 each.

The Spirit of Refreshment

Coca-Cola hosts the miniature Moonliner soda shop. The rocket is reminiscent of the TWA rocket during Disneyland's early days. The original Rocket was dismantled years ago, but the twin-sister ship, once stationed at TWA's headquarters, was saved from destruction.

TREASURE & TRIVIA

The fighter pilot in the attraction is actor Denis Lawson. Lawson plays Captain Wedge Antilles in the first three *Star Wars* films. He is also the only cameo role to appear in each of the first three films.

TREASURE & TRIVIA

Listen for the page, "Would the owner of the red and black land speeder vehicle I.D. THX 1138 return to your craft? You're parked in a no-hover area." Sci-Fi buffs know that *THX 1138* was the George Lucas graduate film that won Best Drama at the National Student Film Festival.

TREASURE & TRIVIA

Paul Reubens, better known as Pee Wee Herman, recorded the voice for the Robot Trainee Pilot REX.

Redd Rockett's Pizza Port

Annual pass holders know that Redd Rockett's has great pasta alfredo, spaghetti, and pizza. Hosted by Buitoni, a division of Nestlé, this covered haven sells tasty food during all the seasons.

Gone, But Not Forgotten

Tomorrowland has always had the challenge of staying ahead of the times and many attractions have been sacrificed to make room for new ones. Some of the attractions forever gone are:

- Mickey Mouse Club Circus (1955-1956)
- Space Station X-1 (1955-1960)
- TWA Moonliner (1955-1962)
- Circarama (1955-1964)
- Astro-Jets (1956-1964), AKA Tomorrowland Jets (1964-1967), AKA Rocket Jets (1967-1997)
- Clock of the World (1955-1966)
- Skyway (1955-1966)
- Junior Autopia (1957-1966)
- House of the Future (1957-1967)
- Submarine Voyage (1959-1998) *
- Flying Saucers (1961-1966)
- Circle Vision 360 (1964-1997)
- Douglas Moonliner (1965-1966)
- Flight to the Moon (1967-1975)
- Adventure Through Inner Space (1967-1985)
- Carousel of Progress (1967-1973)
- People Mover (1967-1996)
- America Sings (1974-1988)
- Mission to Mars (1975-1992)
- Magic Journeys (1984-1986)
- Captain EO (1986-1997)

- Rocket Rods (1998-2000)

Original "E" ticket attraction

The monorail glides through Tomorrowland
giving an excellent view of the land.

Lots of entertainment is included in the price of admission. In fact, so many different shows and musicians play here each day that each person may enjoy a unique experience due to the variety. They are private eye entertainers.

Chapter 11

PRIVATE EYE
Entertainers

Disneyland offers a lot of entertainment and entertainers to enjoy. Some are featured events like the parades and shows, while others are called "atmosphere entertainment." Atmosphere entertainers set the mood for a park area, and relieve pressure from waiting in long lines in the park. Many of the live shows and free attractions were created in the days when Disneyland lacked the capacity and attractions to handle the crowds. The price of an admission ticket includes these extra values.

Parades: Disneyland has always provided innovative and imaginative parades, fireworks, musical performances, and stage shows. Disneyland understands how important Disney's characters are and how visible they should be. They've had a lot of practice in making these events truly spectacular. Try to see at least one Disney parade, if for no other reason than to take something inspirational home with you. Disney frequently changes the parade every few years to promote a new film, attraction or theme.

During the busy seasons the day parades often promenade twice. The first time starting from the entrance near It's A Small World and taking a route between the Matterhorn, and down Main Street U.S.A. ending near the Mad Hatter Hat Shop. The evening parade reverses direction and ends near It's a Small World. Special sound equipment is carefully placed, although hidden down the entire parade route. So anywhere along the route is a good place to see the parade, although the Main Street Train Station is one of the best.

During the holiday season which typically runs from the end of November until the first week in January, the Christmas Fantasy Parade runs, including a large cast of Disney characters all dressed in holiday clothing. Mr. and Mrs. Claus usually make an appearance, too. The great part about the holidays is not just the parade, but that the

Parades feature amazing floats, costumes, and a plethora of Disney characters.

entire park is decked out in garland and wreaths and the holiday spirit. One Christmas parade is sure to get even the worst Scrooge sufferers in the mood.

Fireworks: To keep the fireworks shows fresh, they too change for the season, and periodically every few years to incorporate new music and theming. More than 200 pyrotechnic shells are fired, carefully synced to music. The shows usually last about 30 minutes and are best viewed anywhere you can easily see Sleeping Beauty Castle. Incidentally, Disney is one of the largest users of fireworks in the world. Lately, a Hidden Mickey is sure to be part of the show, and also special fireworks that when they explode create a smiley face or heart. The shells from England appear as if they are poured from a pitcher, while the shells that come from Japan and China display great color and symmetrical star shapes.

The fireworks are launched from behind ToonTown, so this area is closed during the firework display. Shooting the fireworks off from behind this site provides a beautiful effect as they light up the sky directly above the castle.

Always check the resort map and schedule to find out when the fireworks occur. During the off season, the fireworks may only appear on Friday and Saturday nights.

Main Street U.S.A.

Disneyland Band: has been in the park since opening day. Walt first hired British bandmaster Vesey Walker to assemble a band for a two-week engagement, but the band was so popular that it has been a permanent fixture in the park ever since. Specializing in turn-of-the-century songs and classic Disney music, they also play marches, polkas, jazz, and waltzes. Although they can play almost anything, they are most known for the "Mickey Mouse March." In July of 1982, the band celebrated its 50,000ᵗʰ performance.

Sometimes in the morning, the band plays at the front gates, to greet guests waiting for the park to open. The band may raise the flag on the plaza on Main Street and lower it at the end of the day. Appearing throughout the day, they can usually be seen on Main Street, although on rare occasions they'll play on King Arthur's Carrousel.

The band typically has 15-20 members and has been directed by Vesey Walker, James Christensen, Jim Barngrover and Stanford Freese.

All-American College Band: Since 1971, a special summer band composed of college students from around the country has entertained the crowds. The Collegiate All-Star

Photo by Debbie Smith

Band plays an assortment of music, including rock, jazz and Disney favorites. During the summer months, the College Band sometimes plays "The Star Spangled Banner" at flag retreat. Walt Disney World Florida also has an All-American College Band.

Corner Café Piano Players: Rod Miller has quite a following on Friday and Saturday nights, playing piano at Coke Corner. Many locals come to listen and socialize. Rod has come to be known for playing very fast and specializing in ragtime music.

Jim has been playing the piano with Disneyland for many years as well, sometimes as a solo and sometimes with a band. He's likely to play a blues or boogie tune.

The Dapper Dans: is the barbershop quartet and the official greeters of Main Street U.S.A. This all-male quartet made its first appearance at Disneyland in 1957. Barbershop harmony of tenor, bass, baritone and lead is an American Invention. The Dapper Dans sing with a softer sound than a typical barbershop style. Their humor appeals to the Disneyland audience, especially when it incorporates the straw hat and Deagan organ chimes. You may see the Dapper Dans strolling down the sidewalk of Main Street or riding their bicycle built for four. The custom four-seated Schwinn bicycle was ordered especially for the Dapper Dans by Walt Disney.

The Dapper Dans are not typical cast members; they create their own material, organize themselves, and have more autonomy. Over the years, hundreds of singers have participated in the group. In four-part harmony, they sing classic, turn-of-the-century songs, such as: "In the Good Old Summertime," "Coney Island Baby," "When You Were Sweet Sixteen," "Lida Rose," "Sheik of Araby" and "Cecilia."

ADVENTURELAND

Above the Jungle Cruise you may hear one of two different bands: Alturas or the Trinidad Tropical Steel Drum Band.

Alturas: features South American Indian instruments and plays exotic Inca-inspired music.

Trinidad Tropical Steel Drum Band: plays calypso music at the entrance of the Jungle Cruise. Their colorful costumes and upbeat music are a Disneyland favorite.

Aladdin's Oasis: This 25-minute show features Aladdin, Jasmine, a wise-cracking host and a guest star as Jafar. Using pantomime, this interactive group jokes about current events and tells the story of Aladdin and his lamp. The building was once called the Tahitian Terrace. It was made over in 1993.

LESSON TO LEARN

Before you panic when reading the term pantomime, and begin running as far away from Adventureland as you can get, remember that pantomime is simply acting, using current events for ad lib humor.

TREASURE & TRIVIA

The 1992, the animated film Aladdin won two Oscars. One award was given for Best Song, "A Whole New World," and another for Best Original Score. The intricately patterned flying carpet animated in the movie is set in tile at the entrance of the building. A tiger head symbolizing the cave of wonders appears on the corners of the tile.

NEW ORLEANS SQUARE

The atmosphere in New Orleans is jazz, lots of jazz. Invented around 1900 by black Americans, jazz offers musicians a great deal of freedom to improvise and create while they are playing. Although there are exceptions, jazz is based on the principle that an infinite number of melodies can fit a repeating chord progression while each instrument is featured.

New Orleans is the birthplace of a particular sound, one of the many different kinds of music that make up jazz. In New Orleans jazz, a cornet or trumpet typically carries the melody, while a clarinet plays the counter melody, a trombone performs the rhythmic slides or simple harmony, a tuba or string bass provides the bass line, and drums do what drums always do. New Orleans jazz concentrates on exuberance, and volume while the band members show off their finesse and skills at improvisation.

Royal Street Bachelors: are the crown jewel of the New Orleans bands. This trio plays at the corner of Orleans and Royal Street sporting green vests, checked coats, straw hats and bow ties. The Royal Street Bachelors play a slow, smooth, sultry street jazz. They're sometimes asked to play for dignitaries at special events. Some of the music you may hear include "Blue Moon," "China Town," "What a Wonderful World," and so on. There is rarely a crowd, but definitely worth stopping for a set and enjoying a rest.

The Bayou Brass Band: plays contemporary New Orleans-style seven-piece jazz. They describe their music as hip hop, high energy, classic and contemporary New Orleans-style brass. You can hear it at the French Market Restaurant or sometimes in front of Le Bat en

Rouge shop. They sport black hats and crazy black shoes, a tribute to their CD *In Our Shoes*. The Bayou Brass Band started in fall of 1996 and includes a sousaphone, trombone, tenor sax, bari sax, two trumpets, and cocktail drums. Their goal is to musically recreate Mardi Gras and play some second-line music. You might hear a contemporary funk, or you might hear a little classic *Cantaloop*.

Side Street Strutters:
This sextet plays Dixieland jazz. The Side Street Strutters are often heard at the French Market Restaurant and sometimes for the pre-show of Fantasmic! Then you'll remember them once you hear such favorites as "Alexander's Rag-time Band," "Bill Baily," "Sweet Georgia Brown," or "When the Saints Go Marching In." Typically, the band is made up of saxophone, clarinet, trombone, trumpet, tuba, and drums. Sometimes the piano joins in for this fun, tireless sound. Entertaining Disneyland guests for over a decade, you'll find five Side Street Strutters CDs available to purchase in the park.   .

River Rascals:
can be heard playing at the French Market, the New Orleans balconies, or sometimes on the rafts as part of the pre-show for Fantasmic! The River Rascals have been playing at Disneyland since 1997 and include more electric, more zydeco, rhythm & blues,

and Caribbean/blues in their style. The band includes piano, sax, trumpet, guitar, bass guitar, and drum, although you may hear them or part of their band throughout New Orleans Square. They play songs like "Brown-eyed Handsome Man," "Just Friends," "Back to New Orleans," and "Cajun Rage." In 2003, they released their first CD so you can take a little of their energy home with you.

Variety Atmosphere:
New Orleans Square wouldn't be complete without street performers, including a mime, tap dancers, jazz soloists, face painters and artists. Some of the most treasured keepsakes from Disneyland are the portraits of the children who visit the park.

Fantasmic!:
(1992): Long after guests have departed Tom Sawyer Island every evening, lights continue to shine from the deserted island. Since 1992, Mickey Mouse has appeared dressed as the sorcerer's apprentice to conjure up images from 60 years of Disney animation.

Fantasmic! incorporates scenes and music from *Fantasia*, featuring *The Sorcerer's Apprentice*, by Paul Dukas and *Night on Bald Mountain* by Modeste Mussorgsky. Other Disney classics featured are: *Dumbo*, *Pinocchio*, *Jungle Book*, *Peter Pan*, *Snow White*, and many more. Bruce Healy's Orchestra plays the dramatic score.

LESSON TO LEARN

I n New Orleans, a funeral procession is a very big deal. Led by a Grand Marshal, the band wearing top hats or derbies is followed by the hearse. The sisters of the church, all dressed in white, typically follow the hearse. The Grand Marshal usually wears a broad satin sash over his shoulder and across his chest. The name of the band or the church is normally emblazoned on the sash. The sash often has a purple border or gold braid.

On the way to the cemetery, the band plays solemn and slow music, songs like "Just a Closer Walk with Thee." This music is called first line. After they "turn the body loose," the parade marches back to church, this time playing ragtime or jazz music, referred to as second line. People would dance and celebrate in honor of the person who died. Bands play songs like "Oh Didn't He Ramble," and "When the Saints Go Marching In." Sometimes they would play a song called, "I'm Glad You're Dead, You Rascal You."

Incidentally, in New Orleans bodies can't be buried because the city is below sea level. Bodies are therefore interned above ground in tombs.

FRONTIERLAND

By day, Frontierland appears normal. But at night an amphitheater emerges including movie projectors, speakers, extensive lighting facilities, 30-ft. tall props, dressing rooms, fog machines, fireworks, firing pads and a high-tech control room. The Rivers of America was drained and a three-story subterranean basement was created.

The 22-minute spectacular features live performers, animation projected on three, 30x50-ft. water-mist screens, giant props, floats that really float, and pyrotechnic lasers, fog, and fiber optics. The story is one of good versus evil. It features Mickey and several classic Disney villains, including the 45-ft. fire-breathing dragon from *Sleeping Beauty.* More than 100 cast and crewmembers participate in the show, which may be seen by as many as 12,000 guests. It is so popular, Disney-MGM Studios in Florida built a theater and recreated the show.

Billy Hill & the Hillbillies: have a bluegrass look, a bit of a country sound, but play a variety of song styles. You'll hear a country twist applied to classical, rock, surf, rag, and back to country. The band is made up of guitar, violin, bass, and electric violin all played by brothers whose first names are

Billy. Sporting overalls, handkerchiefs, and long red underwear, you can't miss 'em when you see 'em. You can't help but love 'em once you hear 'em. You are guaranteed to hear cornball and comedy and have a hand clappin', knee slappin' good time. Audience participation is just part of the fun. Billy Hill and the Hillbillies usually play at the Golden Horseshoe, but also out near the Festival Arena behind Big Thunder Mountain Railroad.

Laughing Stock Co.: is a street show where Frontierland Mayor McGillicuddy tries to marry off his daughter Sallie Mae to the Sheriff Clem Clodhopper. This comedy team relies on audience participation, for a hysterically funny good time. Appearing throughout the day, you find Laughing Stock out in front of the Golden Horseshoe.

FANTASYLAND

Sword in the Stone Ceremony:
The Disney Film (released in 1963) and the park event (1983) are both based on T.H. White story, *The Sword in the Stone* (1939). The legend is re-enacted with the Excalibur sword and a member of the audience—perhaps even one of your kids. The legend of Excalibur is inscribed on the anvil: "Who so pulleth out this sword of this stone and anvil is rightwise king born of England." Merlin the magician hosts the event and gives a crown

for the day to anyone able to withdraw the sword.

Fantasyland Theatre: (June 1995) features daily stage shows, special events, and elaborate musical productions with the Disney characters. Another Fantasyland Theater debuted in 1955 showing Disney cartoons. During the holiday season, the Fantasyland Theater hosts the Christmas Candlelight Ceremony and Processional.

To rule this magic kingdom, it's easy, just pull this sword from the stone.

The Candlelight Procession:

This tradition began in 1958. Throughout the year, choirs from local communities, churches, high schools and colleges audition to participate in the event. During a couple of nights in December the lights along Main Street U.S.A. darken for the Christmas holiday spirit to be shared by hundreds of carolers carrying lighted candles. Only one group is a permanent fixture to the scene, the Disney Cast Choir. The Cast Choir is made up, not of professional singers, but interested cast members who audition. They practice for about six months for their appearance in white collars and green robes. They perform in the shape of a Christmas tree each year while a celebrity guest narrates "The Christmas Story." Accompanied by a live orchestra, 800 voices fill the stage.

TOMORROWLAND

Trash Can Trio:

Guests may confuse the group at first as custodians, but when the musical percussion on trash bins rocks the crowd, they'll know they've met the Trash Can Trio. They perform throughout Tomorrowland and often prior to a parade toward the entrance of Tomorrowland. A keen eye will recognize that these so-called custodians move through the crowd pushing bright silver trash cans, unlike the normal refuse removers throughout the park.

Club Buzz Stage:

Once known as the Tomorrowland Terrace Stage it was first built so guests could watch the televised moon landing of Apollo 11 in the summer of 1969. During the evening, different shows may appear, specializing in popular music appropriate for dancing. Typically one of five bands play over the weekend. See schedule for current listing.

Calling all Space Scouts:

is a show featuring Buzz Lightyear and friends. This short program has high energy, fun music, and a lot of audience participation. Several shows a day are available only at the Club Buzz Stage.

Misc. Nighttime Entertainment:

is enjoyed at the Club Buzz Stage every weekend evening. Different bands play each week and the area becomes a hangout for dancing to pop and rock 'n' roll. The dance floor is large, the lights are bright and colorful, and crowds gather to enjoy modern and current hits.

Chapter 12

BEHIND-THE-SCENES
Agents

Imagineering

The word Imagineer is a combination of imagination and engineering, a blend of creative fantasy and technical understanding necessary to build a Disney attraction. This division of Walt Disney Company is a prestigious organization of only about 1000 people. Walt and his original Imagineers transformed 160 acres of orange groves in Southern California into the Magic Kingdom. The responsibility of expanding and creating show elements at Disneyland falls on the Imagineers. The Imagineers come from varied backgrounds. They include engineers, architects, artists, landscape designers, special effects technicians, writers, project managers and more.

The original Imagineers were a group of motion picture artists. John Hench, a key Disney designer once said, "We knew how to create continuity between scenes, and used those filmmaking techniques at Disneyland; as guests progress from land to land, even the ground color changes." This concept is called cross dissolve; a distance, for example from Adventureland to New Orleans Square, may not be very far, but enormous change in theme and story occur. The transition is smooth because there is a gradual blending of themed foliage, sound, music, color, and architecture.

An excellent book, *Walt Disney Imagineering,* describes how the positions were formed and some of the exciting works were done by the highly creative and talented people who became Imagineers.

Gardening

When the park opened, more than $500,000 was spent on landscape and irrigation systems. More than 1,200 full-size trees and 9,000 shrubs were brought to the park. Today, a large staff of gardeners attends to the park's 800 species of plants from more than 40 nations. The landscape includes 4,500 trees and 40,000 shrubs and perennials.

Approximately 1 million annuals are planted. Ninety percent of the landscape at Disneyland is not indigenous to California. Pruning and replanting are continuously required at the park and usually done while it is closed. Perhaps part of the floral beauty of the park is the result of Lilly Disney's interest in the landscape. It took about three years for the park to mature fully.

Bill Evans, the original director of landscape, had several goals in mind as he landscaped Disneyland. Foremost, the park had to be a nice place, and it had to shut out the rest of the world. Each land was to have its own visual mood with an appropriate theme. The 20-ft. berm around the park kept the noise out, and the trees and shrubs were strategically placed to hide the sight of the outside world. The park had to have year-round color. Every three months, flower-beds are replanted with new blooms.

During construction, Walt wanted to save many of the existing trees on the property. He tagged the trees with different color ribbons to identify if they were to be moved, removed, or saved. Unfortunately, most of the trees were accidentally bulldozed—the bulldozer operator was color-blind.

More than 25 different varieties of grasses cover more than five acres. The grass is mowed at daybreak by landscapers wearing miner's helmets. The grounds are watered by more than 50,000 drip emitters and sprinkler heads. Cast members at City Hall and the Information Center keep a file of almost every plant on the property. So if a special plant catches your eye, the staff can more than likely help you identify it.

Main Street was to have a Victorian formality. The landscape is very disciplined with decorative posies and neatly trimmed shrubs. Ruth Shellhour designed the Main Street landscape for the grand opening.

One of the most photographed spots in the world is the Mickey flowers at the entrance of the park. To keep the flowers looking fresh and full, Mickey's face is planted nine times a year. It is important for a well-manicured Mickey to greet visitors at the entrance. Walt once said, "Mickey Mouse represents independence. The life and ventures of Mickey Mouse have been closely bound up with my own personal and professional life. He still speaks for me, and I still speak for him." Mickey's greeting at the entrance to Disneyland is actually a personal greeting from Walt.

Adventureland is undisciplined. It is designed to appear as if there is no gardening in the man-eating jungle. Considering that the site was originally an orange grove, this proved to be no small undertaking. Many plants from around the world were added, including native African and Brazilian trees. With a little bit of landscaping artistic license, fig trees from China, India, and Australia blend perfectly.

Frontierland looks like a southwestern-painted desert down the main strip, filled with cactus of multiple varieties. These plants usually grow at an elevation of several thousand feet in very low humidity. Even the 10-12 inches of Southern California rain is too much for these plants, so special drainage is required. Even then, these plants have to be replaced every two years. Everywhere else in the park, the plants required water pipelines for more water.

Tom Sawyer Island is plush and green with its pine, southern red cedar, carolina cherry, sycamores, and live oak trees. The pine trees are the tallest trees at Disneyland. On occasion, guests write to complain that their children were infected by poison oak while playing on Tom Sawyer Island. The landscape is so natural that guests really believe they are in a natural wilderness. Rest assured, there is no poison oak on Tom Sawyer Island. Every plant is catalogued.

Fantasyland has a bit of whimsy with its topiary figures and decorative patterns in the hedges. The topiaries first made their appearance in 1966. They are made from thugas, junipers, cypress, ficus, and African boxwood trees. Topiaries have been a European tradition for more than 150 years. In the early days, Disneyland didn't have the luxury of time, so they shaped old plants with wiring to assume new shapes. Today's topiaries are the product of between 24 months and 10 years of hard work, with concerns about overwatering, underwatering, too much fertilizer, and too little pest control. Disneyland and Walt Disney World use different methods for making topiaries. Walt Disney World can make theirs in a month since they use sphagnum-moss, but Disneyland cultivates the plants to form a shape, which takes a great deal longer.

Throughout the rest of Fantasyland, elm trees are especially appropriate. They are easily seen through, which makes them perfect for hanging twinkling lights.

The Matterhorn uses all natural trees, mostly Colorado blue spruce trees since their 1-inch needles and blue cast suggest distance. A drip irrigation system waters the trees. They grow rapidly and ruin the scale of the mountain, so the trees need to be replaced every two to five years.

Another area that requires special care is the Storybook Land attraction. Gardeners must devote five times as much attention to pruning here as elsewhere in the park. All the plants are miniatures that must fit to the 1/12 scale, even the 1-foot spruce. A special process of stunting keeps the trees in scale. The plants are kept in small pots to prevent their root systems from expanding.

Don't let the size fool you; some of the plants are very old. A San Diego gardener sold Disneyland the 20- to 35-year old cypress plant that still sits next to Geppetto's toyshop. Near the cottage of the seven dwarves are pine trees from Mendocino County that are 130-180 years old.

Tomorrowland was relandscaped in 1998, when edible plants replaced the foliage. A recent change adds landscape that doubles as a garden, from strawberries, to lettuce, cabbage, coffee plants, and seasonal changes. Most of the trees bear fruit, including orange, lemon, lime, apple, banana, persimmon, olive, pomegranate, avocado, pecan, and date palm.

Kennel Club

Since 1958, Disneyland has offered kennel services for guest's pets. Kevin Corcoran and Old Yeller's son Duke presided over the opening ceremonies of the kennel. There are 127 cages of various sizes. Although most kennel guests are dogs, the kennel has hosted cats, parrots, snakes, hamsters, lizards, ferrets, squirrels, pigs, raccoons, and chimps.

Owners are asked to return two or three times a day to walk and visit their pets. Overnight accommodations are not available. The cast members are not allowed to handle the animals. Stray animals are taken to a nearby shelter. The Disney Kennel is hosted by Friskies.

Animal Care

Located behind Frontierland and Fantasyland is an area known as the *Circle D Corral*. Before 1980, the area was known as the Pony Farm with a little farmhouse that was once the home to one of the original landowners. The farmhouse is now the office for Circle D Corral.

The most familiar residents are the horses. There are French Percherons, and Belgian and English Clydesdales that pull the carriages and parade wagons down Main Street. The largest of these horses is Duke, a Percheron draft horse weighing more than 2,400 lbs. The horses work four-hour shifts, four times a week. They are exercised and fed daily and tended by the blacksmith at Circle D Corral. The horses sport a collection of personalized harnesses created by a vintage 1911 sewing machine.

Other livestock at Circle D Corral include mules, goats, sheep, ducks, chickens, and once even a python. Circle D Corral is also the home of the homing pigeons used in special events and the swans that live in the castle moat.

Custodial

Disneyland is known for being clean. Sweepers with dustpans are visible and always on patrol. They carry park maps to give to guests and are a good resource for directions. Although most of the maintenance is completed at night, more than 600 people work around the clock to clean the park and make repairs by opening time the next day. Every night, steam-cleaning guns scour the streets while every inch of counter, floor, window and sidewalk is being cleaned. The brass on the carousel is polished, the snow on top of the Matterhorn is cleaned, Monstro the Whale in the Story Book attraction gets his teeth brushed, and the Haunted Mansion gets a fresh supply of cobwebs. The kitchens and bathrooms are scrubbed, shelves are dusted, and floors are polished and waxed.

On a busy day, custodians collect and recycle 30 tons of garbage. The resort can recycle 510 tons of paper and 15 tons of aluminum cans in a single year. This saves 1,727,190 kilowatts of energy compared to using virgin materials.

There are more than 19 million gallons of water in Disneyland's 10 water areas. Scuba divers go down to retrieve lost items and inspect mechanical parts and underwater tracking systems.

Lighting

Disneyland maintains a large staff of full-time electricians. One crew's sole job is to change the lights that edge the roofline. There are more than 100,000 light bulbs in Disneyland, including the 11,000 bulbs trimming the buildings on Main Street U.S.A. The lights around Main Street are replaced when they reach 80 percent of their life expectancy. The park takes on a different appearance at night when the theatrical lighting of the castle and other key attractions gives Disneyland a magical glow. Imagineers use light to evoke a certain mood or feeling inside as well as outside all of the attractions. If you think the park is lit up during the year, try coming during the holidays!

Maintenance

The facilities and maintenance teams inspect attraction vehicle and tracks nightly for safety. After the park closes, teams spread throughout the park to conduct point-by-point inspections of electrical connections, motors, fuses, sound systems, lighting, and relays. The wonderful collection of people who maintain Disneyland understand all aspects of old-time craftsmanship—glass blowing, sculpting, mural painting, model making, ship rigging, saddlemaking, woodcarving, weaving, and more.

To keep a better-than-new look, Disney uses more than 20,000 gallons of paint each year. Disney's specialists are masters at making new things look old and old things look new. The maintenance department is also responsible for the 24-karat gilding found on the turrets of Sleeping Beauty Castle and It's A Small World.

They perform frequent checks of the Audio-Animatronic characters to keep them running and to check for wear and tear. The

Audio-Animatronic characters have been known to wear out their clothes from the inside. From time to time, costumers, hairdressers, and makeup artists completely make over these mechanical cast members.

Wardrobe

Cast members and their costumes must add to the experience and not distract from it. This challenge keeps a whole costume department of over 300 professionals very busy. The wardrobe collection includes more than 500,000 pieces, including attraction hosts and parade costumes, maintenance crew uniforms, and Audio-Animatronic figures. From its initial design to its first public view, a new costume takes 37 steps and from six to eight months to produce. Even before the opening of Disney's California Adventure, the Disneyland Costume Division stocked approximately 500,000 yards of 900 different fabrics.

The average life of a costume is nine months. Staff members create, alter, repair, and launder costumes for 20,000 cast members. Every week, more than 20,000 garments are exchanged for cleaning. Cast members always have clean costumes to wear; they can even obtain a freshly cleaned outfit during their shift. Approximately 150,000 individual pieces are replaced each year.

Even the 1,100 Audio-Animatronic figures have costume dressers who check and maintain their wardrobes. Their costumes are created with zippers and Velcro® to make them easy to slip on and off. Most of the soiling of the Audio-Animatronic outfits occurs on the inside thanks to moving parts and leaking oil.

Mickey Mouse alone has an elaborate wardrobe including his sorcerer's apprentice robe and hat, black tuxedo formal look, black and white outfit from his before color days to his most famous red pants.

Cast members

The cast members play an integral role in sustaining the magic. The cast members are famous for being friendly and helpful. From the tram drivers, food service workers, guest services, store clerks, ticket takers, security, and attraction hosts, every employee participates in Disney training called "Traditions." Cast members must follow a strict code of hygiene and practice pleasant and helpful behavior. "Traditions" lasts several days and includes a strong emphasis on the Disney Company culture. Walt insisted that employees treat every customer like a guest.

Parking Structure

The parking structure was built in 1999. It includes 10,240 parking spaces on six levels. It was added to handle the increased parking requirements of Disney's California Adventure and Downtown Disney.

Corporate Sponsors

Throughout the book many non-Disney companies have been noted for hosting restaurants and other attractions. They gently remind guests of the outside world. The support of these companies makes the fantasy of Disneyland stronger, because they allow Disney to try new endeavors. In return, sponsors enjoy the high visibility of association with Disney. Each sponsor corporation is prominent in its field and meets the high quality expectations demanded by Disney. A financial portfolio of all the corporate sponsors of Disneyland would be quite profitable. Among the highly recognizable companies are:

AAA Touring and Travel Services
AT&T
Bank One Visa
Chevron
Coca-Cola and Minute Maid
COMPAQ
Dole Pineapple
Energizer
Federal Express
Kodak
McDonald's
National Car Rental
NESTLE Corporation (Nestlé/Carnation, Nestlé Ice Cream, Nestlé Toll House, Nestlé Carnation Baby Formulas, Stouffer's, Bouitoni, and Friskies)

AAA

The American Automobile Association (AAA) promises "We're Always With You." This is true even if your travels bring you to Disneyland. Visitors to Disneyland will find the Touring and Travel Service Center operated by the Automobile Club of Southern California near the entrance gates in the park. Located on Main Street, U.S.A., guests may inquire about flat tire services, towing, hotel reservations, and many other AAA services.

Once primarily known as a roadside assistance service, AAA has added over the years many more benefits including travel, financial, and insurance services. Members can enjoy auto buying and financing help, ownership & maintenance services, and membership discounts.

AAA has supported United Way, Children's Miracle Network, American Red Cross, American Cancer Society, Law enforcement events, motor sports and community level projects. Children of kindergarten age to second grade may enjoy the "Otto the Auto" web pages where they can print out games, lessons or creative projects relating to traffic safety. Parents may appreciate the safety tips for roller skating, Rollerblading, bicycling, and skateboarding.

The Automobile Club of Southern California has over 5.9 million members, more than 8,000 employees, $3.4 billion in assets, and over 90 locations. To learn more about membership services or perhaps join, you can log onto the website www.aaa-calif.com.

AT&T

AT&T produced special decoder cards when the Indiana Jones attraction first opened. The cards had different pictures on them and are quite collectible today. Some of the Mara Font on the walls of the queue makes reference to AT&T and their former promotion of "choosing wisely." Choose wisely your passageway in the Temple of the Forbidden Eye, but also your phone service.

In the year 2000, AT&T had annual revenues of nearly $66 billion. Backed by research and development, AT&T runs the world's largest, most sophisticated communications network. AT&T is the largest cable operator in the U.S. and is the leading supplier of data and Internet services. In October of 2000, the company announced that it would restructure into four businesses, individually trading as either common stock or tracking stock. AT&T now has separate companies called AT&T Wireless, AT&T Broadband, AT&T Business, and AT&T Consumer. To learn more about AT&T Consumer services, such as long distance, phone cards, DSL and Internet service, check out their website www.consumer.att.com.

Bank1One Visa issued a special Disney credit card in Spring of 2003. The special red card features a Hidden Mickey on the front and special Disney Dream Reward Dollars benefits. For every 100 dollars spent using the Visa, members receive one reward dollar to be redeemed for most Disney merchandise, park tickets, hotel nights, food and more at Disneyland, Walt Disney World theme parks, Disney Cruise Line, Disney catalogs and Disney Stores. Special bonus offers allow card holders to earn double and triple dollars on select purchases.

For members who applied for the Bank One Visa during the launch promotion had "Member since: Day One" printed on their cards.

To apply for the Disney Visa by phone call 1-877-252-6576. Customer service is available 24 hours a day, 7 days a week. To learn more about the APR and special offers, check out their website at www.bankone.com and click on Disney Rewards under Special Offers.

Chevron

Autopia is utopia for the Chevron cars and the guests wishing to drive them. The Chevron sponsorship at Disneyland is very prominent and amusingly effective. The Chevron cars promotional campaign was started to create awareness about Techron. Consistent use of Techron minimizes harmful deposits on the intake system and reduces emissions compared to other gasoline. The Chevron cars with personalities gave Disney's Autopia a new angle and springboard for fun. For families making the road trip to Disneyland, check out the Chevron kids web page with stickers and coloring pages of the Autopia cars at Disneyland. Printable pictures of Suzy, Dusty, Sparky, and Classic Cars are available on www.chevroncars.com/wocc.

Chevron is one of the country's largest refiners and marketers of petroleum products. Primarily serving the west, southwest, and south, they have five refineries in the U.S., and more than 7,900 retail outlets. In 1879, the company started as Pacific Coast Oil Company. In 1900, they merged with Standard Oil and got involved for a short time with John D. Rockefeller. It wasn't until 1931 that the Chevron symbol was chosen as a company identity, but eventually the Standard was dropped and Chevron evolved as the company name.

Chevron is also proud of the continued contributions to aviation. Back in 1926, the company painted the city names on the rooftops of stations from Seattle to San Diego to help pilots navigate. On a clear day the signs could be seen from 3,000 feet up. To learn more about Chevron's products, history, and services, such as their travel club and credit cards, go to www.chevron.com.

Coca-Cola

More than a billion times a day, every day, thirsty people throughout the world reach for a Coca-Cola product. Founded in 1886, Coca-Cola fits in with the turn of the century Main Street U.S.A. Coca-Cola has become the world's leader in manufacturing, marketing, and distributing of non-alcoholic beverage concentrates and syrups. With 230 brands, Coca-Cola offers soft drinks, sports drinks, fruit juices and bottled water to nearly 200 countries. Guests to Disneyland can enjoy Coca-Cola products in the restaurants, outdoor vending, the Coca-Cola Refreshment Corner on Main Street, or in Tomorrowland at The Spirit of Refreshment under the model of the rocket.

Coca-Cola merchandise is very collectible. On the company website, www.coca-cola.com, visitors can purchase apparel, collectibles, games, toys, and home décor. The website also offers a virtual plant tour, youth partnerships and fun activities. Coca-Cola is very proud of their sponsorships with the Olympics, NASCAR, FIFA (Federation International Football Association, aka Soccer) World Ranking and World Cup Tournaments, the American Music Awards among other programs targeted to local communities. To learn more about Coca-Cola and their core values and investor information visit the site.

COMPAQ

COMPAQ merged with Hewlett-Packard (HP) in 2002. The combined forces has over a billion customers, serving 162 countries and 150,000 employees. "The new HP" is the leading provider of access devices, application delivered as Web Services running on infrastructure solutions. HP signed one of their first deals with Walt Disney in 1938 for eight model 200b oscillators, the equipment used for the Fantasia soundtrack. Today, guests who visit Disneyland on the weekend and summer will enjoy "Believe . . . There's Magic in the Star" fireworks spectacular powered by COMPAQ.

The website, http://thenew.hp.com, offers solutions for the home, home office, business, government, education and healthcare arenas. Surfers can browse for products and services, download drivers and software, and get technical support. When you're ready to purchase, you can buy direct or locate retailers nearby.

"The new HP" sponsors a variety of organizations and programs where the company has a significant presence. Including United Way, Junior Achievement, Boys and Girls Clubs of America, Habitat for Humanity, food banks and many others.

Dole

Dole has made the word "Hawaiian" almost synonymous with "pineapple." The Enchanted Tiki Room wouldn't be complete without a little taste of Hawaii or Dole Pineapple. Dole is the largest produce supplier in the world with over $4.5 billion in revenue. Dole is known for high-quality fresh vegetables, fruit, flowers and a line of packaged foods. The company history dates back to 1851 in Hawaii. Dole supports the Tiki Juice Bar and the Enchanted Tiki Room.

When Disneyland guests return home, a quick look at www.dole.com is worth the effort. Surfers will find recipes, coupons, careers and a Fun for Kids page. The children's learning center has games, lessons on nutrition, and ideas for preserving the environment. Dole is a sponsor of the "5 a Day for Better Health" Program and provides learning materials for kids.

Energizer

With high innovation and creativity, it's appropriate that Energizer sponsors the Tomorrowland-favorite Star Tours. Today, Energizer Company is the global leader of portable power and flashlights. Energizer was the first company to develop a zero-mercury battery that's safer and environmentally conscious. The new titanium battery has improved performance and longer life. This is a long way from the company back in 1886 who sold a six-inch battery for home telephones. Energizer continues to use innovation to build better, longer-lasting products, as consumers require more portable power to keep up with the latest technological demands.

Energizer has a great website www.energizer.com that features technical product information about their batteries, and flashlights. The Energizer Learning Center has fun, safe science projects, demonstrations on how batteries and flashlights work, and lessons about weather preparedness. Shoppers can find the Bunny Store featuring apparel and novelties. The Pink Energizer Bunny, beating his drum is one of the top five advertising icons in the U.S., although he only made his debut in 1989. The Energizer Bunny was made into a hot air balloon 166-ft. tall. It's the largest hot air balloon ever made and is easy to track on the website as he makes his travels.

Kodak

Eastman Kodak is one of the few companies that could have been on a Main Street U.S.A. at the turn of the century. Kodak made their first simple camera accessible to the public back in 1888. Today, it is one of the 25 largest U.S. companies. Kodak was built on four business principles: mass production at low cost, internal distribution, extensive advertising, and a focus on the customer.

Thanks to Kodak, visitors to Disneyland have beautiful, free, color souvenir programs. The programs are printed weekly and share the schedule for all the park events. The Main Street Photo Supply Company is a great resource for guests needing film, camera equipment or advice. In Fantasyland, look for the camera kiosk, also sponsored by Kodak, for assistance. Sprinkled throughout the park Kodak has identified seven photo spots to remind families to "Share Moments. Share Life."

The family photographer may want to jump on the Kodak website, www.kodak.com, to see the Picture of the Day, the Kodak e-Magazine, improve photography techniques, and shop at their on-line store. Investor and charitable information is readily available on the site. In 2001, Kodak donated $16.7 million to programs like United Way, American Red Cross, National Urban League, Education, Arts/Culture and Community Revitalization.

McDonald's

There are two American icons that are familiar to almost every person on the planet: Mickey Mouse and Ronald McDonald. Both Disneyland and McDonald's began in 1955 in Southern California and both have had incredible international success. McDonald's is the largest and best-known food service retailer in the world. There are over 30,000 McDonald's restaurants in 121 countries. McDonald's vision is to provide outstanding quality service, cleanliness and value. Visitors to Disneyland can find the McDonald's famous food at Harbour Galley in Critter Country or Conestoga Fries in Frontierland.

TREASURE & TRIVIA

Ronald McDonald made his first television appearance in 1963. Willard Scott dressed up as the first Ronald McDonald.

The McDonald's web surfer can find a lot of valuable and interesting information by visiting www.mcdonalds.com. Children can interact with Ronald McDonald & Friends with games and activities, including the current Happy Meal promotions often featuring Disney partnerships. Older and career-minded family members may find job opportunities, and join the long list of successful business people who started their first job at McDonald's. Remember that 70 percent of McDonald's restaurants are independently owned and operated, so potential franchisers may find guidance and resources. For the investor in the family, financial information is readily available.

More information is available about how Ronald McDonald House Charities (RMHC), support families of critically ill children. At Ronald McDonald Houses, families can stay near their children while they're getting the appropriate medical care. Current promotions and donations are available online for the RMHC.

National Car Rental

Visitors to Disneyland may enjoy free, one-way transportation on Main Street, U.S.A. courtesy of National Car Rental. National sponsors the fire engine, horse-drawn streetcar, horseless carriage, and omnibus. Outside of Disneyland, National Car Rental is the official car rental company with Walt Disney World Resort. This strong affiliate is why you may see Mickey Mouse, Goofy and other Disney characters on the airport buses taking guests to the car rental station.

The website for National Car Rental helps travelers check rates and reservations, choose vehicles, take advantage of promotional specials, join the Emerald Club for frequent travelers or answer a multitude of questions about renting automobiles. National Car Rental is also affiliated with a lot of frequent traveler programs. The website even has suggestions for reading material under their Travel Partners and the Amazon Bookstore web page.

Nestlé, *N-E-S-T-L-É-S—Nestlé makes the very best.* This jingle is almost as familiar as M-I-C (see ya real soon) . . . The relationship between Nestlés and Disneyland goes back to Disneyland's infancy when Carnation Company was involved. Today, Carnation is part of the Nestlé franchise. In fact, Nestlé U.S.A. is the world's largest food company. In February 2002, Fortune Magazine named Nestlé U.S.A., America's most admired Food Company for the fifth consecutive year. One reason may be that Nestlé understands and anticipates their customers needs in order to fulfill them. Nestlé's food and beverage sales in the U.S.A. totaled nearly $12 billion in 2001. Visitors at Disneyland may want to enjoy some of the many restaurants sponsored by Nestlé U.S.A. including Blue Ribbon Bakery, French Market, Rancho del Zocolo, and Redd Rockett's Pizza Port. In the California sun, it's almost tradition to splurge and enjoy Nestlé Ice Cream to cool yourself down. When you return home, take a little Nestlé with you by checking out the www.Nestleusa.com website. Many Disneyland visitors may not realize that Nestlé sponsors the baby care center and kennels as well.

Nestlé USA's website is amazing with five separate consumer programs. Visitors can find more than 13,000 recipes on www.mymeals.com. Web surfers can also make a grocery list, develop a meal plan and keep a recipe box online. The children's website, www.verybestkids.com, has crafts, games, activities, and fun cooking and baking ideas. The baking website, www.verybestbaking.com, has contests, recipes, newsletters, E-cards and chat rooms for kitchen talk. For mom's and mom's-to-be, Nestlé's www.verybestbaby.com website includes a free magazine subscription, easy interactive tools related to nutrition for moms, babies, and families.

BIBLIOGRAPHY

"All Aboard for Mickey's Santa Fe
Express" by Dore Redfern, *Disney
News,* Fall 1993, page 47.

"Did you hear the One About . . . " by
Ryan A. Harmon & David Mumford,
Disney News, Spring 1992, pages
33–35.

"FANTASMIC!" by John McClintock,
Disney News, Spring 1992, pages
8–10.

*The Updated Official Encyclopedia
Disney A to Z* by Dave Smith, pages
9–10, 15, 24, 36, 37, 46, 64, 68, 69, 77,
91, 93, 101, 105, 108, 120, 123, 128,
130, 132, 134–135, 142, 146–148,
150, 151, 154, 162, 173, 181, 185,
186, 191, 193, 197, 206, 210, 218,
220, 226, 229, 231, 234–235, 240,
242–243, 244, 245, 260, 270, 273,
279, 280, 286, 287, 289, 291, 292,
296, 300, 303–304, 311, 315, 320,
324, 327, 340, 341, 345–346, 351,
353, 356, 361, 368, 373, 375, 399,
400, 405, 409, 413, 431, 437, 451,
476, 480, 503–505, 513, 515, 521,
526, 528, 534, 535, 545, 550–551,
561–562, 582, 593, 601, 602, 603.

"Predicting the Future" by Ryan A.
Harmon, *Disney News,* Fall 1991,
pages 32–35.

"Toon In Tomorrow, Imagineering
Mickey's Toontown for Disneyland"
by Jeff Kurtti, *Disney News,* Summer
1992, pages 29–30.

Disneyland the Nickel Tour by Bruce
Gordon and David Mumford, July
1995, pages 14, 18, 21, 23–25, 29,
50, 55, 58, 59, 63, 67, 76, 90, 102,
118, 122, 136, 149, 151, 157, 162,
167–169, 171, 175, 188, 189, 226,
228, 229, 230, 234, 238, 253, 255,
256, 262–265, 278, 279, 284, 285,
288, 293, 322, 326, 328, 329, 334,
335, 336, 345, 347.

*The Man Behind the Magic, The Story
of Walt Disney* by Katherine and
Richard Greene, July 1991, pages
123, 125, 138, 156.

The Ultimate Disney Trivia Book 1 by
Kevin Neary and Dave Smith, 1992,
pages 133–146.

The Ultimate Disney Trivia Book 2 by
Kevin Neary and Dave Smith, April
1994, pages 169–171.

The Ultimate Disney Trivia Book 3 by
Kevin Neary and Dave Smith, 1997,
pages 128–151.

"Yo Ho A Pirate's Life for Every Disney
Guest" by David Fisher, *Disney
News,* Fall 1992, pages 23–25.

"Remembering Walt Marc Davis,
Animator, Imagineer, Friend" by
Libby Slate, *Disney News,* Fall 1992
page 26.

"92803 Toon Town: A Zip Code With
Character at Disneyland" by Ryan A.
Harmon, *Disney News,* Winter 1992,
pages 8–12.

"A First For Disneyana Collectors;
Walt Disney World Hosts Its First
Disneyana Convention" by David R.
Smith, *Disney News,* Winter 1992
pages 14–15.

"Euro Disneyland Trivia Part Deux" by
Ryan A. Harmon, *Disney News,* Fall
1993, pages 16–21.

*Mouse Tales: A Behind–the-Ears Look
at Disneyland,* by David Koenig,
Bonadventure Press, 1994, pages
41–45, 49–50, 53.

"Ask Dave" by Dave Smith, *Disney News,*
Fall 1997, pages 109–111, 114, 117.

Internet: www.hiddenmickey.org
Disneyland: Main Street.

Internet: www.hiddenmickey.org
Disneyland: Adventureland.

Internet: www.hiddenmickey.org
Disneyland: New Orleans Square.

Internet: www.hiddenmickey.org
Disneyland: Critter Country.
Internet: www.hiddenmickey.org
Disneyland: Fantasyland.
Internet: www.hiddenmickey.org
Disneyland: Frontierland.
Internet: www.hiddenmickey.org
Disneyland: Toon Town.
Internet: www.hiddenmickey.org
Disneyland: Tomorrowland.
*More Mouse Tales: A Closer Peek
Backstage at Disneyland,* by David
Koenig, 1999, pages 77, 81, 96.
"Munching on the Job" by Angela
DeCarlo, *Disney News,* Spring 1993,
page 46.
"From Our Mailbox, Letters," *Disney
News,* Spring 1993, page 6.
"Mickey's ToonTown is Open" by
Mickey Mouse, *Disney News,* Spring
1993, page 22.
"Crafting a Cast of Characters" by Jean
Lee, *Disney News,* Spring 1993, page
43.
"Secrets of Walt Disney World" by
David J. Fisher, *Disney News,*
Summer 93, pages 8, 9, 11, 13.
"Going for a Spin on Roger Rabbit's New
Ride" by David J. Fisher, *Disney News,*
Summer 1993, pages 18, 19, 20.
"Disneyland Celebrates 40 Years of
Adventures" by Jean Lee, *Disney
News,* Summer 1995, pages 15–24.
"Silence, Please!" by Leonard Shannon,
Disney News, Summer 1995, page 48.
"If the Job Fits . . . " by Dan Persons,
Disney News, Winter 1999–2000,
page 17.
*Where in Disneyland Attractions? A
Pictorial Souvenir Book,* by Shani &
Scott Wolf, 1997.
*Birnbaum's 2000 Disneyland: Expert
Advice from the Inside Source,* by
Alice Garrard, 2000, pages 25, 56,
62–90, 92–98.
Disneyland Tour "Walk in Walt's
Footsteps," Cast Member: Jason.
"Window-watching on Main Street,"
Disney News, Fall 1995, page 11.

"Windows on Main Street" Handout
compliments of City Hall, Main
Street U.S.A., Disneyland.
"Acting Idle," *The Disney Magazine,*
Fall 1995, page 13.
"So you Want to Be an Imagineer" by
David J. Fisher, *The Disney
Magazine,* Fall 1995, pages 38–40.
"2000 A Disney Scrapbook—An
Intimate Look at the First 100
Years," *The Disney Magazine,* Fall
1999, page 30.
"Ask Dave Disney's Archives Director
Answers All Your Questions!" *The
Disney Magazine,* Fall 1999, page 80.
"Horses (in alphabetical order)"
Handout compliments of City Hall,
Main Street U.S.A., Disneyland.
The Official Mickey Mouse Club Book
by Lorraine Santoli, Hyperion, 1995,
pages 4, 13, 181.
"Ancient Temple Unearthed at
Disneyland! Indiana Jones Reveals
the Legend of Mara and the
Forbidden Eye" by Bob Kumamoto,
The Disney Magazine, Fall 1994,
pages 28-29.
"The Disney Gallery, Disneyland's
Second Floor Surprise," by Angela
Rocco DeCarlo, *The Disney
Magazine,* Fall 1994, pages 37–39.
"Nautilus Redux, Captain Nemo's
Fantastic Submarine Surfaces at Euro
Disneyland" by Jeff Kurtti, *The Disney
Magazine,* Fall 1994, pages 48-49.
"Frank G. Wells, In Celebration of an
Extraordinary Life" by Anne K. Okey,
The Disney Magazine, Fall 1994,
page 12.
"Mailbox—Letters to the Editor," *The
Disney Magazine,* Fall 1994, page 8.
"Hot Cross Buns," *The Disney
Magazine,* Spring 1998, page 22.
"Ask Dave," by Dave Smith, *The Disney
Magazine,* Spring 1998, page 89.
"The Fathers of Invention," by Jeff
Kurti, Leonard Shannon and Pippen
Ross, *The Disney Magazine,* Fall
1996, pages 62–67.

"The Ultimate Insider, Because It's There," by Alexandra Kennedy, *The Disney Magazine*, Fall 1996, pages 86–88.

"Destination Disneyland: A Boy's First Romp Through the Magic Kingdom," by Dan Parsons, *The Local Concierge™ Destination Orange County*, Spring 2000, pages 38–39.

"Great Moments with Mr. Lincoln© The Walt Disney Company," Brochure.

The Keys to the Kingdom, by Kim Masters, 2000, page 150.

"Disneyland Celebrating 45 years of Magic," by Tim O'Day, *Disney Editions*, 2000, pages 18, 19, 21–23, 26, 29–33, 39, 41, 42.

Conversation with Rod Miller, Cast Member, Disneyland, May 20, 2000.

Panel Discussion at Pirates of the Caribbean Special Event, May 20, 2000.

"Rod Miller Ragtime," 1995, Creative Entertainment Productions, (Record Sleeve).

"A World of Differences," *The Disney Magazine*, Spring 2000, pages 38–52.

"Eyes & Ears," *The Disney Magazine*, Spring 2000, page 73.

"Disneyland's Keel's Boats," by Jack E. and Leon J. Janzen, *The "E" Ticket*, Spring 2000, page 41.

Work in Progress, by Michael Eisner published 1998, pages 148, 149, 173, 182, 202, 203, 210.

"A Mint Julep Moon and All That Jazz…" by Lori A. Wildrick, *The Disney Magazine*, Winter 1995, pages 52–53.

"From the Earth to the Moon and Back Again!" by Patrick Alo, *The Disney Magazine*, Winter 1995, pages 26–28.

"Disney News—It Was Thirty Years Ago Today!" by Nick Paccione, *The Disney Magazine*, Winter 1995, page 30.

"Rolly Crump," by Leonard Shannon, *The Disney Magazine*, Winter 1995, page 50.

"ON: TIME Disney's Rail Roads," *The Disney News*, Winter 1990, page 32–34.

"Feasting Amid Medieval Magic," by Scott Richter, *The Disney News*, Winter 1990, page 42.

"Legends Set in Stone" by Anne Okey, *The Disney News*, Winter 1990, pg. 48.

"Milt Albright," by Mike Mallory, *The Disney News*, Winter 1990, page 50.

"Ask Dave," by Dave Smith, *The Disney Magazine*, Spring 1997, pages 84–89.

"Mailbox," by Anne K. Okey, *Disney News*, Winter 1993, page 8.

"A Fan for All Seasons," by Bob Kumamoto, *Disney News*, Winter 1993, pages 36–37.

"Disney Legends 1993, A Spectrum of Talent Honored," by Jeff Hoffman, *Disney News*, Winter 1993, pages 49–51.

Designing Disney's Theme Parks, The Architecture of Reassurance edited by Karal Ann Marling, page 48.

"From Our Mailbox, We Get Letters," by Anne Okey, *Disney News*, Spring 1990, page 4.

"The Disneyland that Never Was, Art That Predicts History at the Disney Gallery," by Ryan Harmon, *Disney News*, Spring 1990, page 24.

"Star Tours, The Movie, Now Departing from Walt Disney World," by Anne Okey, *Disney News*, Spring 1990, page 16.

"Orange Groves to Theme Park," by Anne Okey, *Disney News*, Spring 1990, page 24.

"Dick Nunis, Creating Happiness for Walt," by Anne Okey, *Disney News*, Spring 1990, page 27.

"Disneyland, Walt Disney Biography" brochure #29149, October 1994.

Internet: www.Laughingplace.com, "Space Mountain—The First 25 Years," June 18, 2000.

Disneyland Line, by Melissa Britt, Volume 28, July 12, 1996, Celebrating 41 Years of Happiness, pages 2, 5.

"Disneyland, Disneyland Fun Facts," brochure handed out at City Hall.

Walt Disney's Disneyland Pictorial Souvenir, Disney's Kingdom Editions.

"Disneyland Secrets, You Just Have to Know Where to Look," by Brad Andrews, *Disney News,* Spring 1989, page 27–29.

The Illustrated History of NASA by Robin Kerrod, Gallery Books, W.H. Smith Publisher, 1986, pages 18, 20, 39, 40.

One Day At Disney, edited by Wendy Lefkon, Hyperion, 1999, pages 56, 80, 117, 148, 160.

The Music of Disney, A Legacy In Song, ©The Walt Disney Company 1992 Buena Vista Pictures Distribution, Inc., pages 6, 19, 20, 23–25, 29, 48, 49, 51, 52, 53.

"The Disney Traveler, Parks and Beyond: What's New, What's Great, What a Deal" by Lisa Oppenheimer, *The Disney Magazine,* Summer 1998, page 24.

"All That Glitters," by Lisa Oppenheimer, *The Disney Magazine,* Summer 1998, page 26.

"Disney's Animal Kingdom, On Safari," by Alexandra Kennedy, *The Disney Magazine,* Summer 1998, page 40.

"Jurassic Walt," by Alexandra Kennedy, *The Disney Magazine,* Summer 1998, page 100.

"Making Scents the Disney Way" by Christopher Lentz, *Disney News* Spring 1984, pages 2–3.

"New Adventures with Alice in Wonderland" by Les Perkins, *Disney News,* Spring 1984, page 6.

"Space Station," by Alexandra Kennedy, *The Disney Magazine,* Winter 1998–1999, page 26.

"Helping Hands," by Alexandra Kennedy, *The Disney Magazine,* Winter 1998–1999, page 28.

"The Ink & Paint Girls" by Pippin Ross, *The Disney Magazine,* Winter 1998–1999, page 58.

"Eyes & Ears, On the Beat: Books, Music, Art, Interactive and Online" *The Disney Magazine,* Winter 1998–1999, page 87.

"Ask Dave, Disney's Archived Director Answers All Your Questions!" by Dave Smith, *The Disney Magazine,* Winter 1998–1999, pages 90, 92.

"Cat Burglar," by Alexandra Kennedy, *The Disney Magazine,* Winter 1998–1999, page 100.

"Voices of the Kingdoms" by Michael Mallory, *Disney News,* Winter 1991, pages 20–24.

"Sounds Like Fun" by Joe Burns, *Disney News,* Winter 1991, pages 20–24.

"The Secrets of Walt Disney World, Mickey, Mickey Everywhere" by David Fisher, *Disney News,* Winter 1991, pages 43–46.

Internet: www.laughingplace.com, "Interview with a Legend: Bob Gurr [Bash and Bash]" June 18, 2000.

Internet: www.laughingplace.com, "Interview with a Legend: Bob Gurr Broggie's Pickup." June 18, 2000.

Remembering Walt, Favorite Memories of Walt Disney, by Amy Boothe Green and Howard. E. Green, Hyperion, 1999 Disney Enterprises, pages 15, 149, 155, 156, 163, 165, 166, 169, 171, 172, 182, 203.

Designing Disney's Theme Parks, The Architecture of Reassurance edited by Karal Ann Marling, Flammarion, 1997, pages 29, 55, 87, 105, 113, 116, 118, 120, 130, 132, 134, 140, 182, 197.

The Art of Walt Disney From Mickey Mouse to the Magic Kingdoms, Concise Edition by Christopher Finch, Harry N. Abrams, Inc., Publishers, 1999, pages 138–145.

The Musical World of Walt Disney by David Tietyen, Hal Leonard Publishing Corporation, 1990, pages 32, 58, 65, 94, 114, 118–120.

Building a Company Roy. O. Disney and the Creation of an Entertainment Empire by Bob Thomas, Hyperion, 1998, page 266.

Internet: www.schweitzer.org A brief biography in English of Albert Schweitzer.

Internet: www.laughingplace.com Walt Disney's Miniature Locomotive Lilly Belle Turns 50.

Disney the First 100 Years, by Dave Smith and Steven Clark, published by Hyperion, 1999, pages 71–101, 102, 104, 106, 107, 112, 114, 117, 131, 133, 135, 138, 145, 146, 150, 154, 164, 166, 171, 178, 184.

"Jack of All Trades, Master of Fun" by Patrick Alo, *The Disney Magazine,* Spring 1994, page 20.

"Roger Takes A Spin as the Toontown Easter Bunny" *The Disney Magazine,* Spring 1994, page 32.

"At the Disney Kennels, It's a Dogs Life . . . " by Libby Slate, *The Disney Magazine,* Spring 1994, pages 43–45.

A Legacy of Animation by Leonard Maltin, *The Disney Magazine,* Winter, 1997–1998, pages 40–45.

"Watching the Mouse" reprint from *The Mickey Mouse Watch* by Robert Heide and John Gilman.

"Our Favorite Things: Watching the Mouse," *The Disney Magazine,* Winter 1997–1998, pages 64–68.

"The Disney Traveler, A New Game at Disneyland," by Lisa Oppenheimer, *The Disney Magazine,* Spring 1999, page 21.

"Eyes & Ears, Online:" by Alexandra Kennedy, *The Disney Magazine,* Spring 1999, page 77.

"Ask Dave" by Dave Smith, *The Disney Magazine,* Spring 1999, page 86.

Disneyland, The First Quarter Century, ©1979 Walt Disney Productions, pages 7, 12, 13, 16, 17, 18, 19, 24, 26, 27, 28, 33, 38, 42, 43, 44, 47, 48, 54, 57, 59, 61, 69, 75, 76, 80, 96, 97, 100.

Internet: www.laughingplace.com/ Info-ID-DL-Windows.asp, Disneyland Windows on Main Street, July 30, 2000.

Walt Disney Imagineering: A Behind the Dreams Look at Making the Magic Real by The Imagineers, published by Hyperion, 1996, pages 11, 43, 49, 50, 57, 63, 84, 90, 94, 118, 122, 130, 138, 140, 141, 144, 149, 156, 160, 190.

"Blaine Gibson, Capturing the Spirit" by Scott Elmore, *Disney News,* Summer 1991, page 23.

"For Our Children" by Robyn Flans, *Disney News,* Summer 1991, pages 25–26.

"The Future Isn't What it Used to Be" by Ryan A. Harmon, *Disney News,* Summer 1991, pages 43–45.

"Ask Dave Smith" by Dave Smith, *The Disney Magazine,* Summer 1996, pages 14, 16, 17.

"Space Mountain Rides a New Music Wave," by Alexandra Kennedy, *The Disney Magazine,* Summer 1996, page 26.

"The Hunchback of Notre Dame—A Time Line" by Pippin Ross and Lisa Stiepock, *The Disney Magazine,* Summer 1996, page 52.

"Searching for A Bright New Tomorrowland" by Susan Roth, *The Disney Magazine,* Summer 1996, pages 65–66.

"Backstage Pass: Our Roving Photographers Take You There," by Alexandra Kennedy, *The Disney Magazine,* Fall 1998, page 16.

"On Track Creating a Coaster for the Millennium" by Pippin Ross, *The Disney Magazine,* Fall 1998, page 47.

"Ask Dave" by Dave Smith, *The Disney Magazine,* Fall 1998, page 85.

Inside the Magic Kingdom, Seven Keys to Disney's Success by Tom Connellan, Bard Press, April 1997, pages 60, 152, 171, 172.

"Along with Walt," by Jack E. and Leon J. Janzen, *The "E" Ticket*, Fall 2000 pages 11–13, 34–39.

Walt Disney's Railroad Story by Michael Broggie, Pentrex Media Group, 1998, pages 13, 27–112, 114, 120, 121, 180, 197, 198, 200, 204, 210, 223, 226, 227, 242, 248, 253, 254, 256, 261, 265, 266, 268, 269, 274, 283, 284, 292, 294, 300, 390–392.

"Mousetalgia," by Paula Sigman, *Sketches*, Volume 1, Number 1, Spring 1993, pages 6–7.

"Train Crazy" by Julie Schlax, *Sketches*, Vol. One, No. One, Spring 1993, pages 8–9.

"You Can Fly! You Can Fly! You Can Fly!" by Julie Schlax, *Sketches*, Vol. One, No. Four, Winter 1993 pages 2–3.

"A Daughter Remembers, He Was So Much Fun" by Diane Disney Miller, *Sketches*, Vol. Two, No. One, Spring 1994, pages 8–9.

"Walt and the Environment A True-Life Adventure" by Jim Fanning, *Sketches*, Vol. Two, No. Three, Fall 1994, pages 4–5.

"Making a Splash for 5 Years!" *Sketches*, Vol. Two, No. Three, Fall 1994, page 8.

"Memorable Moments from Mary Poppins, 30th Anniversary Celebration" by Leonard Shannon, *Sketches*, Vol. Two, No. Four, Winter 1994, pages 6–7.

"Mr. Lincoln & Mr. Disney" by Julie Schlaz-Patrick, *Sketches*, Vol. Three, No. Three, Fall 1995, pages 8–9.

"Walt's Little Wonders" by Emily Dodi, *Sketches*, Vol. Three, No. Two, Summer 1995, page 1.

"Fifty–Four Years and Still Imagineering" by Jeff Kurtti,

Sketches, Vol. Two, No. Two, Summer 1994, pages 4–5.

"The Candlelight Procession—A Disney Theme Park Tradition" by Paula Sigman, *Sketches*, Vol. Four, No. Four, 1996, pages 8–9.

"Potpourri Disney News at a Glance, Disney Days," *Sketches*, Volume 5, Number Two, 1997, page 7.

"Yo Ho, Yo Ho, A Pirate's Life for Me!" by Paula Sigman, *Sketches*, Volume Five, Number Two, 1997, pages 8–9.

"As Nasty As They Want to Be: by Michael Lyons, *Sketches*, Volume 5, Number Two, 1997, pages 10–11.

The Disney Way, by Bill Capodagli and Lynn Jackson, McGraw-Hill, 1999, pages 15, 19, 36, 37.

Inside Disney by Eve Zibart, IDG Books Worldwide, 2000, pages 83, 105–111, 140, 177.

George Lucas Close Up, The Making of His Movies, by Chris Salewicz, Thunder's Mouth Press, 1998, pages 13, 17, 66-67, 87.

Vinyl Leaves, Walt Disney World and America by Stephen M. Fjellman, Westview Press, 1992, pages 59, 67, 73–77, 191–193, 225, 251, 275, 357.

Short lecture by Maggie Irvine Elliot at the Ryman Carroll Young Artists Charity, September 23, 2000.

The Ultimate Disney Trivia Book 4 by Kevin Neary and Dave Smith, Disney Editions, 2000, pages 152–160, 200–206, 220–228.

Microsoft Encarta '97 Encyclopedia: Davy Crockett, Albert Schweitzer, Alexander Graham Bell, Pearl Buck, Andrew Carnegie, George Washington Carver, Thomas Edison, Albert Einstein, Henry Ford, Robert H. Goddard, David Sarnoff, Wright Brothers, Flags of the United States, John Cabot, Saint George, Saint Andrew, Battle of Bunker Hill, George Washington, Betsy Ross, and Star Spangled Banner, Abraham Lincoln, Gettysburg Address,

Matthew Brady and Frederick Douglass.

The Illusion of Life—Disney Animation by Frank Thomas and Ollie Johnston, Hyperion, 1981, pages 306, 388, 512, 517, 528.

Email from Walt Disney Archives.

Flags of the U.S.A. by David Eggenberger, Thomas Y. Crowell Company, 1964, pages 16–18, 32.

"Dazzled in Disneyland," by Aubrey Menen, *Holiday Magazine,* July 1963, pages 68–75, 106.

"Pioneers Carl Barks, Eyvind Earle," by Alexandra Kennedy, *The Disney Magazine,* Winter 2000–2001, page 71.

"Eyes & Ears, Music and Books," by Alexandra Kennedy, *The Disney Magazine,* Winter 2000–2001, page 83.

"Ask Dave," by Dave Smith, *The Disney Magazine* Winter, 2000–2001, pages 86, 88, 90.

Walt Disney's Snow White and the Seven Dwarfs, An Art in Its Making, by Martin Krause and Linda Witkowski, Hyperion, 1994, pages 7–31, 151–179.

Mouse Under Glass by David Koenig, Bonadventure Press, 1997, pages 32, 33, 41, 42, 52, 63, 68, 78, 93, 105, 121, 181, 188, 189, 190, 260, 271, 272.

"Swiss Family Treehouse," *The "E" Ticket, Collecting Theme Park Memories,* Number 23, Spring 1996, pages 20–29.

"Jungle Cruise Journeys," by Jack E. and Leon J. Janzen, *The "E" Ticket, Collecting Theme Park Memories,* Number 23, Spring 1996, pages 30-35.

"Fantasyland's Theatre," by Jack E. and Leon J. Janzen, *The "E" Ticket, Collecting Theme Park Memories,* Number 23, Spring 1996, pages 28–40.

"Creating the Disney Landscape, An Interview with Bill Evans," *The "E" Ticket, Collecting Theme Park Memories,* Number 23, Spring 1996, pages 4–15.

"Wathel Rogers and Audio Animatronics," by Jack E. and Leon J. Janzen, *The "E" Ticket, Collecting Theme Park Memories,* Number 25, Winter 1996, pages 26–34.

"Disney's Mechanized Magic," by Jack E. and Leon J. Janzen, *The "E" Ticket, Collecting Theme Park Memories,* Number 25, Winter 1996, pages 6–19.

"King Arthur Carrousel," by Jack E. and Leon J. Janzen, *The "E" Ticket, Collecting Theme Park Memories,* Number 35, Spring 2001, pages 6–17.

"Disneyland Art Director . . . Bill Martin," *The "E" Ticket, Collecting Theme Park Memories,* Number 20, Winter 1994–1995, pages 10–19.

"Mr. Toad's Wild Ride," by Jack E. and Leon J. Janzen, *The "E" Ticket, Collecting Theme Park Memories,* Number 20, Winter 1994-1995, pages 20–33.

"Disney's Peter Pan Flight," by Jack E. and Leon J. Janzen, *The "E" Ticket, Collecting Theme Park Memories,* Number 26, Spring 1997, pages 10–25.

"Peter Pan, Captain Hook . . . Frank Thomas," by Jack E. and Leon J. Janzen, *The "E" Ticket, Collecting Theme Park Memories,* Number 26, Spring 1997, pages 26–40.

"Dapper Dans of Disneyland," by Jack E. and Leon J. Janzen, *The "E" Ticket Collecting Theme Park Memories,* Number 27, Summer 1997, pages 4–7.

"Bob Gurr's Main Street GurrMobiles," by Jack E. and Leon J. Janzen, *The "E" Ticket, Collecting Theme Park Memories,* Number 27, Summer 1997, pages 8–11.

"Dapper Dans of Disneyland," by Jack E. and Leon J. Janzen, *The "E" Ticket, Collecting Theme Park Memories,* Number 27, Summer 1997, pages 12–27.

The Disney Version, The Life, Times, Art and Commerce of Walt Disney by Richard Schickel, Simon and Schuster New York, 1968.

A Brush with Disney, An Artist's Journey Told Through the Words and Works of Herbert Dickens Ryman, edited by Bruce Gordon and David Mumford, Camphor Tree Publishers, 2000, pages 143-144, 147-148, 193, 205, 209, 244.

"The World's Fifth Largest Navy," by Margery Lee, *Disney News*, Summer 1979, pages 2–3.

"Big Thunder Strikes," *Disney News*, Summer 1979, pages 4–5.

"Timepieces with Character," *Disney News*, Summer 1979, pages 8–9.

"Bob Sewell . . . the Model Shop, and much more," by Jack E. and Leon J. Janzen, *The "E" Ticket*, Issue 29, Spring 1998, pages 4–13.

"The Disneyland Mine Train Story," by Jack E. and Leon J. Janzen, *The "E" Ticket*, Issue 29, Spring 1998, pages 16–31.

"Pirates of the Caribbean . . . More Gems from this Disney Treasure," by Jack E. and Leon J. Janzen, *The "E" Ticket*, Issue 32, Fall 1999, pages 24–37.

"In the Emporium . . . Disneyland's Book Store," by Jack E. and Leon J. Janzen, *The "E" Ticket*, Issue 32, Fall 1999, pages 38–41.

"The Hatbox Ghost, Too Scary for the Haunted Mansion??" by Jack E. and Leon J. Janzen, *The "E" Ticket*, Issue 32, Fall 1999, pages 19–21.

"A Marc Davis Pirates Sketchbook," by Jack E. and Leon J. Janzen, *The "E" Ticket*, Issue 32, Fall 1999, pages 4–15.

"Fast Track," by Alexandra Kennedy, *The Disney Magazine*, Spring 2001, page 92.

"Ask Dave," by Dave Smith, *The Disney Magazine*, Spring 2001, pages 85, 89.

"Claude Coats Prototypical Imagineer,"

by Jack E. and Leon J. Janzen, *The "E" Ticket*, Issue 31, Spring 1999, pages 4–15.

"Alice in Wonderland," by Jack E. and Leon J. Janzen, *The "E" Ticket*, Issue 31, Spring 1999, pages 24–37.

Alamo Flag Company Catalog, Historical Flags, pages 8–9.

"The Indian War Canoes," by Jack E. and Leon J. Janzen, *The "E" Ticket*, Issue 28, Winter 1997, pages 4–7.

"Planning the First Disney Parks . . . A Talk with Marvin Davis," by Jack E. and Leon J. Janzen, *The "E" Ticket*, Issue 28, Winter 1997, pages 8–19.

"Disneyland . . . The First Twelve Months," by Jack E. and Leon J. Janzen, *The "E" Ticket*, Issue 28, Winter 1997, pages 20–35.

"Disney's Space Mountain," by Jack E. and Leon J. Janzen, *The "E" Ticket*, Issue 30, Fall 1998, pages 30–41.

Sotheby's Guide to Animation Art by Christopher Finch and Linda Rosenkrantz, An Owl Company Henry Holt and Company, 1998, pages 80–81, 89–91.

Inside the Mouse, Work and Play at Disney World, The Project on Disney, by June Kuenz et al Duke University Press, 1995.

The Story of Walt Disney, Maker of Magical Worlds by Bernice Seldon, Bantam Doubleday Dell Books for Young Readers, 1989, page 74.

The Disney Villain by Ollie Johnston and Frank Thomas, Hyperion, 1993, page 56.

People to Know, Walt Disney Creator of Mickey Mouse by Michael D. Cole, Enslow Publishers, Inc., 1996.

The Hand Behind the Mouse by Leslie Iwerks and John Kenworthy, Disney Editions, 2001, pages 189, 214–215, 226–227.

Horizon Bound On A Bicycle, The Autobiography of Eyvind Earle, published by Earle and Bane, 1990, pages 247–252.

Walt's Time from Before and Beyond, by Robert B. Sherman and Richard M. Sherman, Camphor Tree Publishers, 1988, pages 37, 51, 63, 68–69, 144, 145, 147, 216, 227.

Storyboard, The Art of Laughter, vol. 4 #4 Aug/Sept. '93, Walt Disney—The Real Man.

Window on Main Street, by Van Arsdale France, Published by Laughter Publications, Inc., 1991, pages 6, 7, 19, 33, 37–39, 42, 46, 48, 53, 78, 96, 97, 111.

Walt Disney His Life in Pictures by Russell Schroeder, Disney Press 1996, pages 10–15.

Original Soundtrack from Walt Disney World's Country Bear Jamboree, 1972, Walt Disney Productions.

Walt Disney Disneyland World of Flowers by Morgan Evans, Walt Disney Productions, 1965, pages 5, 7, 8, 11, 27, 32, 45, 55.

"Early Days of the Monorail" by Jack E. and Leon J. Janzen, *The "E" Ticket,* Issue 36, Fall 2001, pages 10–20.

"Walt Disney's 100th Birthday Celebration in Marceline, Missouri," by Dan Viets, *NFFC FantasyLine Express,* Vol 10, Number 8, August 2001, pages 1, 10–11.

Pocket Guide to Depression Glass & More, Tenth Edition by Gene Florence, Collectors Books, 1997, page 88.

The Magic Kingdom, Walt Disney and the American Way of Life by Steven Watts, Houghton Mifflin Company, 1997, pages 238–274.

The Disneyland Resort Line, Volume 33, Number 8, February 23, 2001. "In Memory of Hideo Amemiya," page 2.

The Disneyland Resort Line, Volume 33, Number 40, October 5, 2001. "Hideo Honored with Window."

Wally Boag Tells of Frontierland, by Jack E. and Leon J. Janzen, *The "E" Ticket,* Number 15, Spring 1993, pages 5, 10, 12.

"Disneyland's Queen of the River . . . The Mark Twain," *The "E" Ticket,* Number 15, Spring 1993, pages 12, 20–22, 24–25.

Jazz New Orleans Style by Bobby Potts, Terrell Publishing Co.,1998, pages 13, 15, 49.

"Santa Fe and Disneyland Railroad," *The "E" Ticket,* Issue 19, Summer 1994, page 3.

"Theme Park Adventure, Walt Disney's Pirates of the Caribbean," by Rick West, *Theme Park Adventure Magazine,* page 58.

"Evolution of a Mascot, Born 2 Ride," *"O" Oregon 2001 Football Game-Day Magazine,* November 3, 2001, Oregon vs. Arizona State, pages 78–79.

"One Score and 17 Years Ago . . ." by Alexandra Kennedy, *The Disney Magazine,* Winter 2001–2002, page 22.

The Big Little Book of Disney, by Monique Peterson, Disney Editions, New York, 2001, pages 22, 39, 41.

Inside the Dream, the Personal Story of Walt Disney by Katherine and Richard Greene, Disney Editions, New York, 2001, pages 61, 63, 68, 74, 107, 160, 170.

The Garden Within, The Art of Peter Ellenshaw by Peter Ellenshaw, Mill Pond Press, page 10.

Walt Disney's Nine Old Men & The Art of Animation by John Canemaker, Disney Editions, New York, 2001, pages 10–11, 24, 265–293.

GLOSSARY

Attractions: Disney's term for the rides. Each ride is more like an experience than simply a ride.

Audio-Animatronics: Hydraulics, cams and other methods of enabling sculptures to move in a realistic fashion. Walt Disney and WED Enterprises developed the process with inspiration from an antique bird found in New Orleans. Audio-Animatronics is now the mainstay for many of the Disneyland attractions.

In the simplest terms, Audio-Animatronics combines and synchronizes sound and animation by means of electronic systems. Every movement of each member of the cast is "programmed" into a sequence of action that can be repeated over and over again throughout the day."

Berm: One of the first elements to be constructed was a 15-ft.-high berm surrounding the site. Walt didn't want people to see anything of the real world while they were in the park. Therefore, it would be far easier for guests to believe they were in the jungle, the old west, fantasyland or the future.

Cast Members: Disney's term for employees who work in view of the public, each is cast a part in their duty.

Disney Legends: Created in 1987, it is an award to recognize lifetime contributions to Disney. Over 91 people have been awarded the prestigious honor. A Hollywood Hall of Fame was built to recognize the winners. A monument in Burbank showcases the handprints, and signatures of every legend is cast in bronze and inlaid. Anchoring the plaza is a 2,000-lb., 14-foot bronze replica of the Legends trophy.

Forced Perspective: The movie-making ability to make sets appear farther, taller or longer than they actually are. Objects are created smaller in size as they go away from the viewing.

Guests: Disney's term for customers who enter the park. Each person is to be treated as a special visitor.

Inbetweener: This is a position in the animation department. The animator would decide which key poses a character would make for a certain scene. The Inbetweener would animate the subtle movement changes between the key actions. Disney typically uses 24 drawings per second in a film.

Imagineer: An employee of Walt Disney Imagineering Department. The name plays off of the words imagination, engineering and maybe even Ears, since Mickey's ears are the trademark of the Disney Franchise.

Imagineering: Is the department of Imagineers, based in Glendale, Calif. These people are designers, architects, technicians, and engineers who create the park attractions. In 1953, the first Imagineers were selected for a department named WED Enterprises. WED changed its name to Imagineering in 1986 when there was too much confusion with marital arrangements.

MAPO: This was a department of WED

Enterprises incorporated in 1965. It would be best described as the machine shop and manufacturing area. It's named for the film *Mary Poppins*, released in 1964.

Queue: The line area waiting to board an attraction.

RETLAW Enterprises: In 1965, Walt Disney sold his WED Enterprises holdings to Walt Disney Productions and Retlaw was formed to handle the family interests. The name comes from Walter spelled backwards.

WED Enterprises: In 1952, Walt Disney founded this design and development team to help him create Disneyland. WED stands for Walter Elias Disney. Walt was the sole owner until 1965, when he sold his interest to Walt Disney Productions. It's been renamed Walt Disney Imagineering (WDI) and its employees are now called Imagineers.

INDEX

The Author

Kendra Trahan was born and educated in Southern Oregon. As a child her family would make the long drive to Southern California every few years to visit all the major theme parks, saving Disneyland, perceived as the best, for last. She remembers Disneyland as always being the most beautiful, impeccably clean, and having the best attractions. Her interest in Disney multiplied when she created a marketing assignment in college that studied the synergy of the Walt Disney Company.

Spending most of her professional career in pharmaceutical sales, she has moved to San Diego Calif.; Wilmington, Dela.; and finally to Orange County, Calif. Kendra's first books were about hospital selling, managed care, and pharmaceutical training manuals.

While in Delaware, she missed the opportunity to visit Disneyland and began reading everything she could get her hands on about the park. Kendra discovered that the more research she did, the more it proved that the Disney artists and Imagineers had done their research too. She began looking for a single resource that included movie props and Hidden Mickeys in Disneyland. Unable to find one, she started a focused effort to research the subject and write the resource herself.

Her (sales) career eventually moved her back to California affording her the opportunity to get involved with some Disney interest groups. There she was encouraged to meet the Disney Legends and Honorees who built the park. She has met many original designers of Disneyland and/or their families, conducted several personal interviews, and wrote chapter three as a special tribute for them. Kendra volunteers once a month as a docent at Walt Disney's barn museum in Los Angeles' Griffith Park as well as being a member of the board of governors of the Carolwood Pacific Historical Society. She is a member of NFFC Chapter at the park and collects books about Disney.

In her spare time, she enjoys visiting wineries with her husband Russell, rafting the Rogue River in Oregon, learning to surf, and taking her golden retriever for walks.

Photographer **Dave Hawkins** was born in Pasadena, Calif. He remembers visiting Knott's Berry Farm and Disneyland at a very young age. His family moved away from all that in 1959 and Dave grew up in Southern Oregon. There he married, started a family, and developed an artistic eye with the camera. Dave moved his family to Alaska for seven years, where he began his professional photography career. Currently, he owns *Dave Hawkins Photography* in Medford, Ore., where his work is well known regionally. You may have seen his work in catalogs, magazines, or especially around the cars at Reno's Hot August Nights. Dave and his wife still live in Southern Oregon and is the father of two grown children.

Brian McKim was born and raised in Southern Calif. He grew up in a Disney family as his father, Sam McKim, spent 32 years at Walt Disney Imagineering. Brian would hear stories at the dinner table about the development of Disneyland and the different projects his father was working on with Walt. At the age of seven, Brian went to the studio to meet his father and just barely missed meeting Walt in person by only a moment. Brian is a great choice for creating the Main Street U.S.A. window illustrations because he grew up knowing and admiring many of the people mentioned in this book. Brian earned his Bachelor of Arts from California State University at Northridge, and B.F.A. from the Art Center College of Design in Pasadena. Brian then went on to work at Walt Disney Studios for 15 years in feature animation. He especially likes painting landscapes and portraitures in oils. For relaxation he likes to spend time with his wife Dorothy, son Tyler, and daughter Natalie. Whenever Brian has some free time, he likes to take the family and go fishing.

Karl Yamauchi

◄ **Karl Yamauchi** is the artistic talent behind all the flags and shield illustrations in the book. His art isn't limited to the designs shown here, but is usually more abstract and fresh. Since childhood, he has been especially interested in pencil drawings and watercolors. Karl is a former bridge architect by profession, and a fervent Disney fan by choice. He remembers watching Walt Disney describe Disneyland on television back in 1954 and like so many of his contemporaries found a special affection for the park. He wasn't able to make his first trip to Disneyland until 1972, but a trip in the mid 1980s with his wife renewed his Disney fascination. He has a special interest in Imagineering due to his architecture background. He is pleased to contribute to the park experience through his art in *Disneyland Detective*. Karl and his wife Nancy are members of Carolwood Pacific Historical Society and volunteers at the Walt Disney barn in Griffith Park. He later retired in his home in Celebration, Fla.

Photographer **Debbie Smith** has two lifelong hobbies: photography and visiting Disneyland. This made her the perfect choice for contributing to *Disneyland Detective*. When you review her work, you'll see she has amazing patience, as she'll wait for hours for that perfect shot. She looks for the perfect angle, light and action to capture her subjects perfectly. Her favorite photos are of the Disney Characters who recognize her and give her just a couple of extra minutes to get the photo just right. Debbie lives in Hanford, Calif., with her husband Martin of 24 years. Both are regular volunteers of the Carol-wood Pacific Historical Society at Walt's Barn in Griffith Park, Ca.

ORDER FORM

If this is a library copy, please photocopy this page.

Ship Books to:

Name:_____

Address: _____

City:_____State: _____Zip:_____

Quantity   _____   Disneyland Detective (soft cover $19.95)

              $ _____   Postage add $2 for first book

              $ _____   Add $1 each additional book

              $ _____   Sales Tax:
                        California Residents only, please add 7.75%

              $ _____   **Amount Enclosed**

Checks, Money orders, Major credit cards Visa accepted.

Credit Card # _____
Exp. Date _____ / _____

Name on Card_____

PermaGrin
Publishing, Inc.
27758 Santa Margarita Parkway #379
Mission Viejo, CA 92691

ORDER FORM

If this is a library copy, please photocopy this page.

Ship Books to:

Name:_____

Address:_____

City:_____State: _____Zip:_____

Quantity _____ Disneyland Detective (soft cover $19.95)

$ _____ Postage add $2 for first book

$ _____ Add $1 each additional book

$ _____ Sales Tax:
California Residents only, please add 7.75%

$ _____ **Amount Enclosed**

Checks, Money orders, Major credit cards Visa accepted.

Credit Card # _____
Exp. Date _____ / _____

Name on Card_____

 PermaGrin
Publishing, Inc.
27758 Santa Margarita Parkway #379
Mission Viejo, CA 92691